LUNARBABOON
The Daily Life of Parenthood

LUNARBABOON
The Daily Life of Parenthood

Remember not having kids?
Not really.
SHH! Quiet you two!

Chris Grady

Andrews McMeel Publishing®
a division of Andrews McMeel Universal

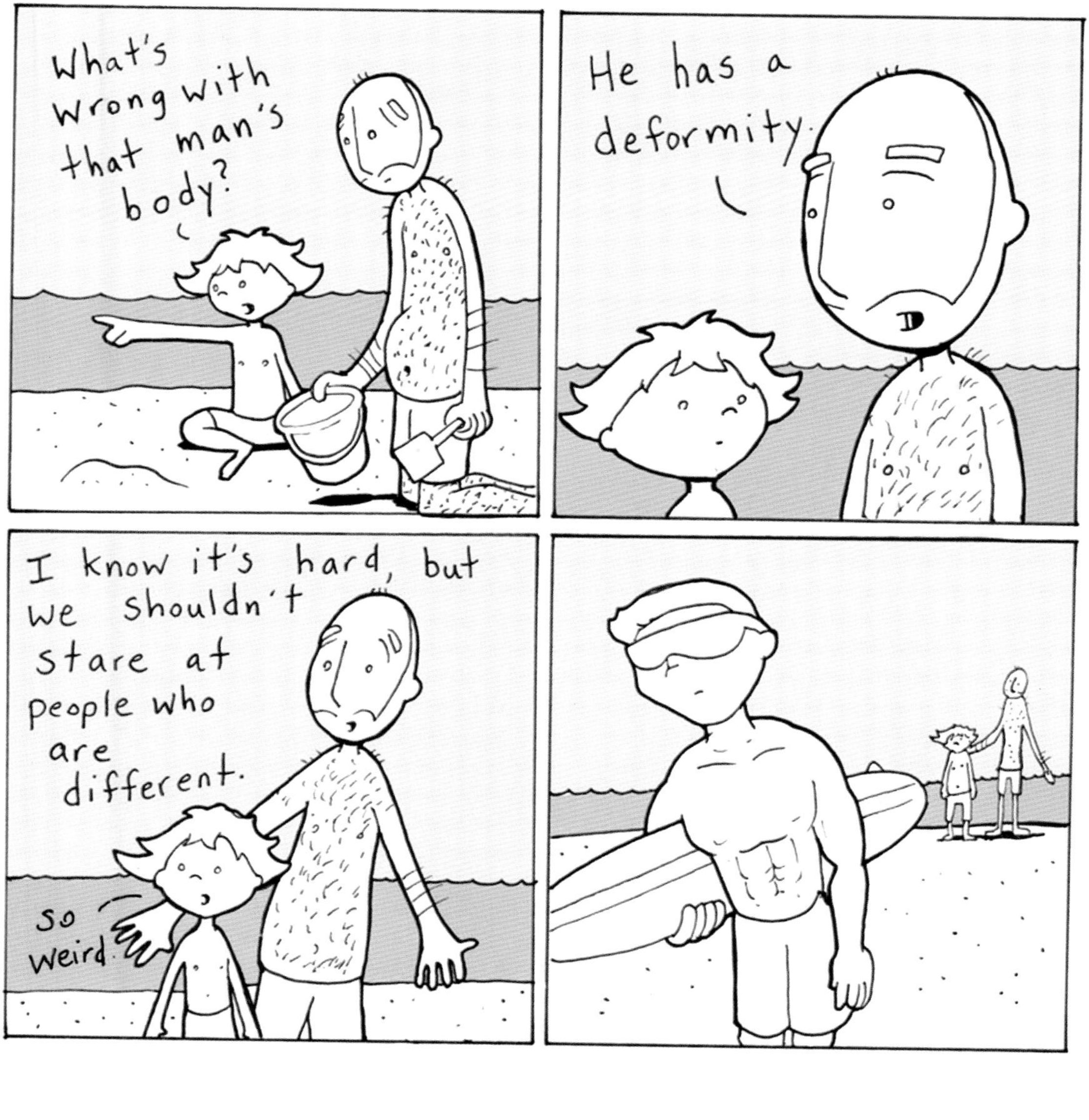
What's wrong with that man's body?
He has a deformity.
I know it's hard, but we shouldn't stare at people who are different.
So weird.

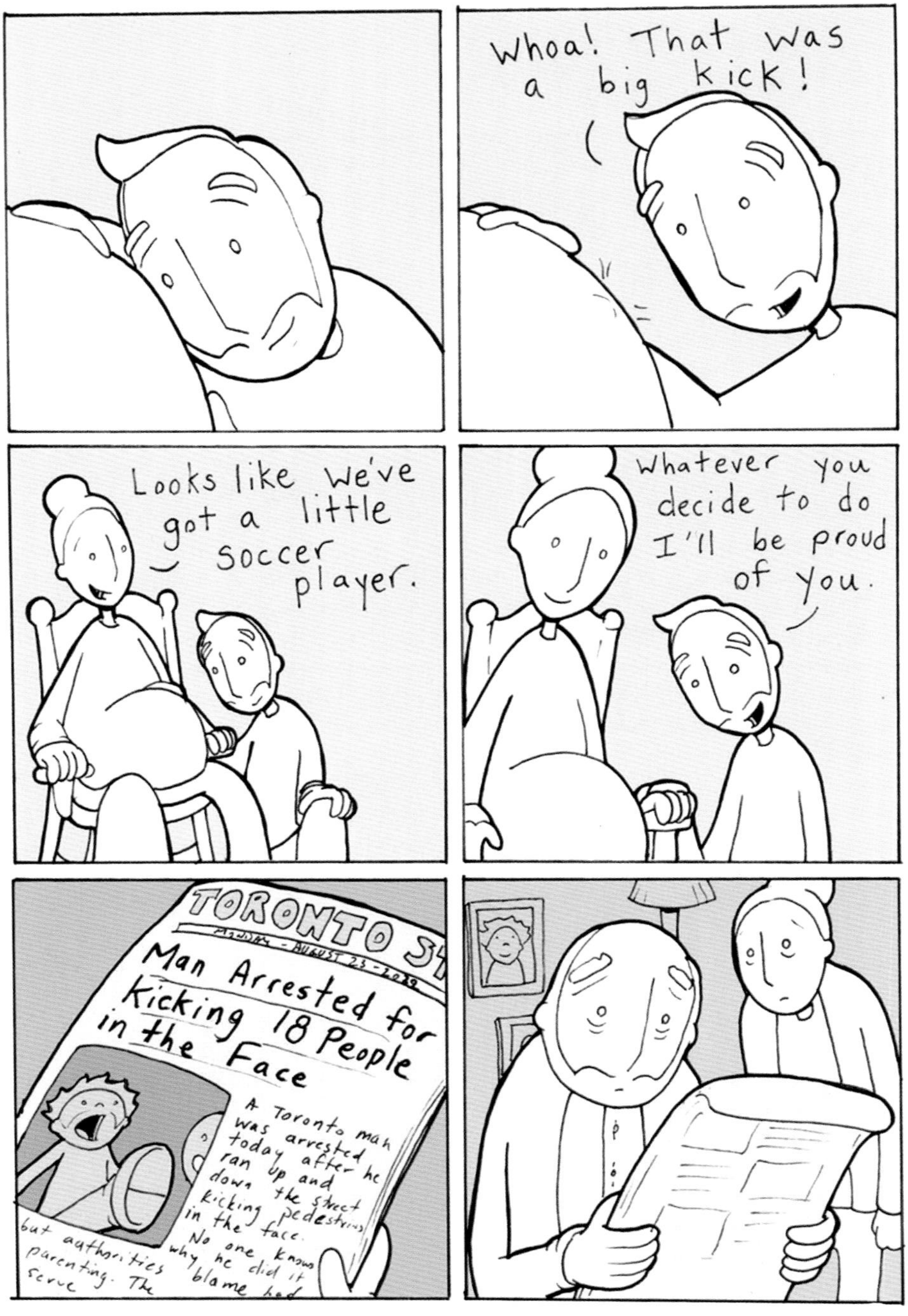

Whoa! That was a big kick!
Looks like we've got a little soccer player.
Whatever you decide to do I'll be proud of you.
TORONTO ST
Man Arrested for Kicking 18 People in the Face
A Toronto man was arrested today after he ran up and down the street kicking pedestrians in the face.
No one knows why he did it but authorities blame bad parenting. The

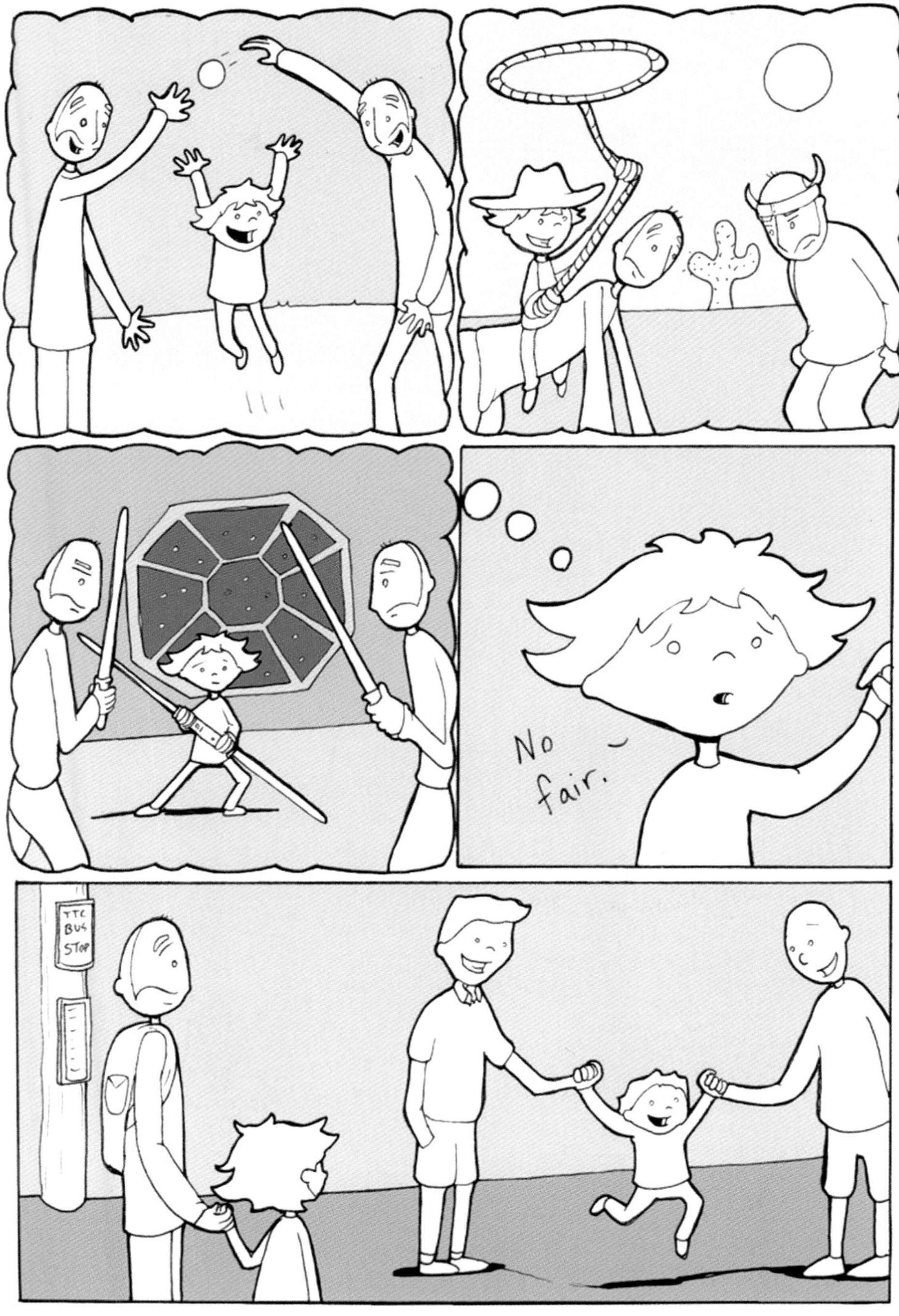
No fair.
TTC BUS STOP

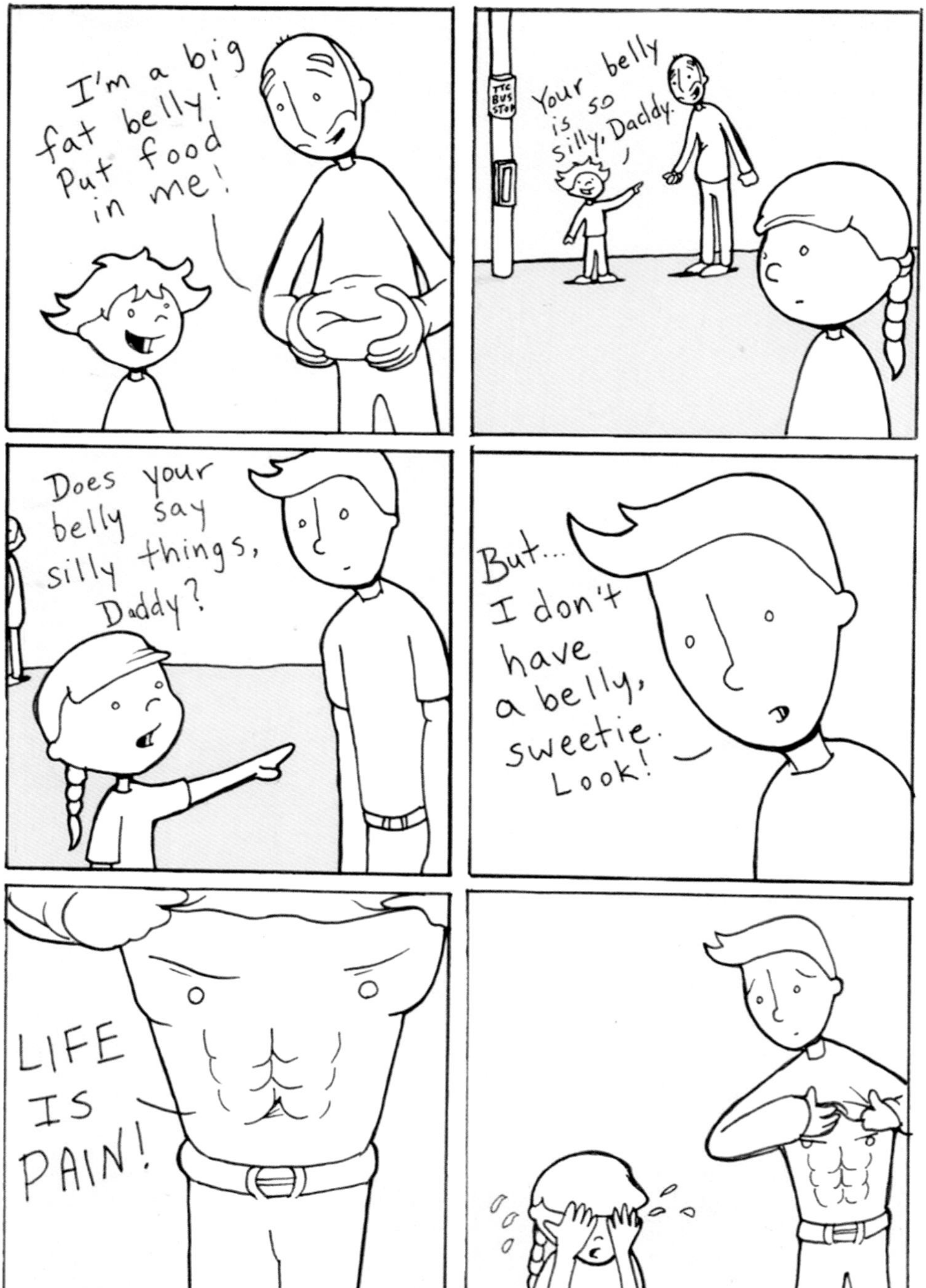
I'm a big fat belly! Put food in me!
TTC BUS STOP
Your belly is so silly, Daddy.
Does your belly say silly things, Daddy?
But... I don't have a belly, sweetie. Look!
LIFE IS PAIN!

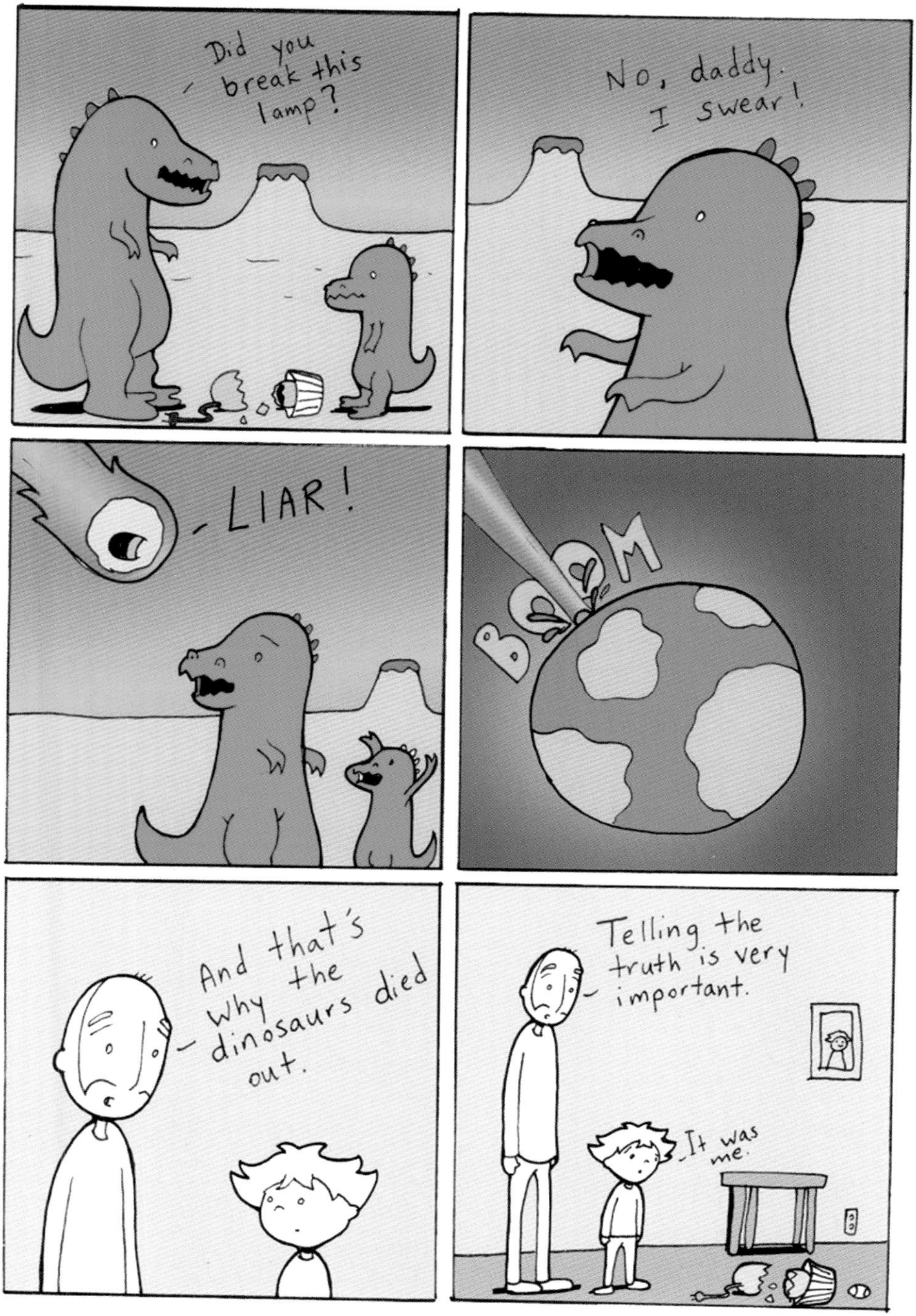
Did you break this lamp?
No, daddy. I swear!
LIAR!
BOOM
And that's why the dinosaurs died out.
Telling the truth is very important.
It was me.

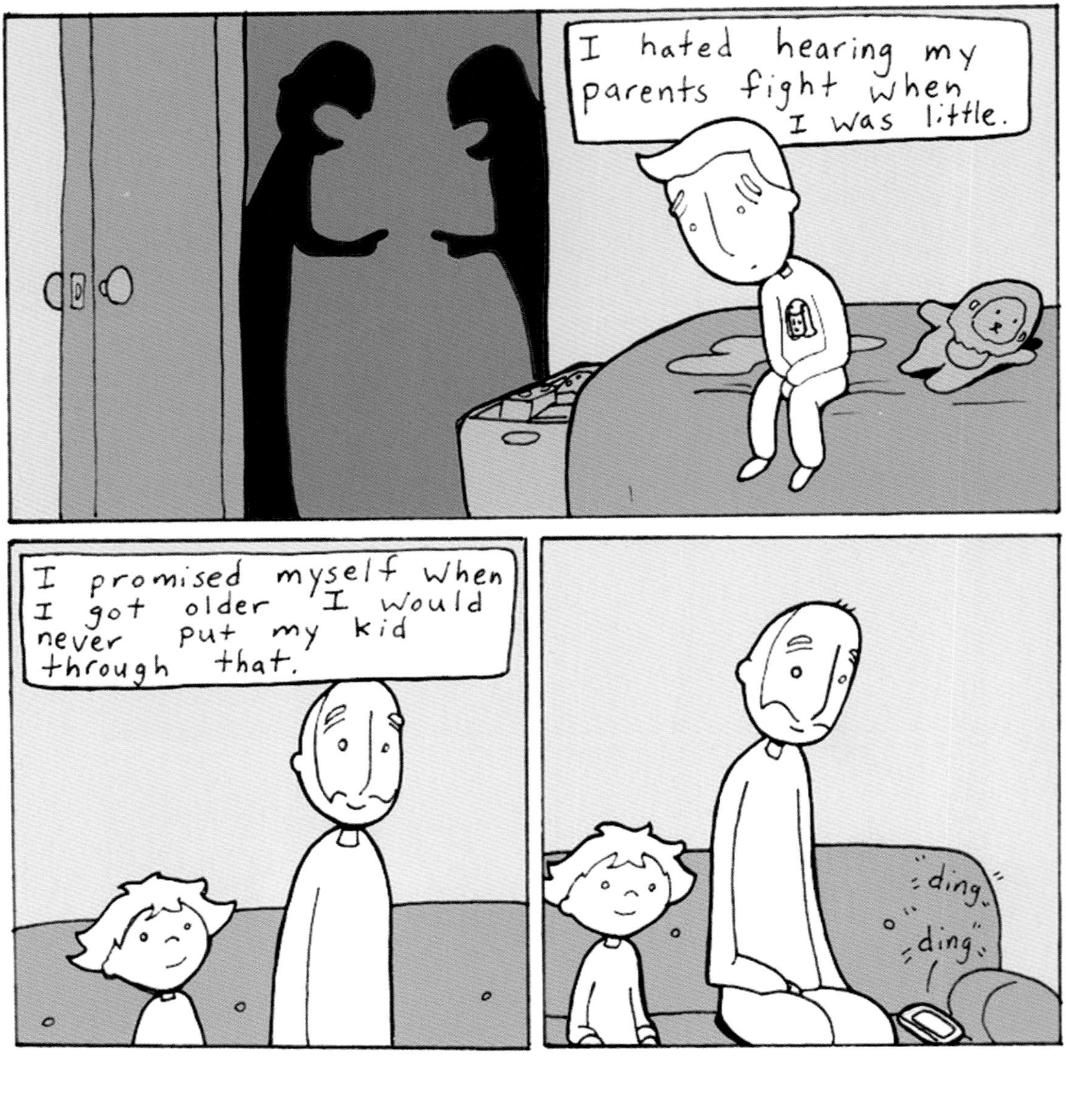
I hated hearing my parents fight when I was little.
I promised myself when I got older I would never put my kid through that.
ding
ding

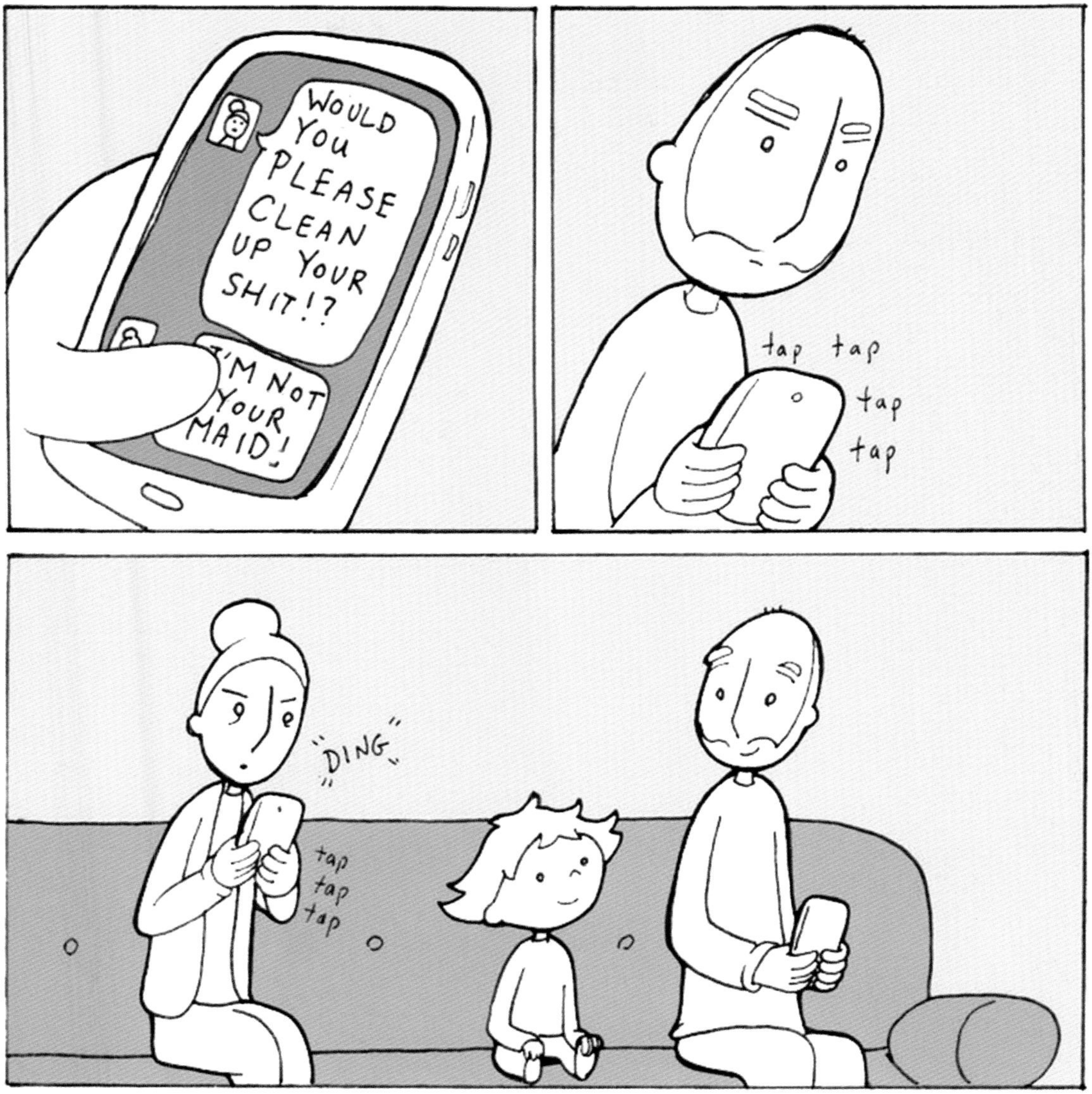
WOULD YOU PLEASE CLEAN UP YOUR SHIT!?
I'M NOT YOUR MAID!
tap tap
tap
tap
DING
tap
tap
tap

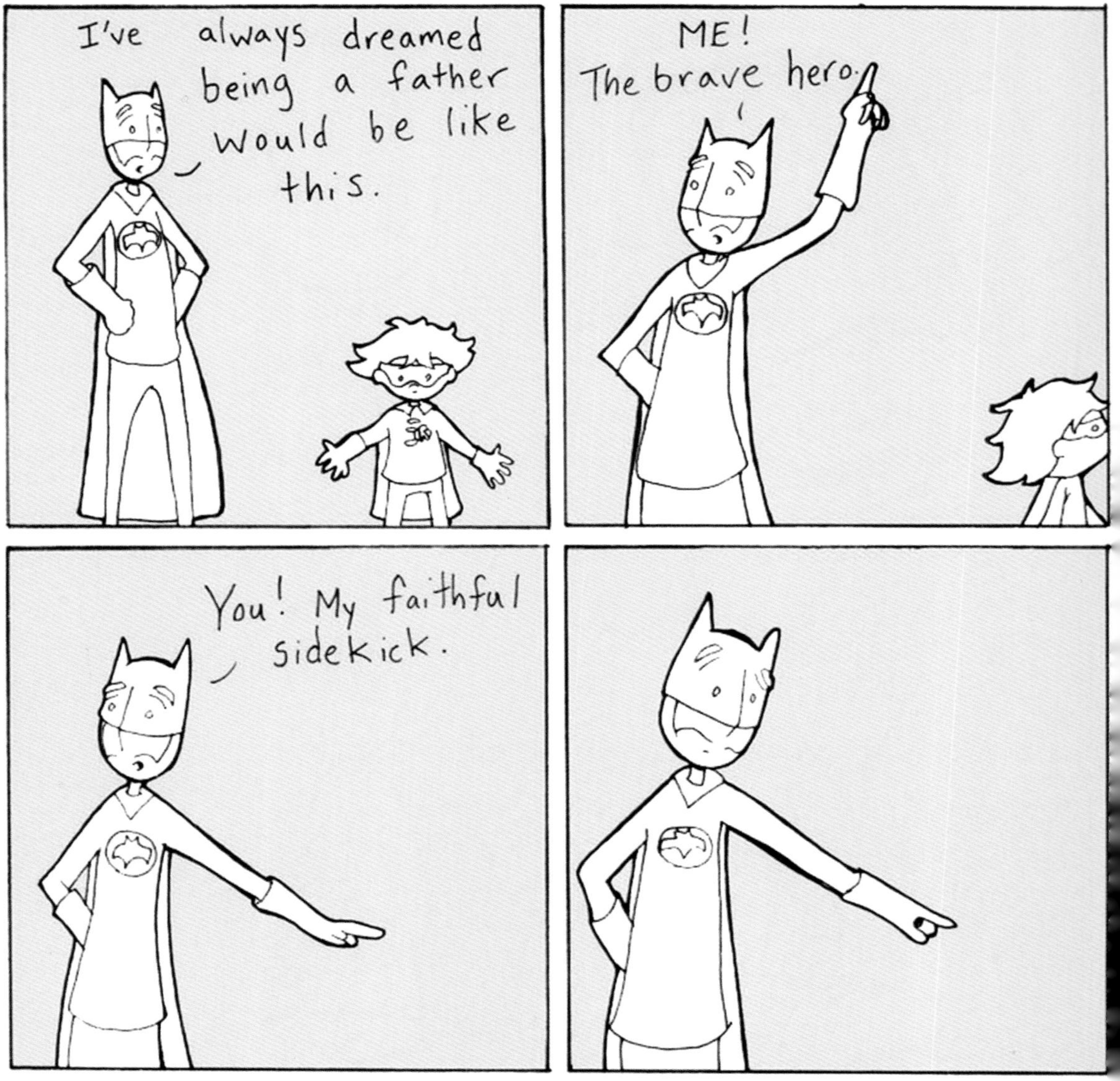
I've always dreamed being a father would be like this.
ME! The brave hero.
You! My faithful sidekick.

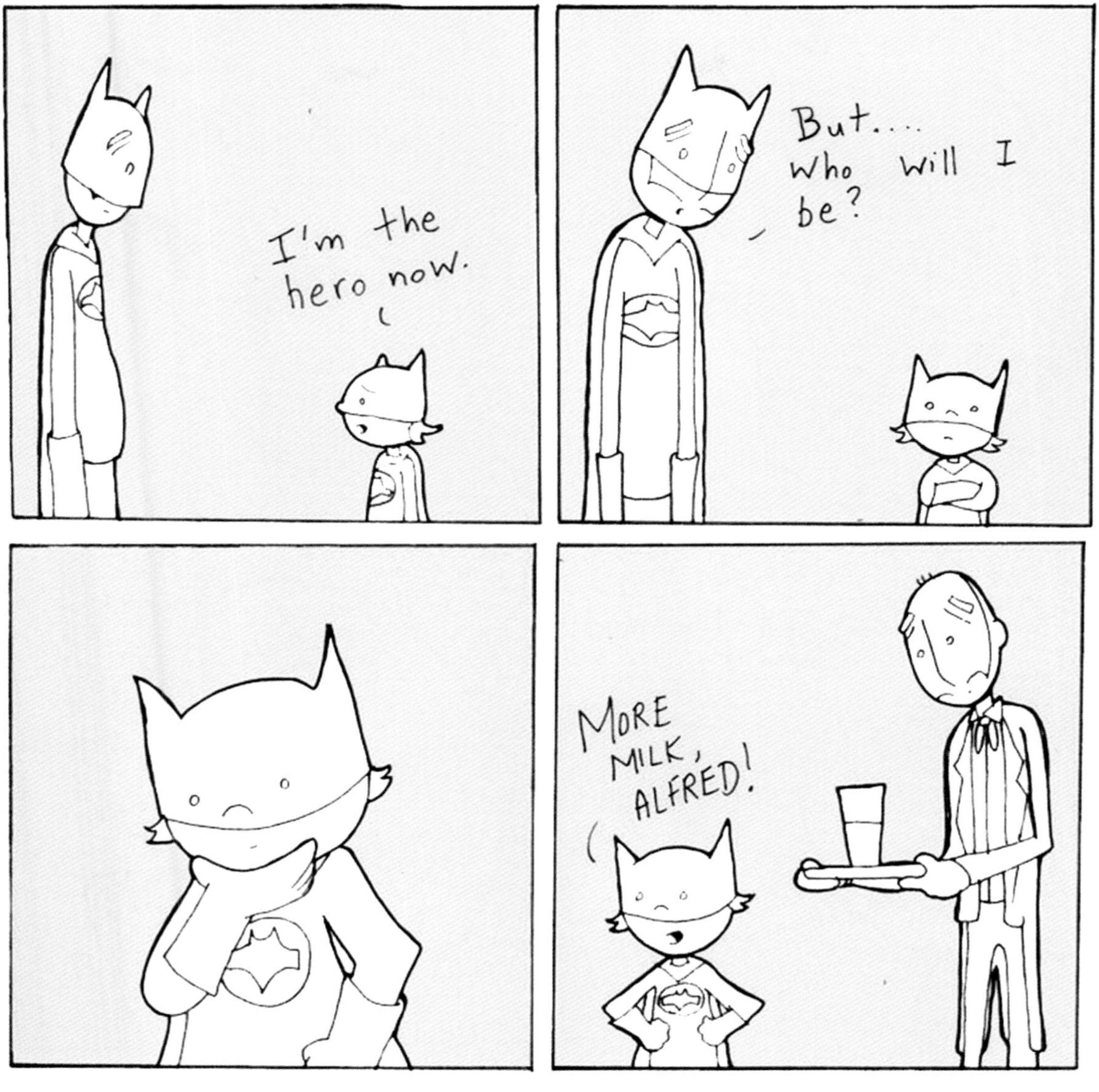
I'm the hero now.
But.... Who will I be?
MORE MILK, ALFRED!

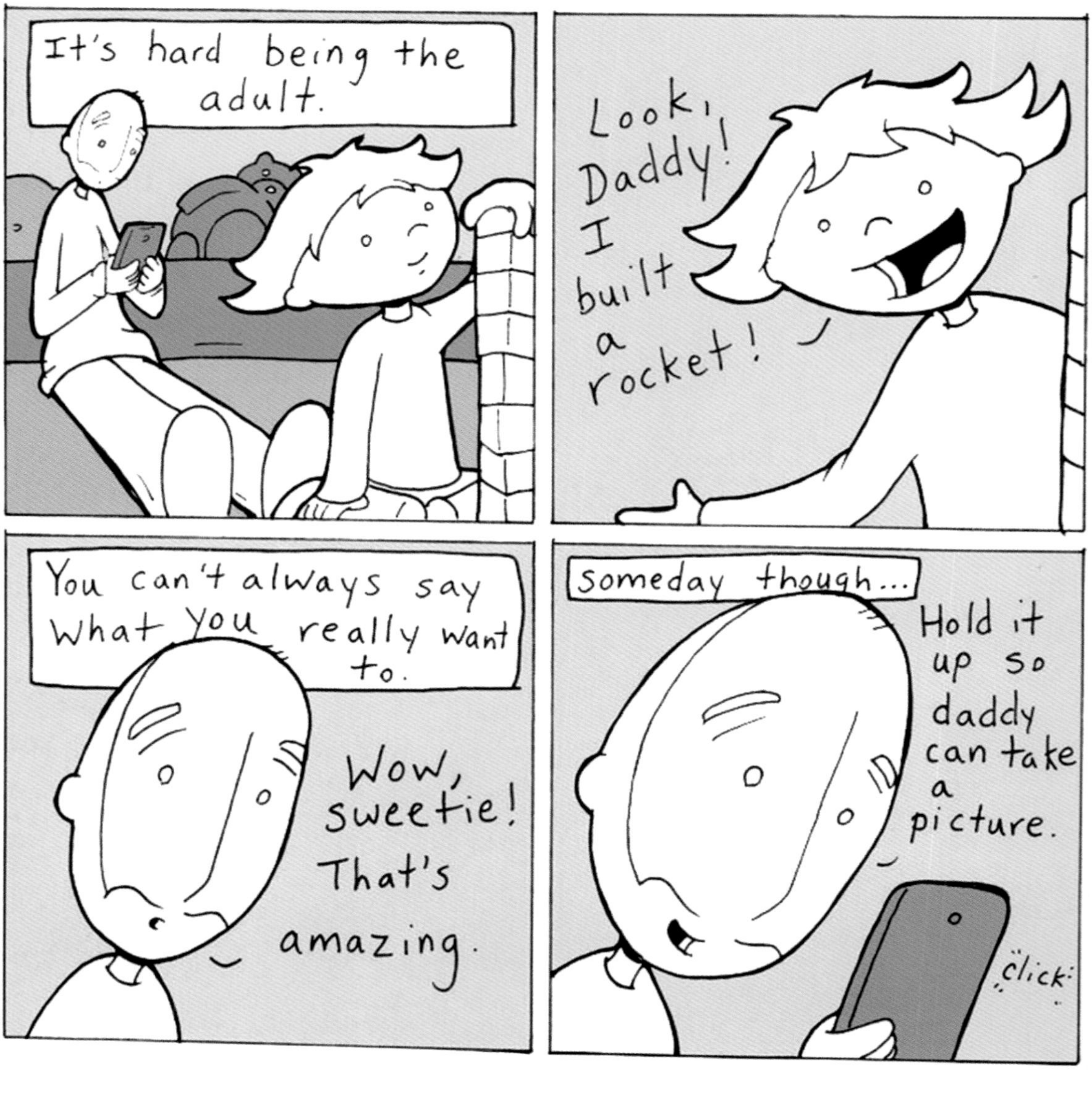
It's hard being the adult.
Look, Daddy! I built a rocket!
You can't always say what you really want to.
Wow, sweetie! That's amazing.
Someday though...
Hold it up so daddy can take a picture.
click

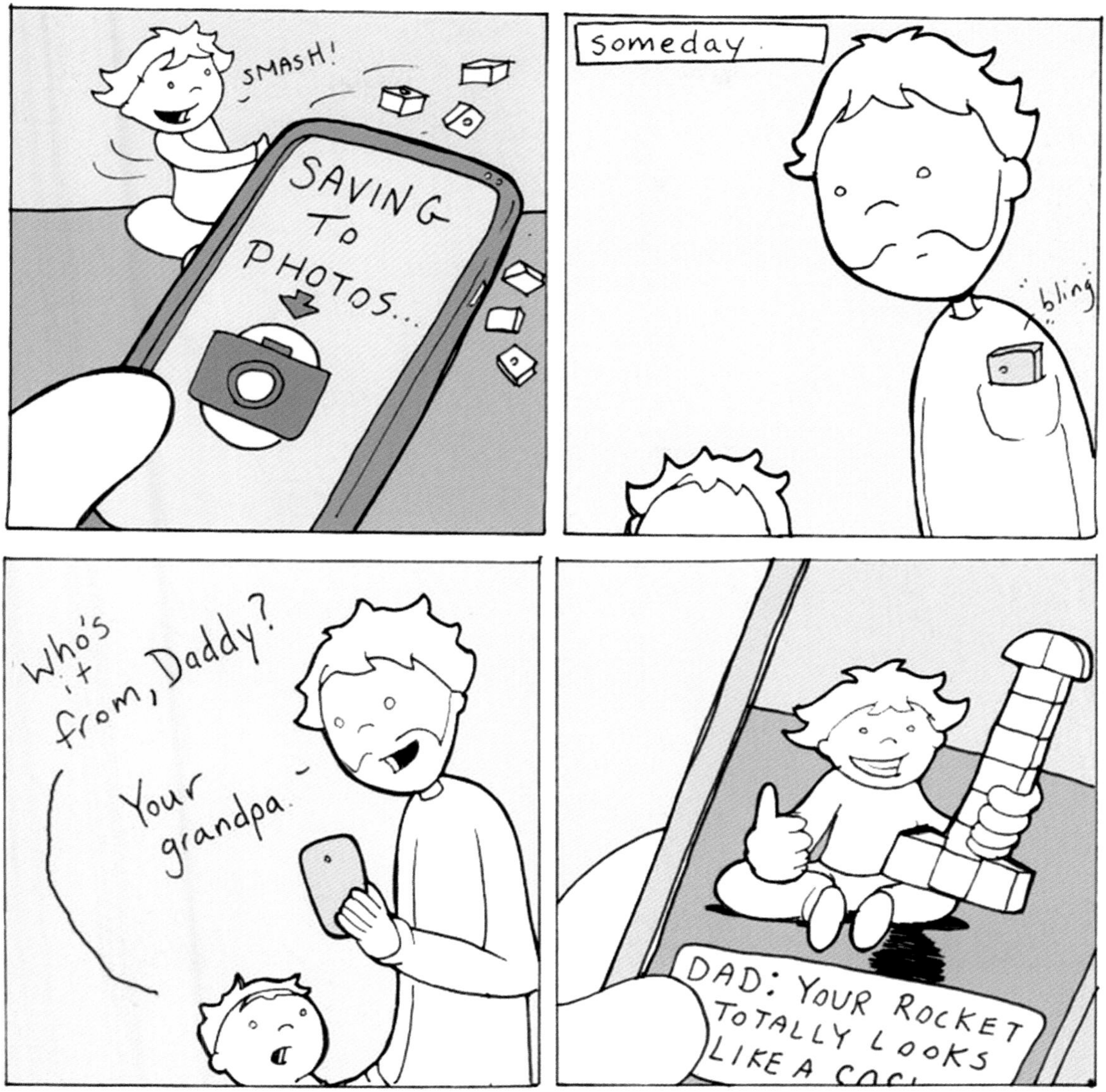
SMASH!
SAVING TO PHOTOS...
someday.
bling
Who's it from, Daddy?
Your grandpa.
DAD: YOUR ROCKET TOTALLY LOOKS LIKE A

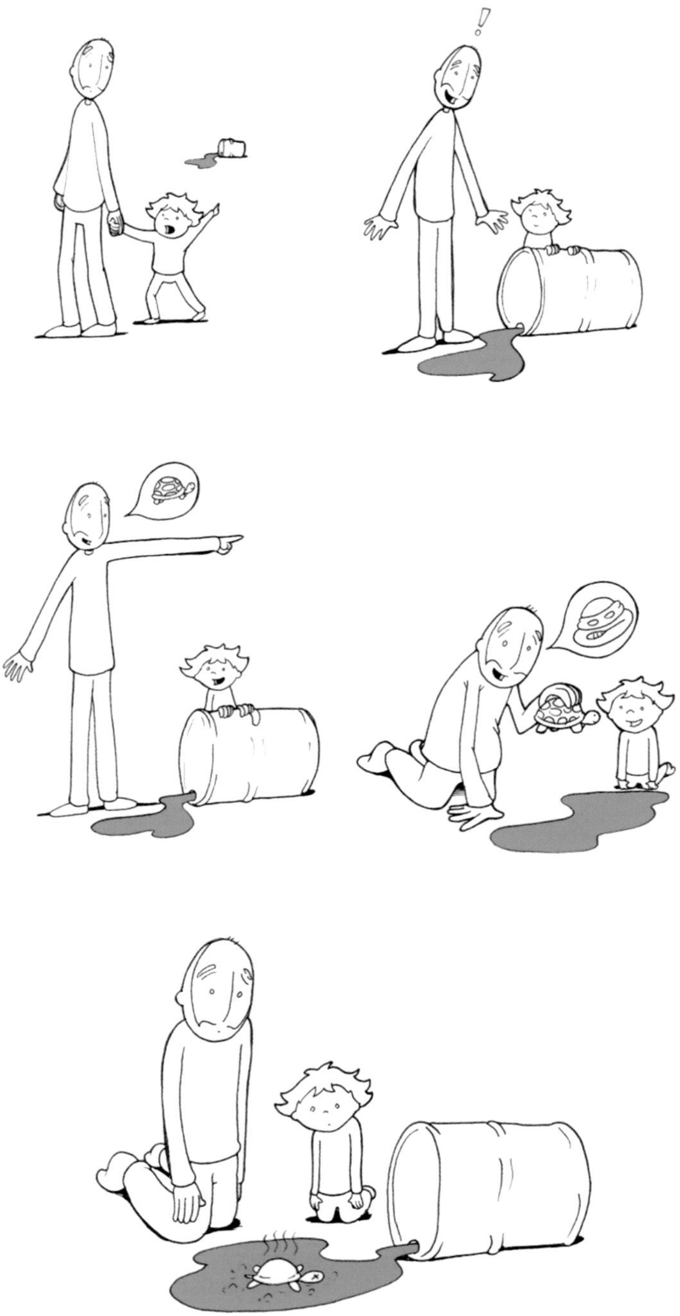
!

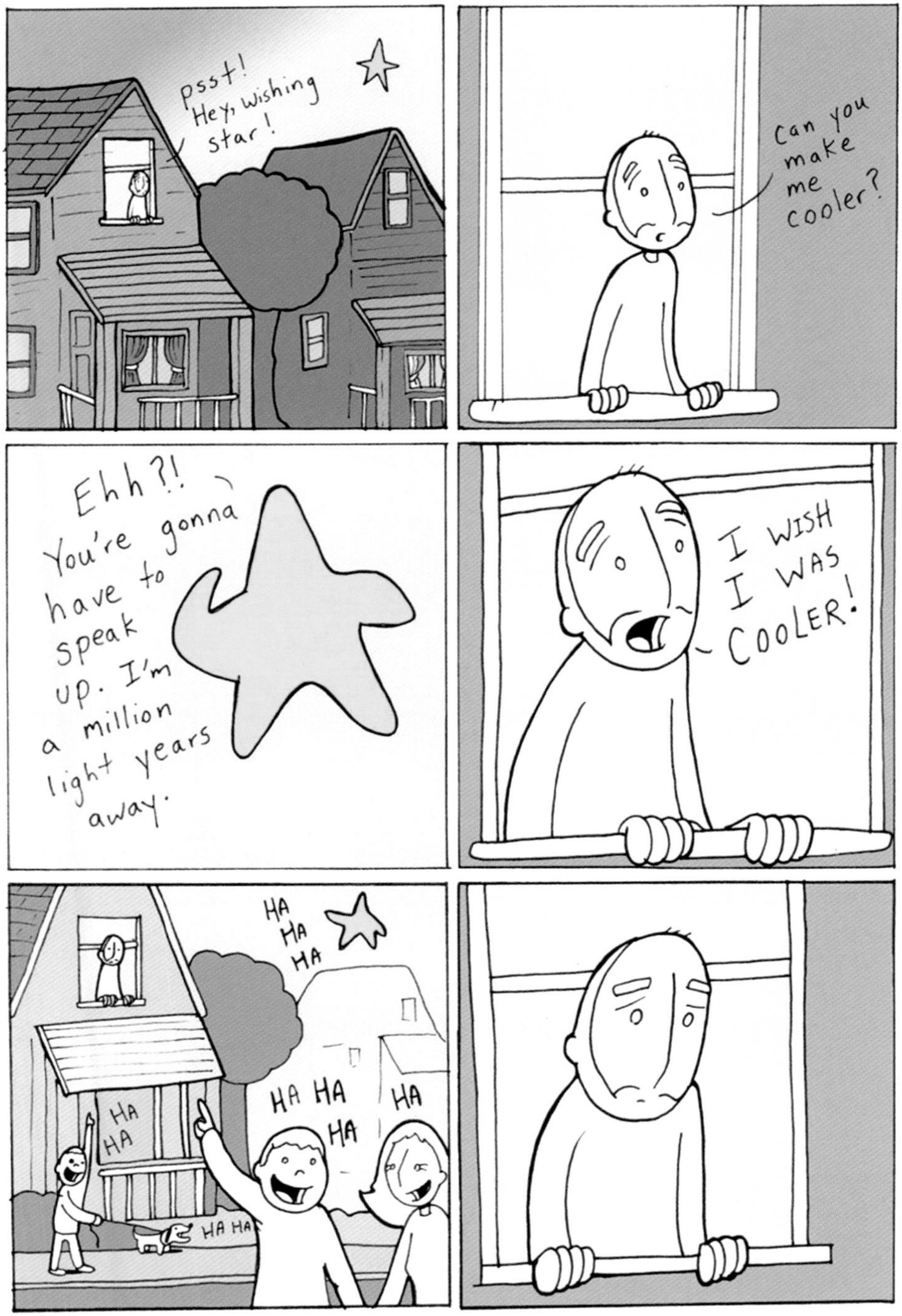
psst! Hey, wishing star!
Can you make me cooler?
Ehh?! You're gonna have to speak up. I'm a million light years away.
I WISH I WAS COOLER!
HA HA HA
HA HA
HA HA
HA HA
HA
HA HA

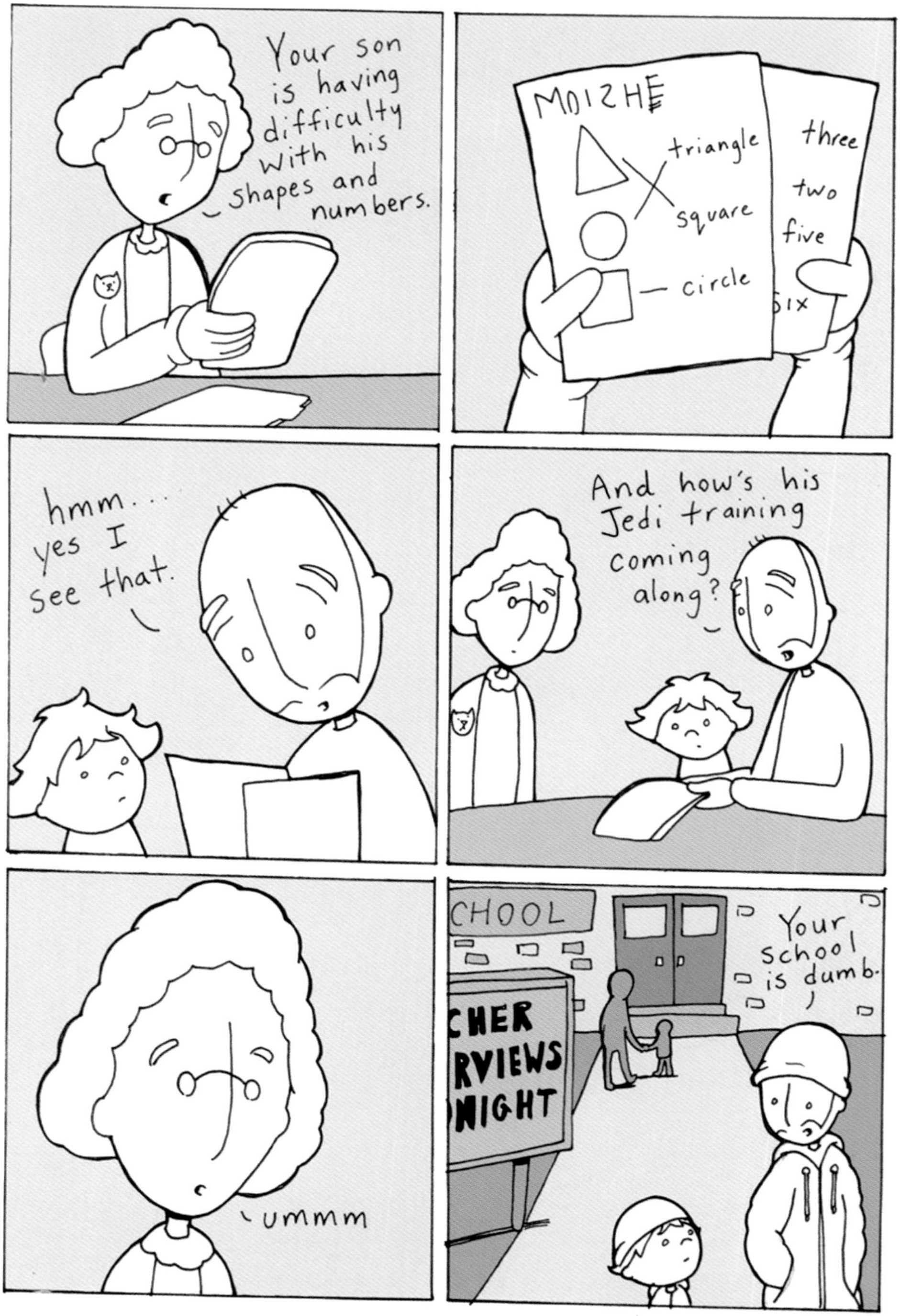
Your son is having difficulty with his shapes and numbers.
MOIZHE
triangle
square
circle
three
two
five
six
hmm... yes I see that.
And how's his Jedi training coming along?
ummm
CHOOL
CHER
RVIEWS
NIGHT
Your school is dumb.

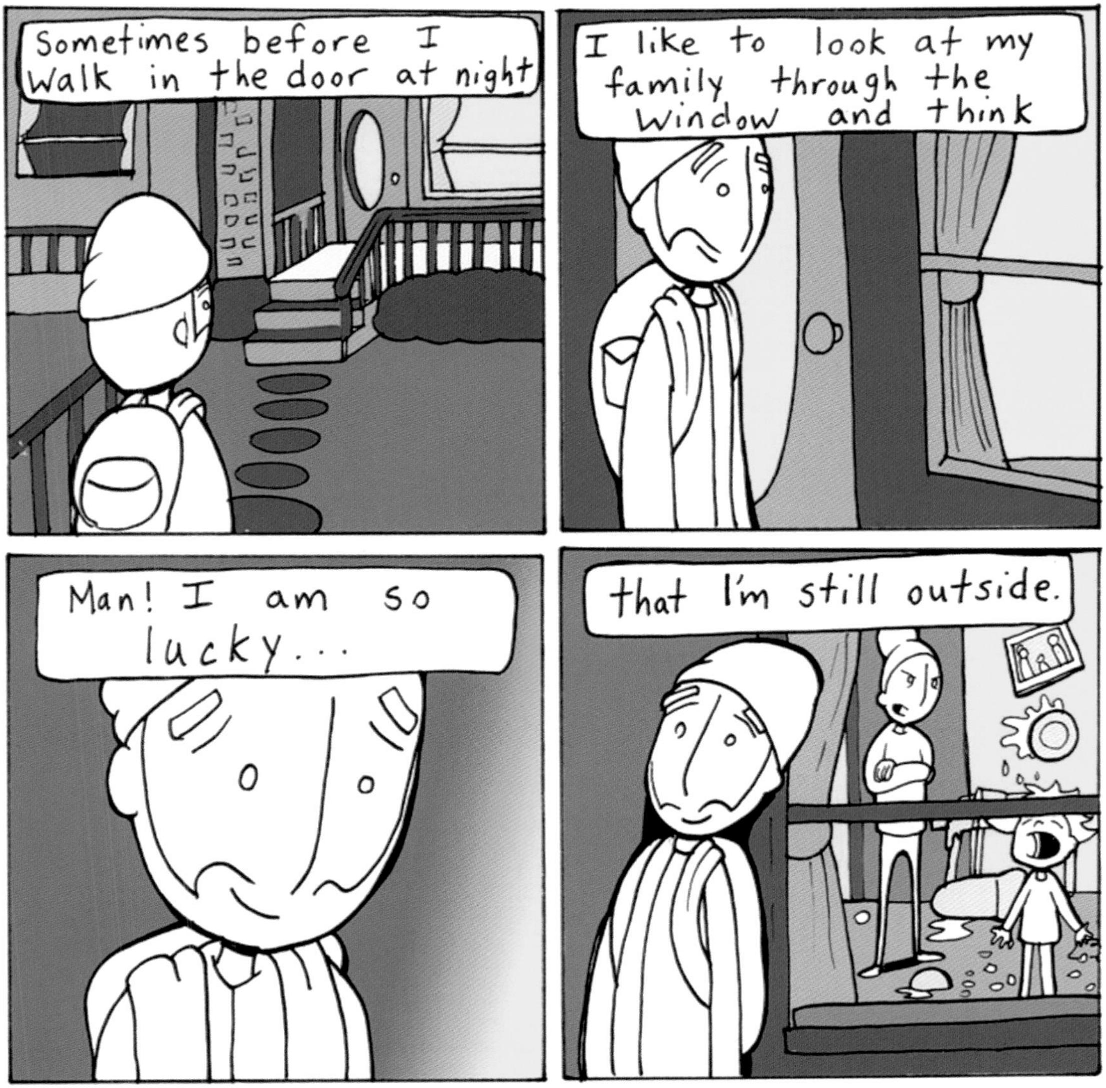
Sometimes before I walk in the door at night
I like to look at my family through the window and think
Man! I am so lucky...
that I'm still outside.

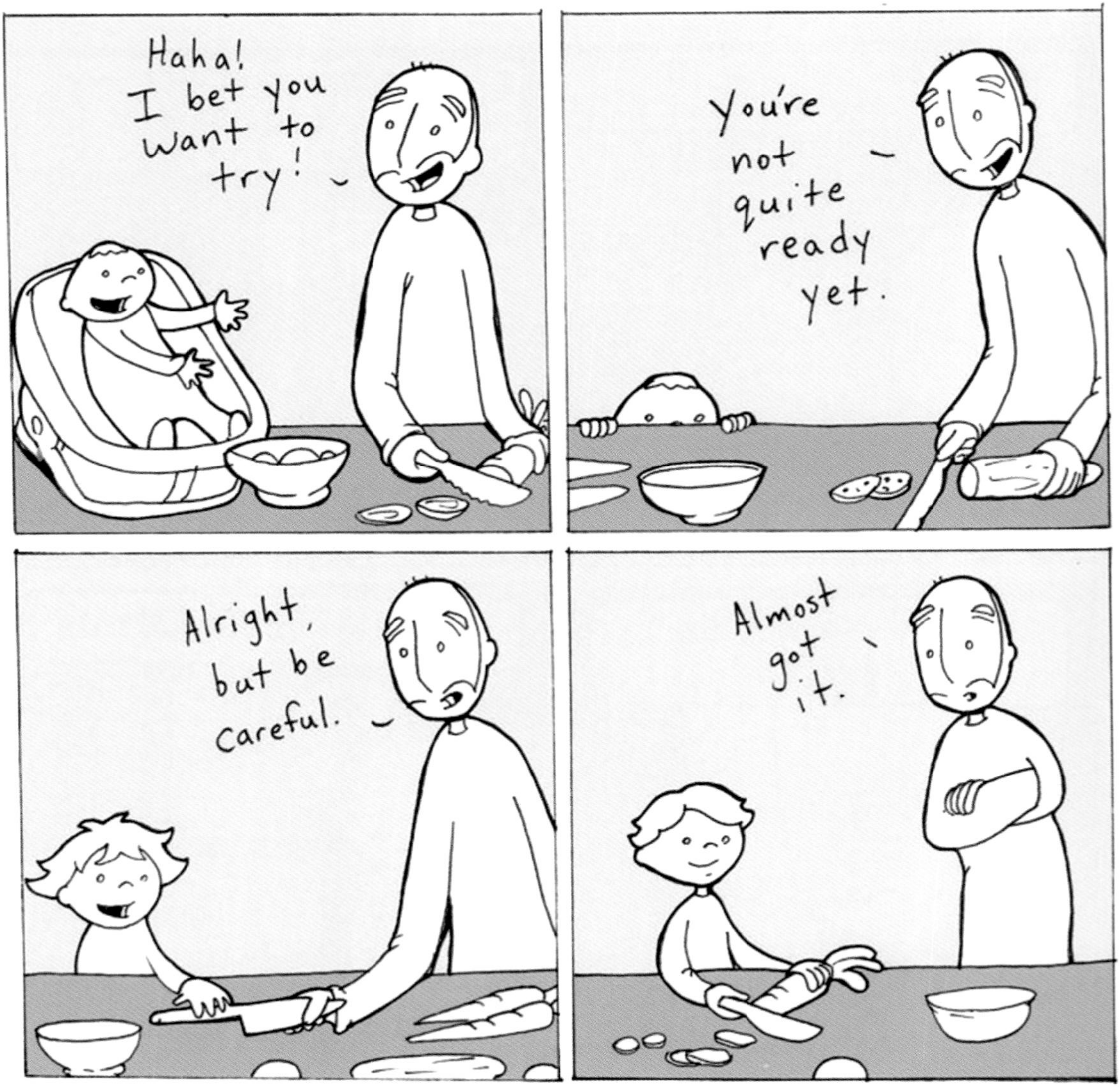
Haha! I bet you want to try!
You're not quite ready yet.
Alright, but be careful.
Almost got it.

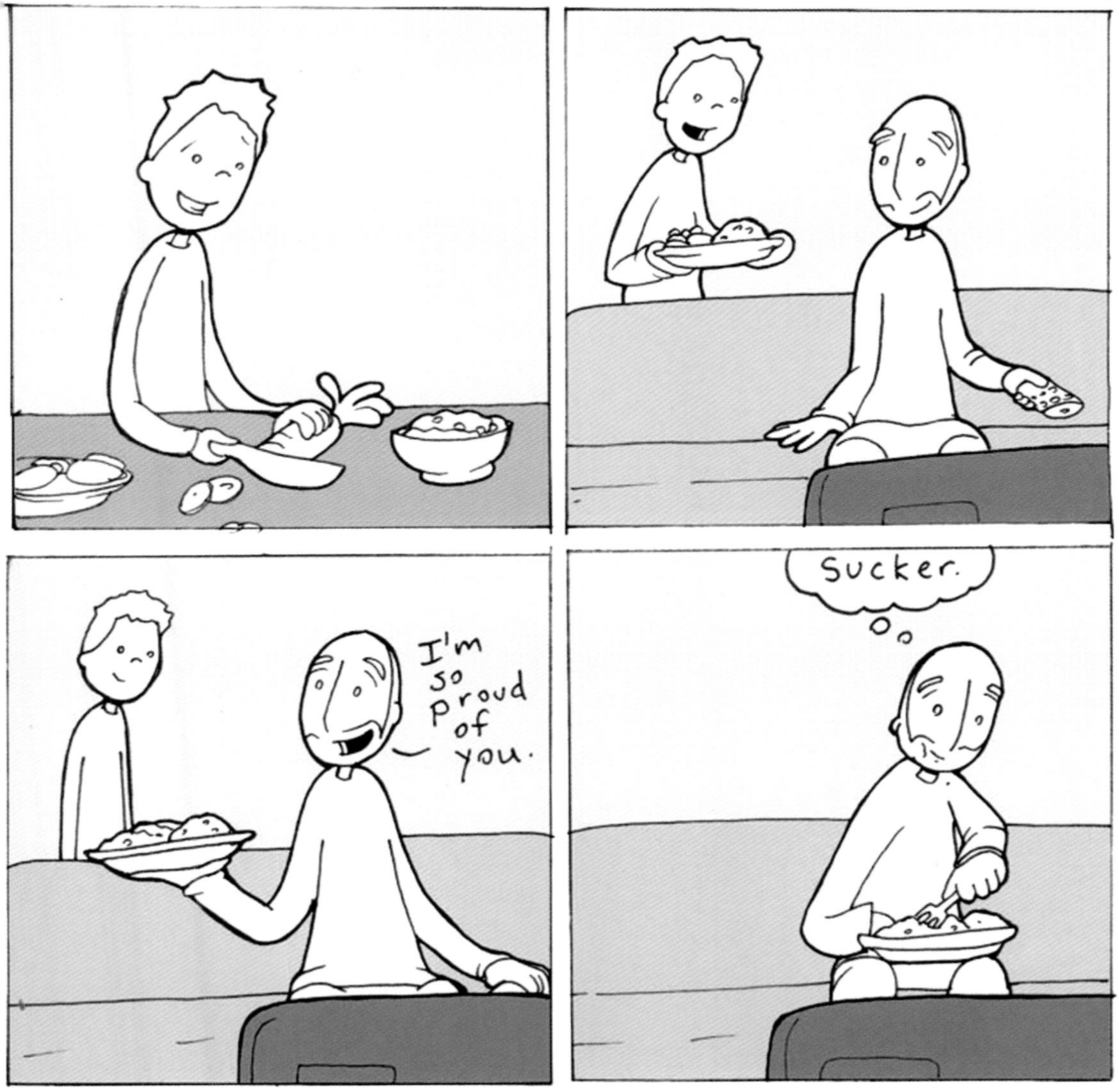
I'm so proud of you.
Sucker.

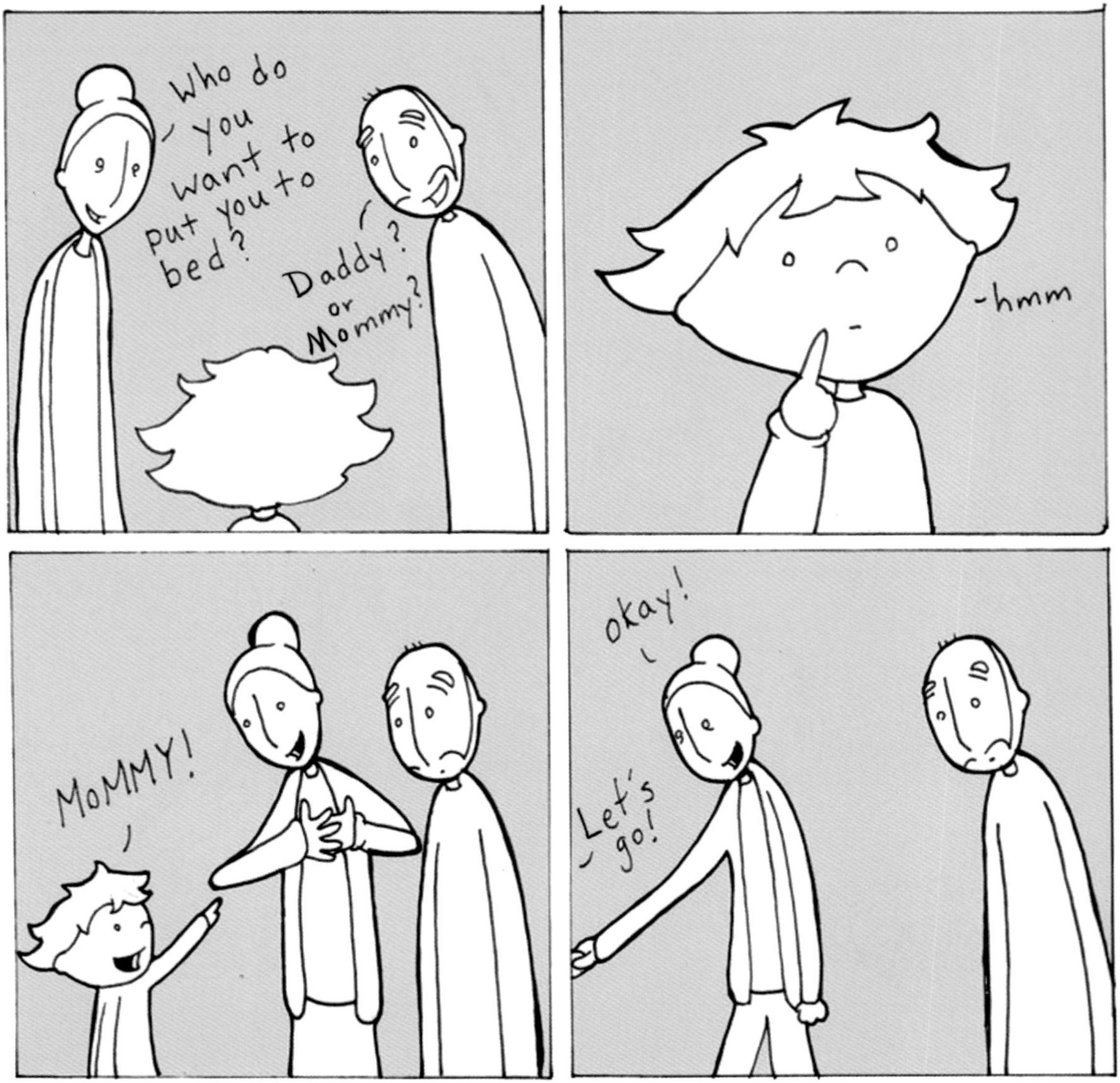
Who do you want to put you to bed?
Daddy? or Mommy?
-hmm
MOMMY!
okay!
Let's go!

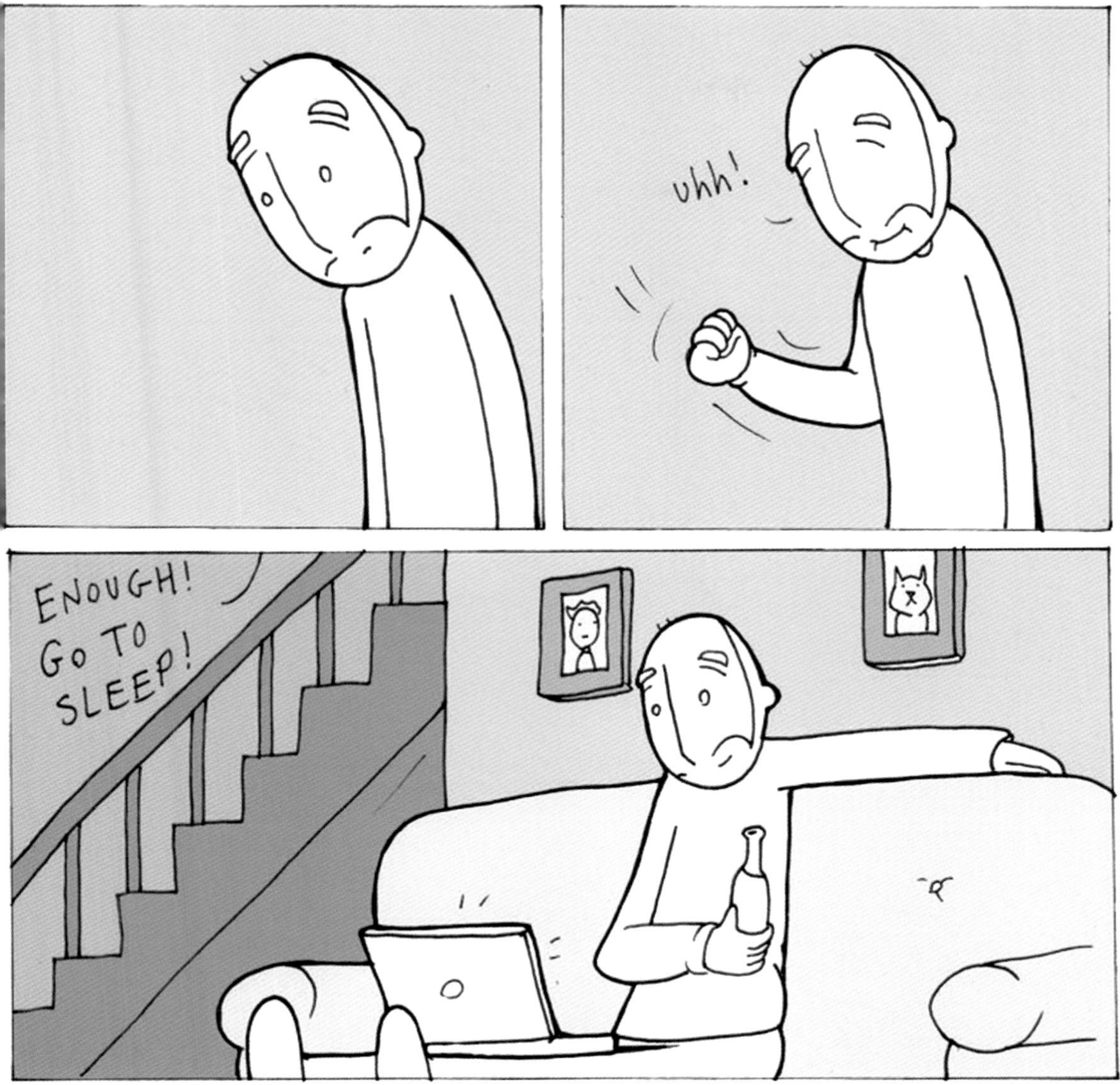
uhh!
ENOUGH! Go TO SLEEP!

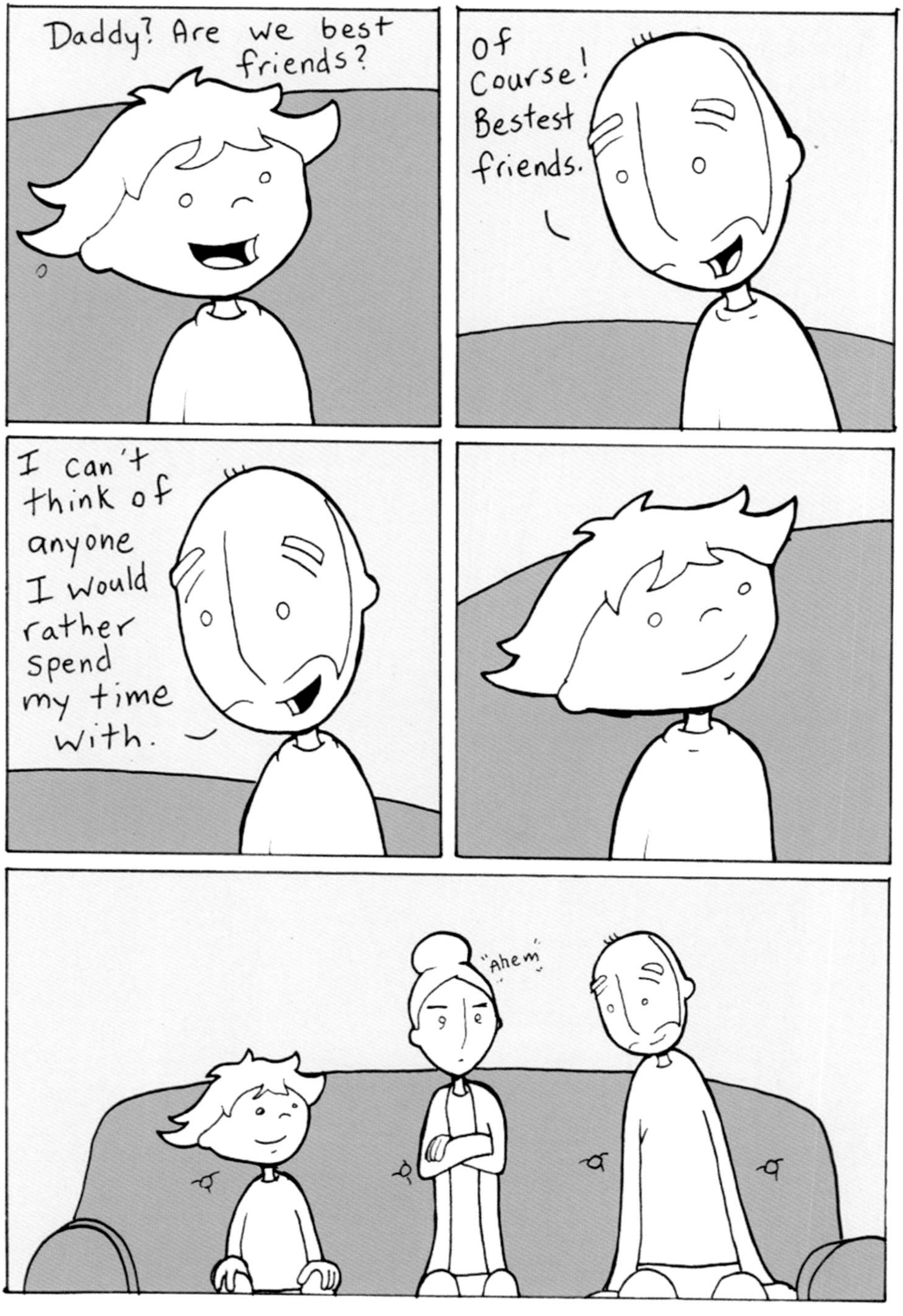
Daddy? Are we best friends?
Of Course! Bestest friends.
I can't think of anyone I would rather spend my time with.
"Ahem"

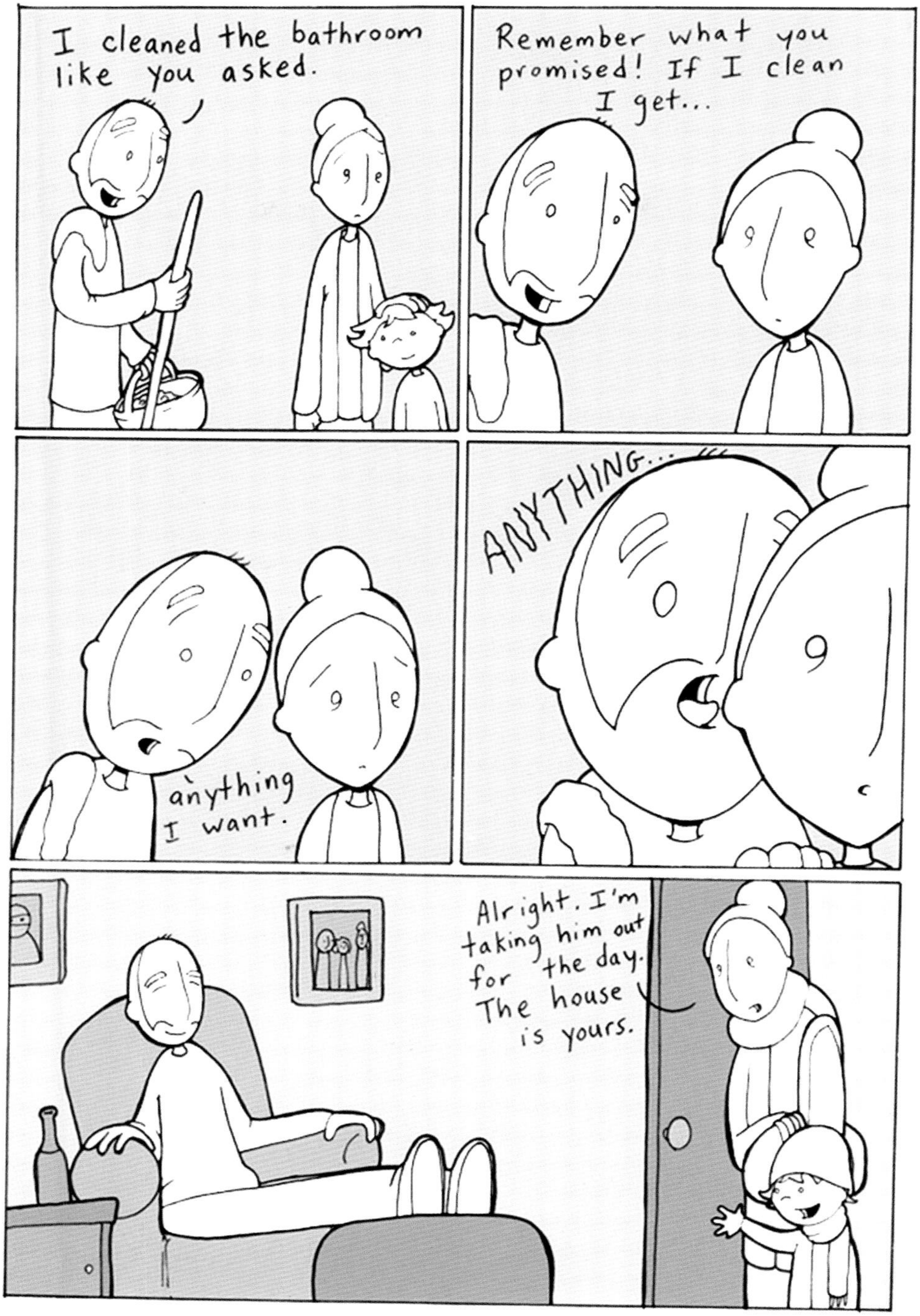
I cleaned the bathroom like you asked.
Remember what you promised! If I clean I get...
anything I want.
ANYTHING...
Alright. I'm taking him out for the day. The house is yours.

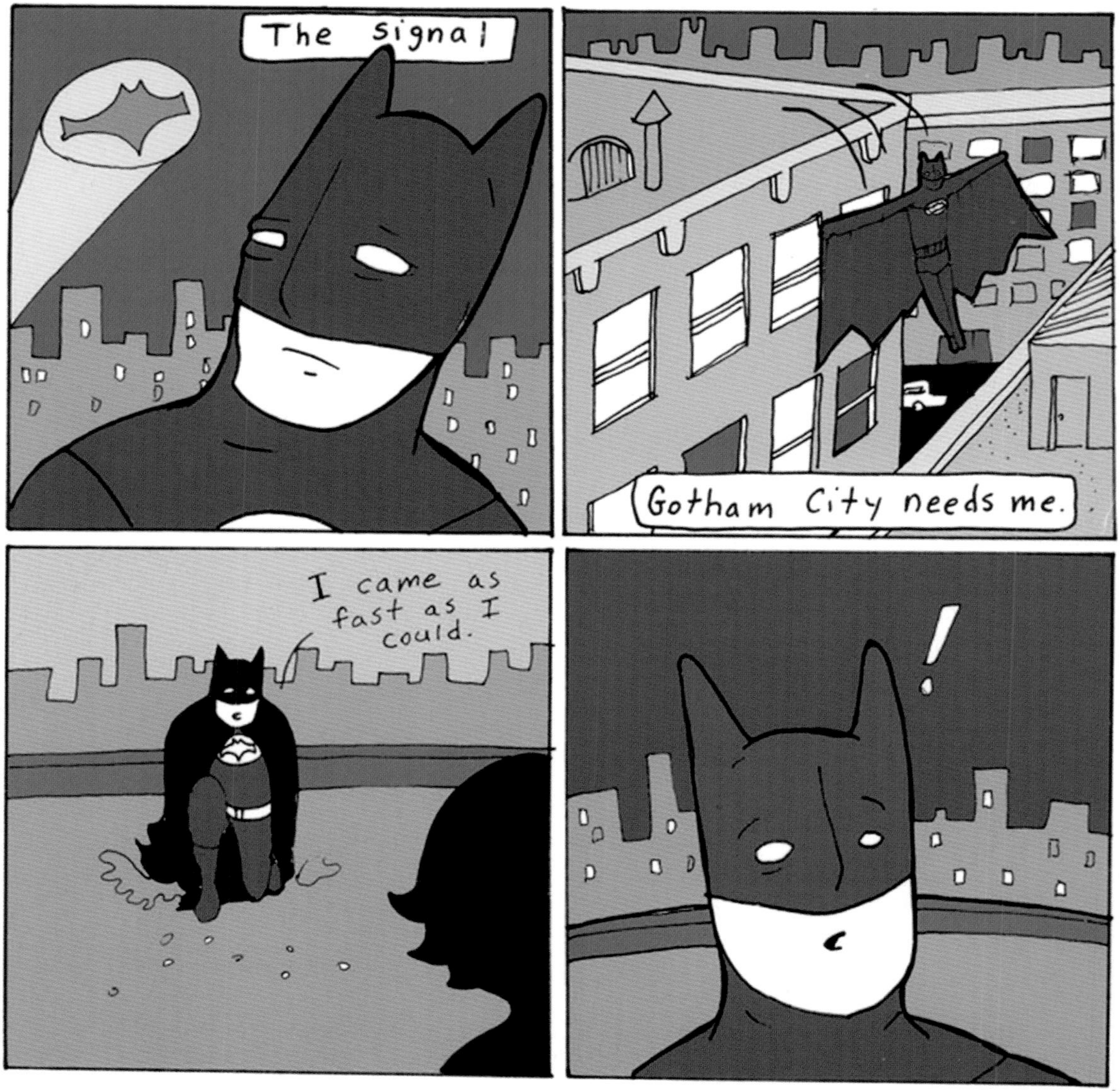
The signal
Gotham City needs me.
I came as fast as I could.
!

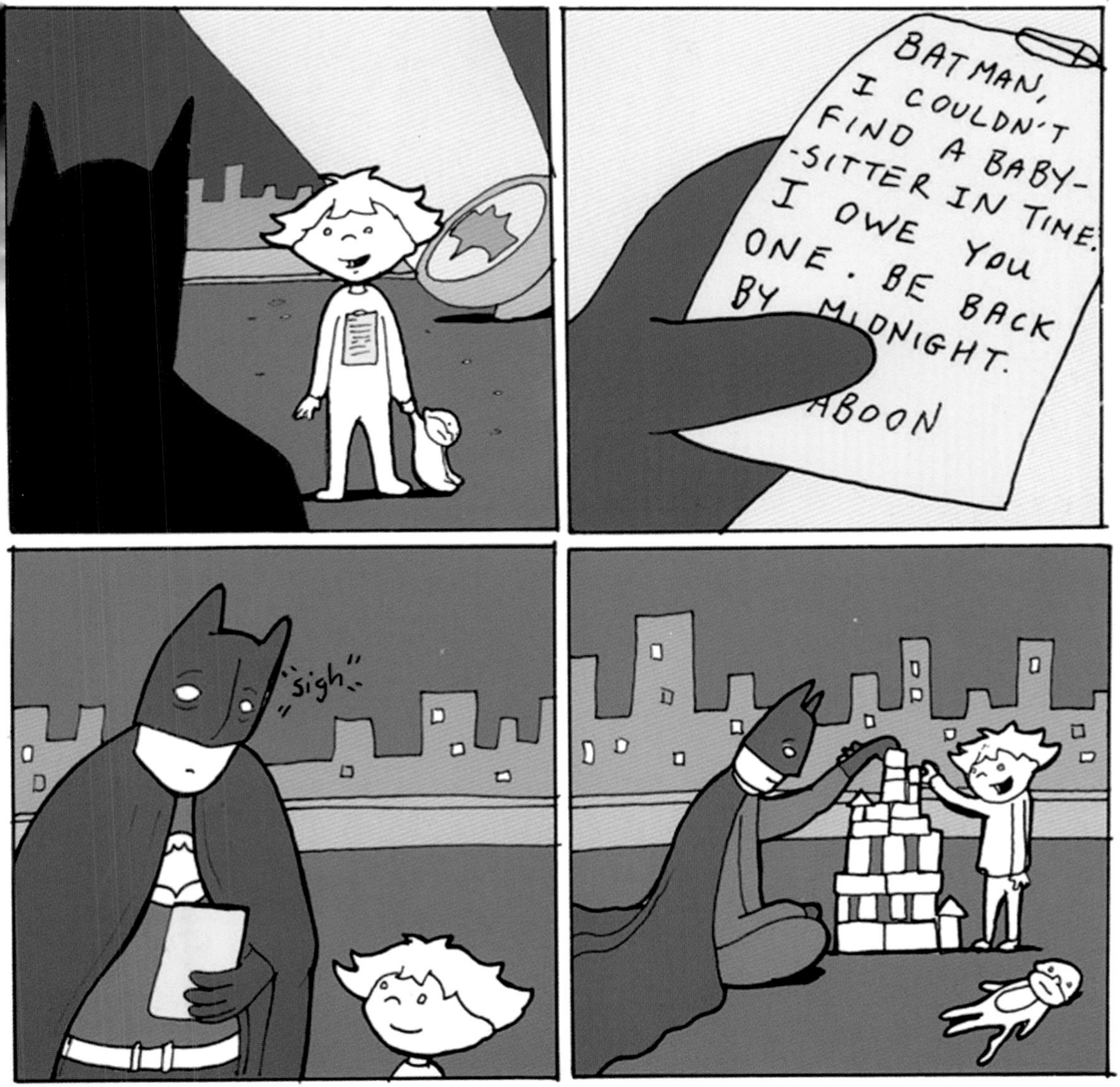
BATMAN,
I COULDN'T
FIND A BABY-
-SITTER IN TIME.
I OWE YOU
ONE. BE BACK
BY MIDNIGHT.
ABOON
sigh

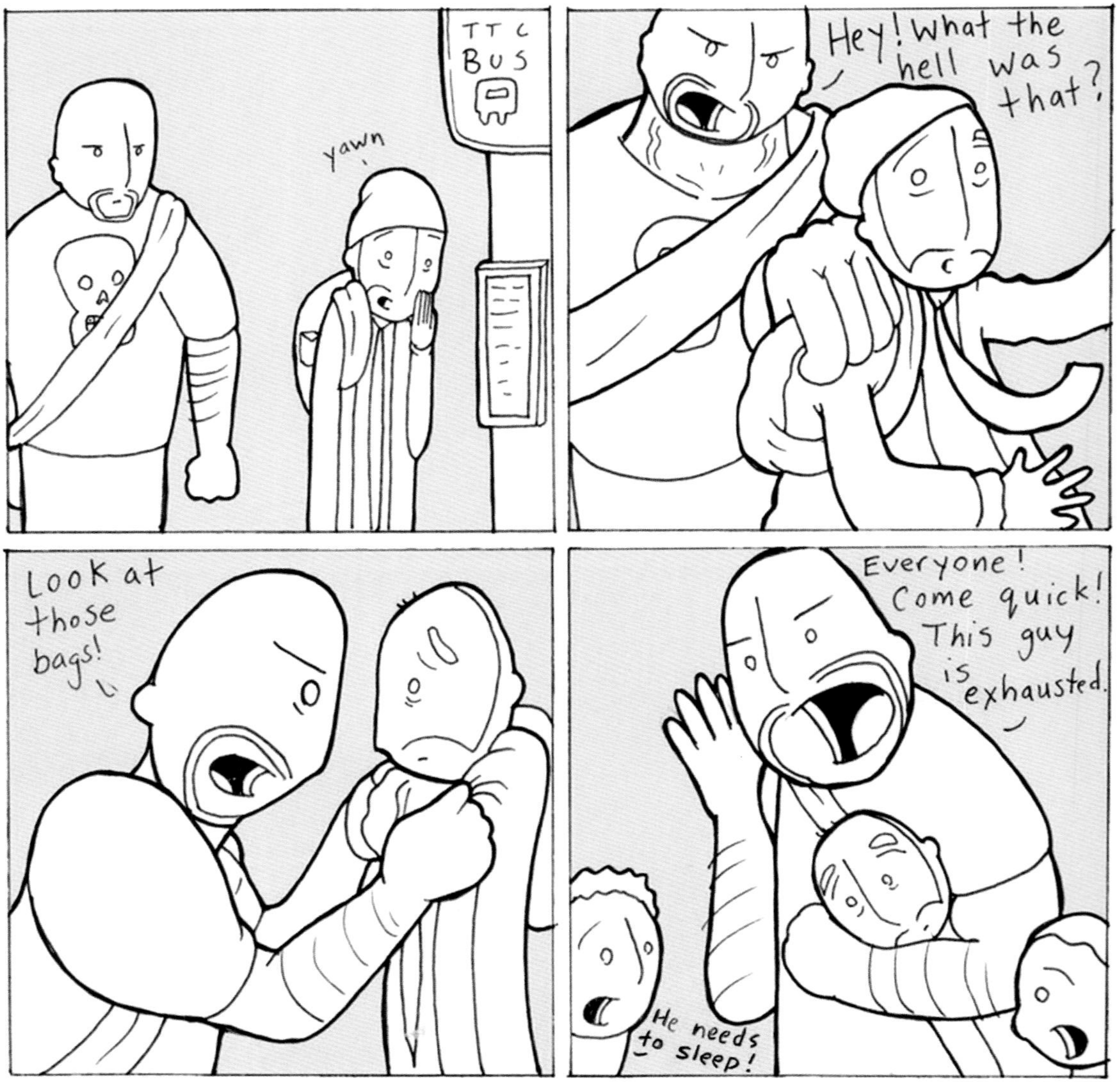

TTC BUS
yawn
Hey! What the hell was that?
Look at those bags!
Everyone! Come quick! This guy is exhausted.
He needs to sleep!

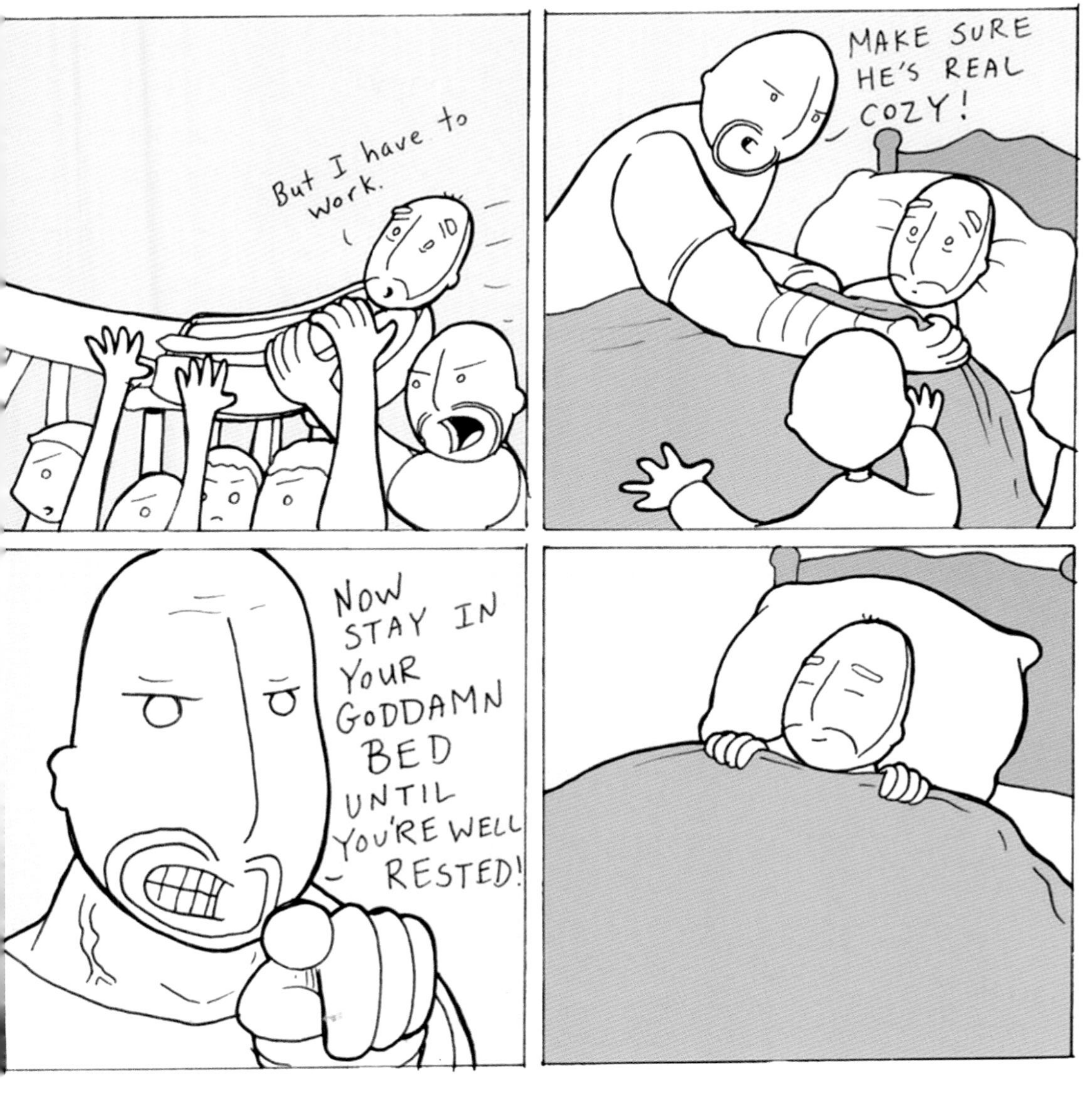
But I have to work.
MAKE SURE HE'S REAL COZY!
NOW STAY IN YOUR GODDAMN BED UNTIL YOU'RE WELL RESTED!

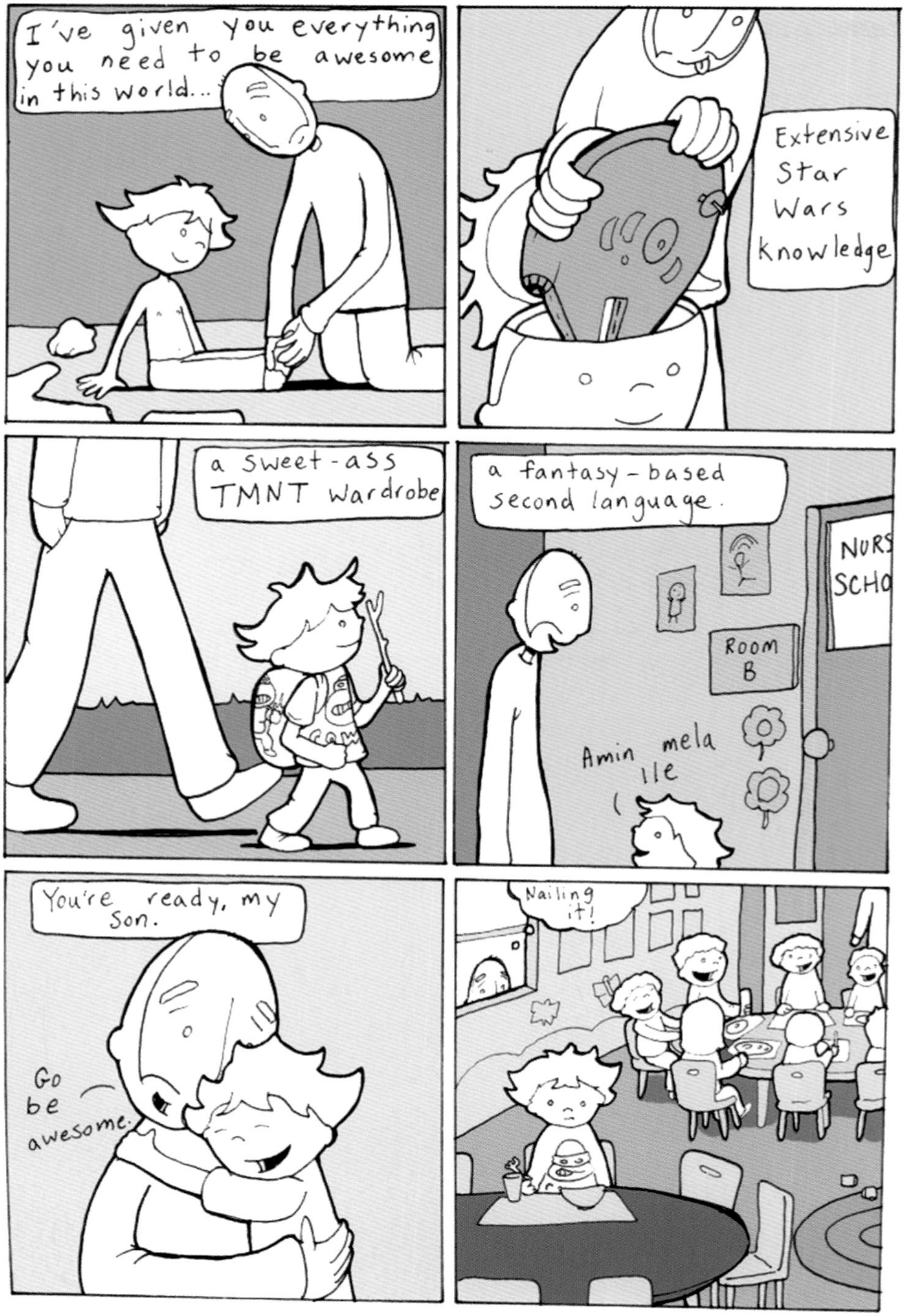

I've given you everything you need to be awesome in this world...
Extensive Star Wars knowledge
a sweet-ass TMNT wardrobe
a fantasy-based second language.
NURS SCHO
ROOM B
Amin mela lle
You're ready, my son.
Go be awesome.
Nailing it!

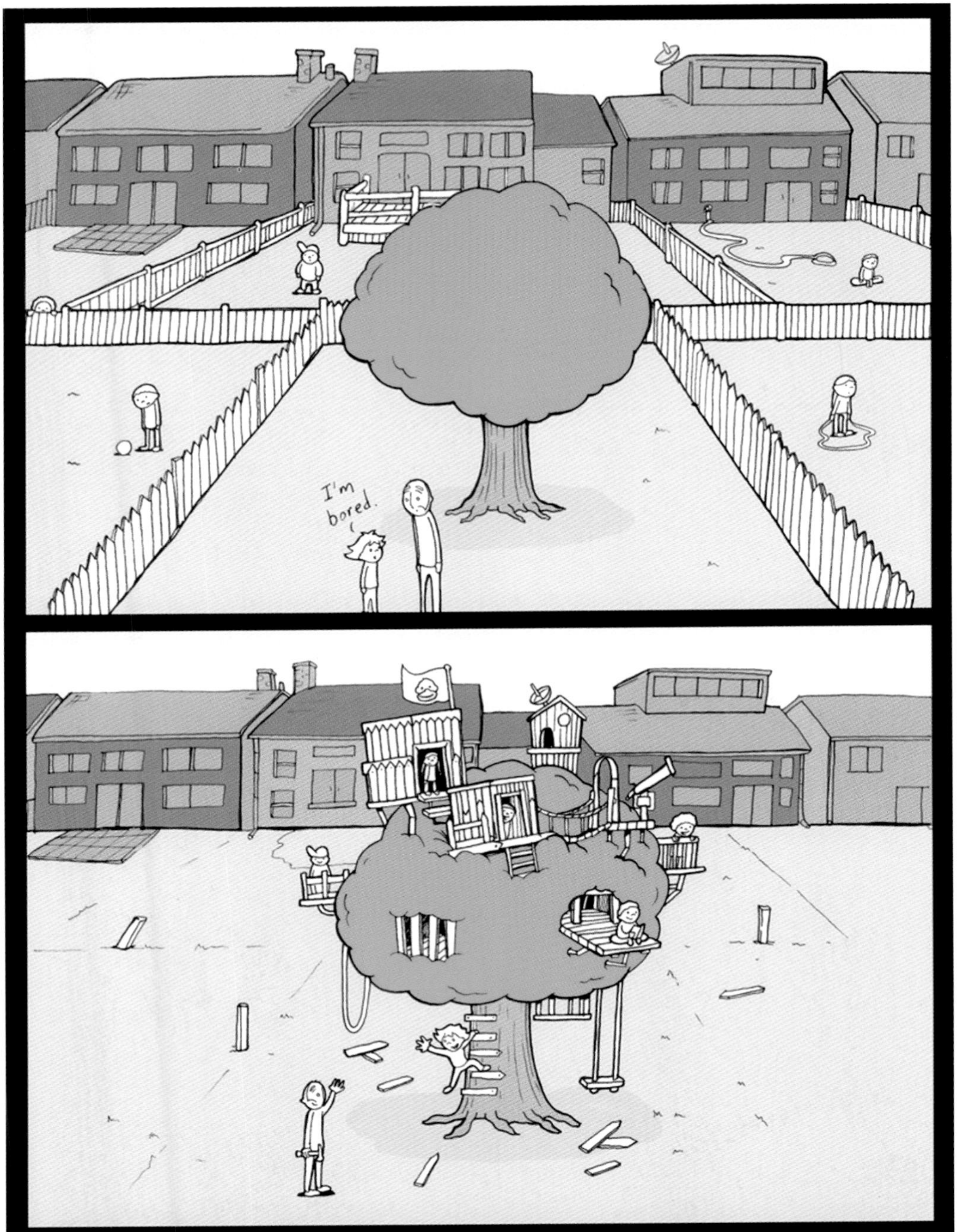
I'm bored.

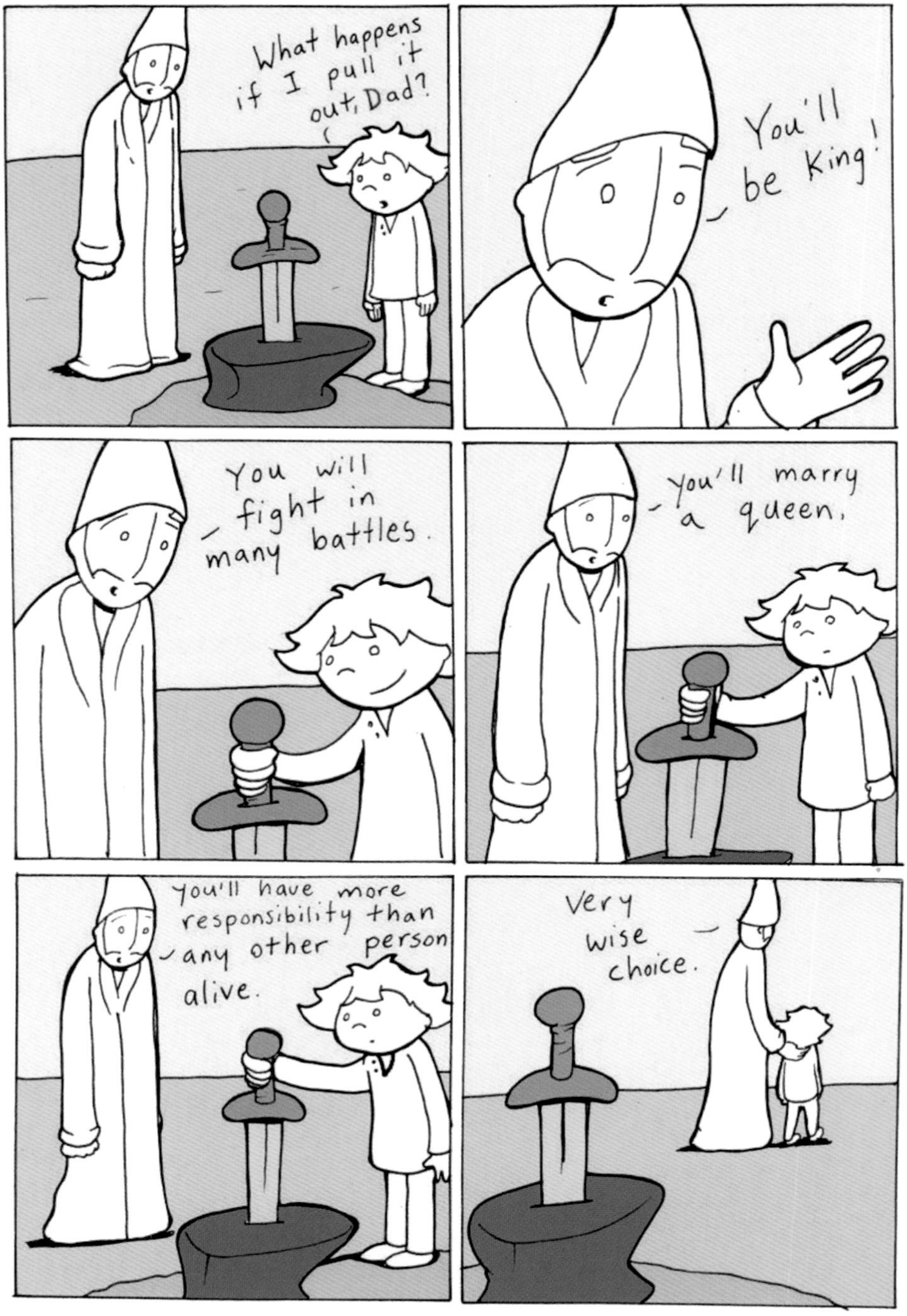
What happens if I pull it out, Dad?
You'll be King!
You will fight in many battles.
You'll marry a queen.
You'll have more responsibility than any other person alive.
Very wise choice.

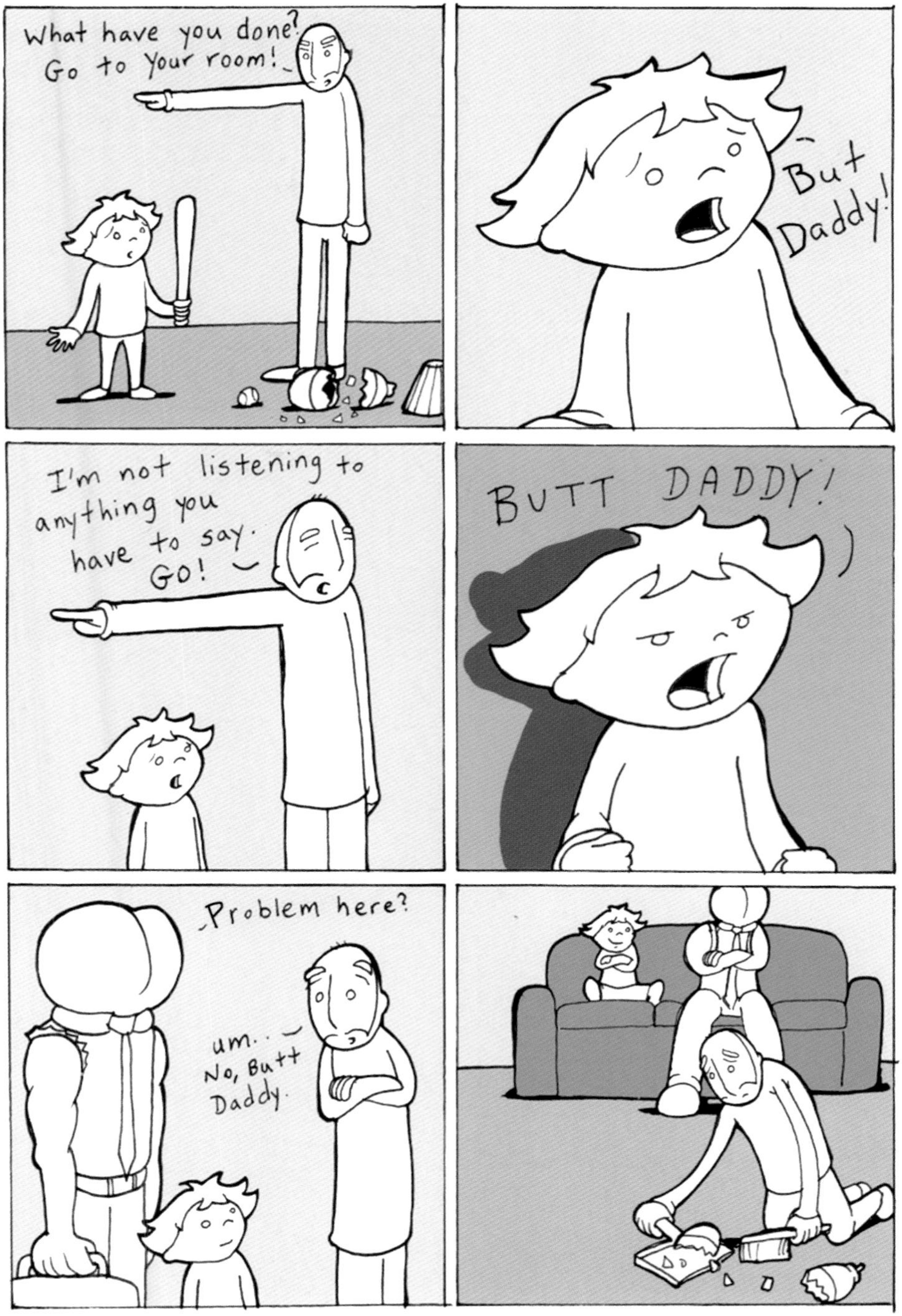
What have you done? Go to your room!
But Daddy!
I'm not listening to anything you have to say. GO!
BUTT DADDY!
Problem here?
um... No, Butt Daddy.

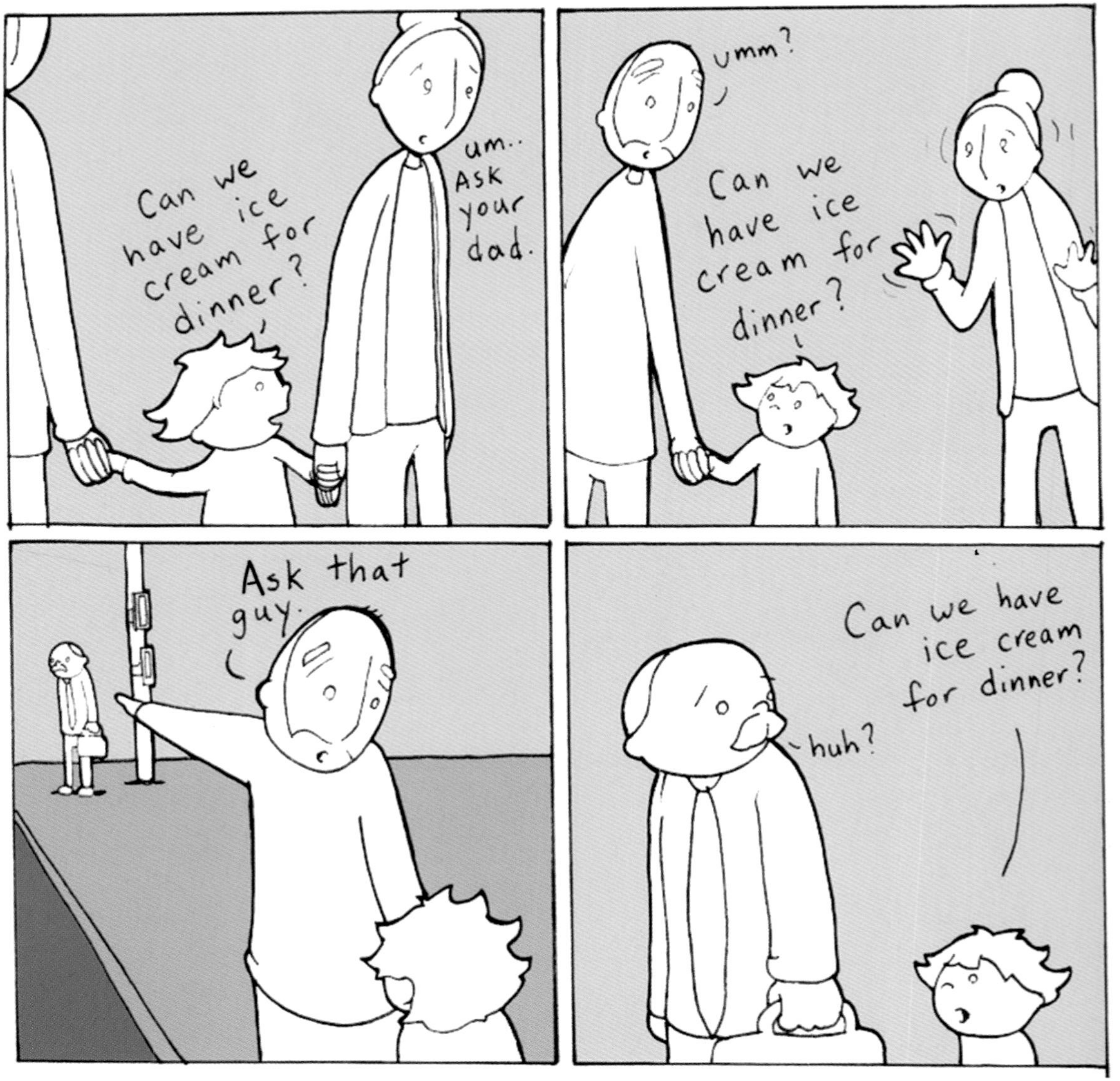
Can we have ice cream for dinner?
um.. Ask your dad.
umm?
Can we have ice cream for dinner?
Ask that guy.
huh?
Can we have ice cream for dinner?

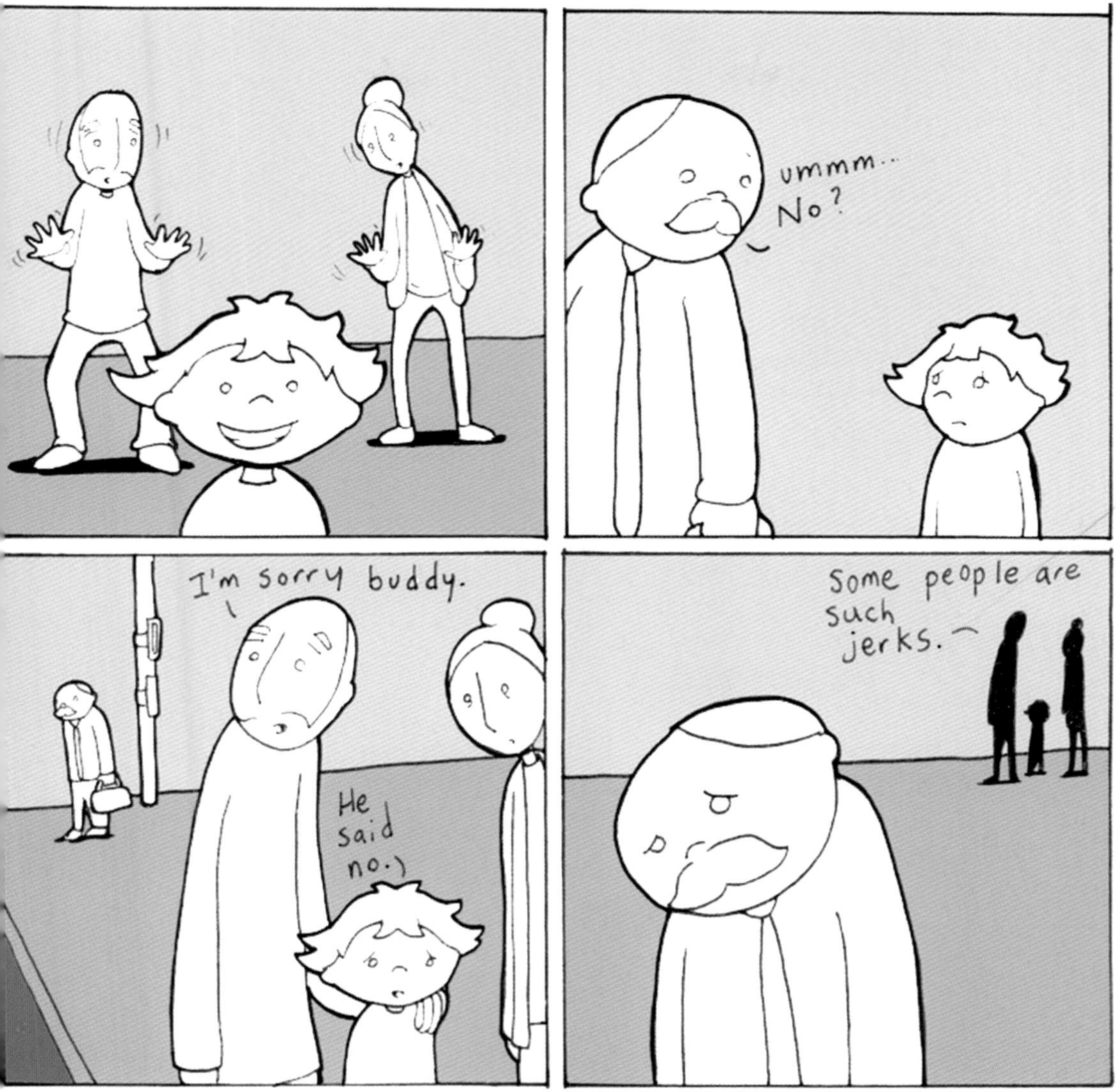
ummm..
No?
I'm sorry buddy.
He said no.
Some people are such jerks.

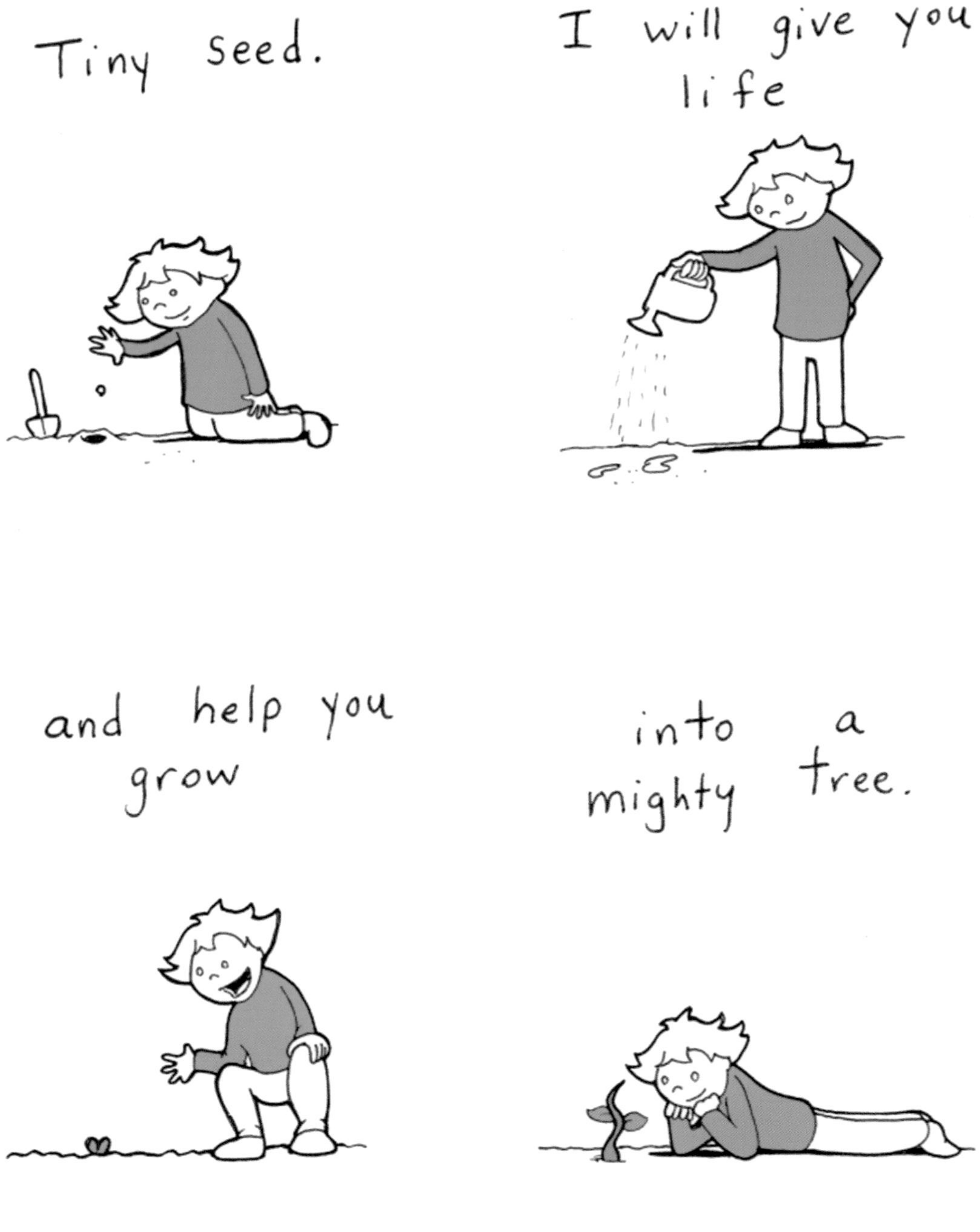
Tiny seed.
I will give you life
and help you grow
into a mighty tree.

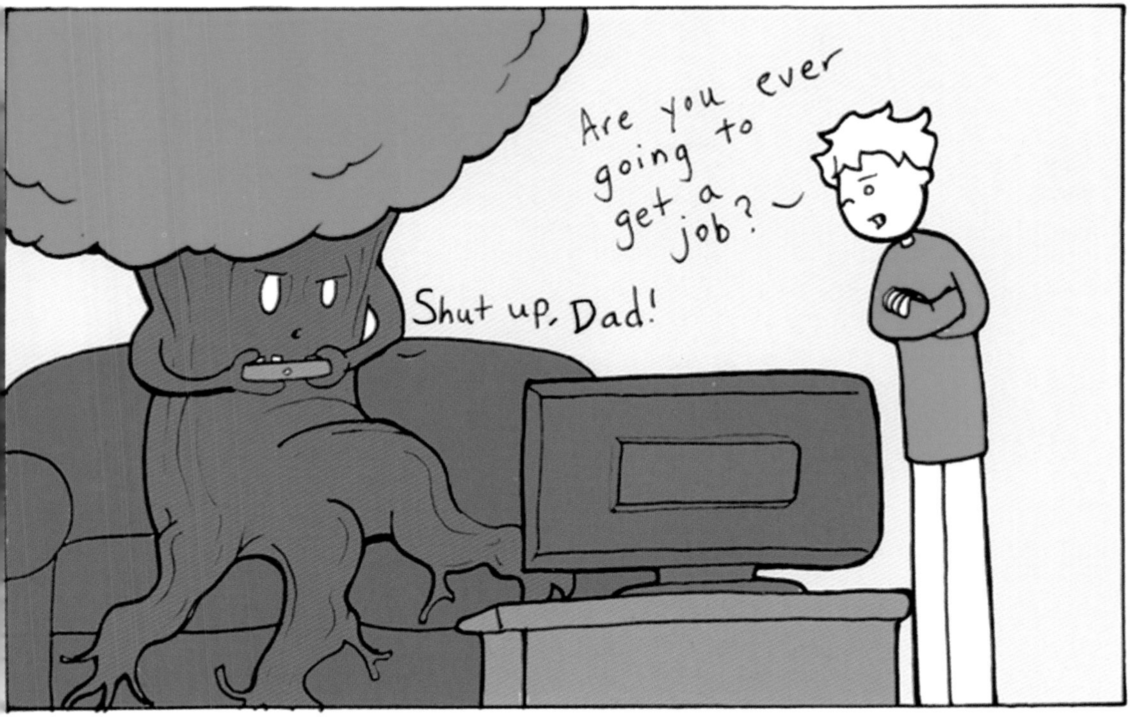
Are you ever going to get a job?
Shut up, Dad!

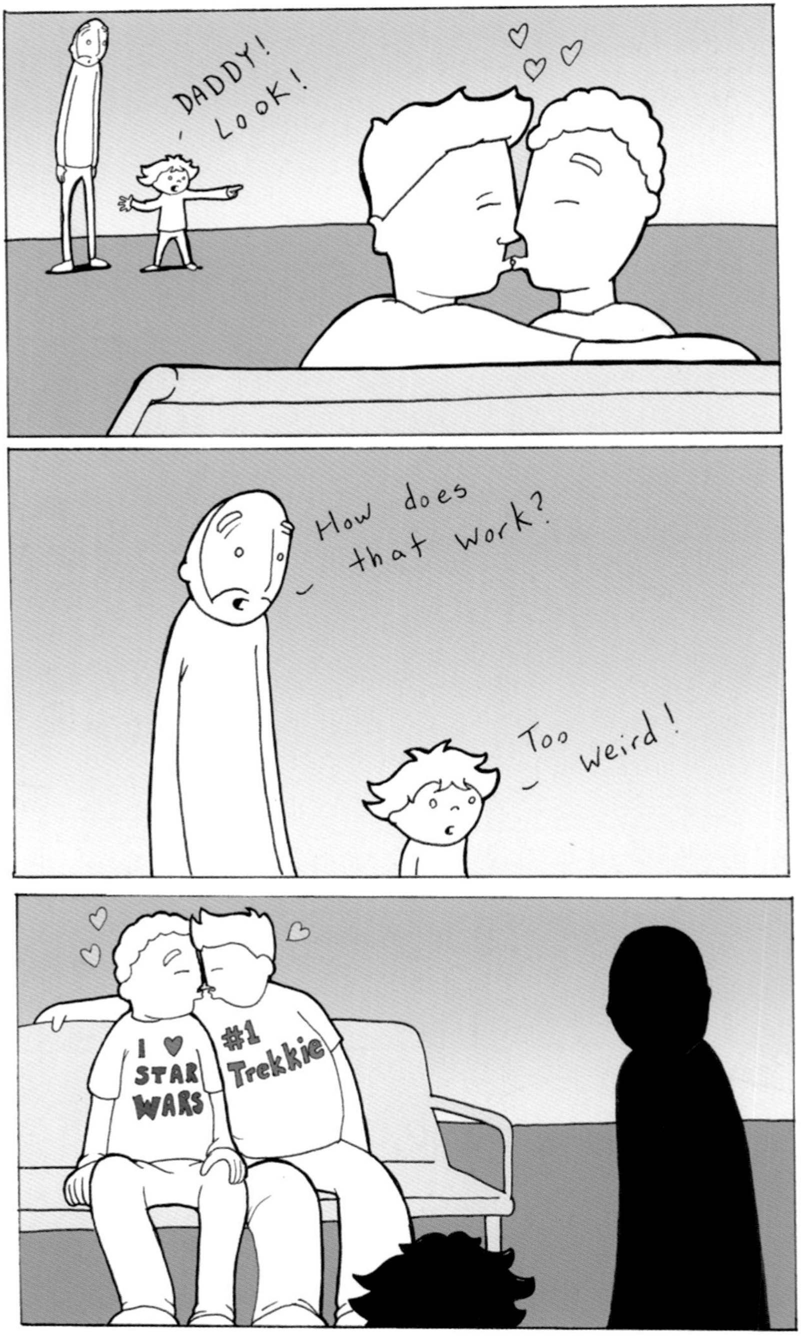
DADDY! LOOK!
How does that work?
Too weird!
I ♥ STAR WARS
#1 Trekkie

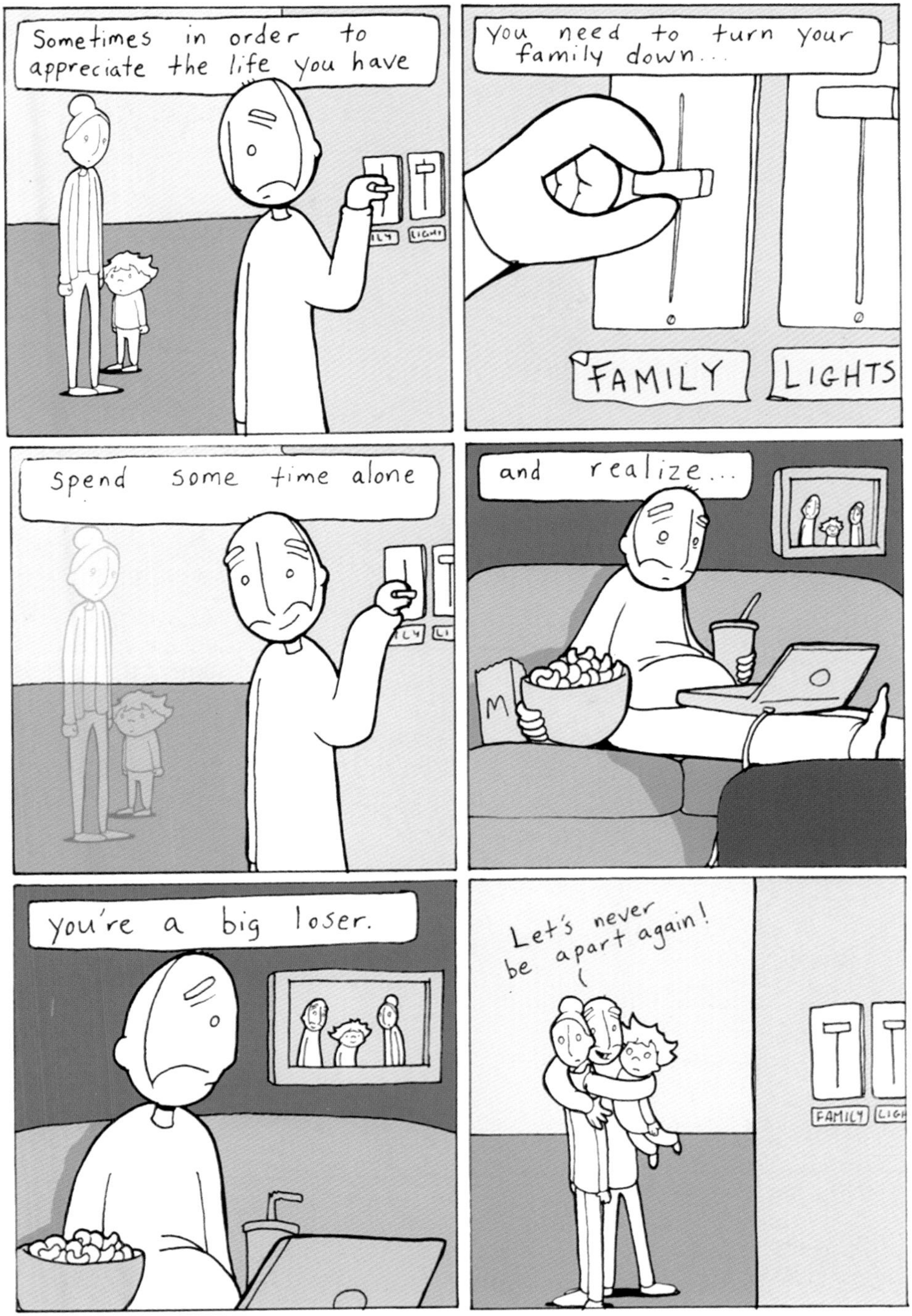

Sometimes in order to appreciate the life you have
You need to turn your family down...
FAMILY
LIGHTS
spend some time alone
and realize...
you're a big loser.
Let's never be apart again!
FAMILY

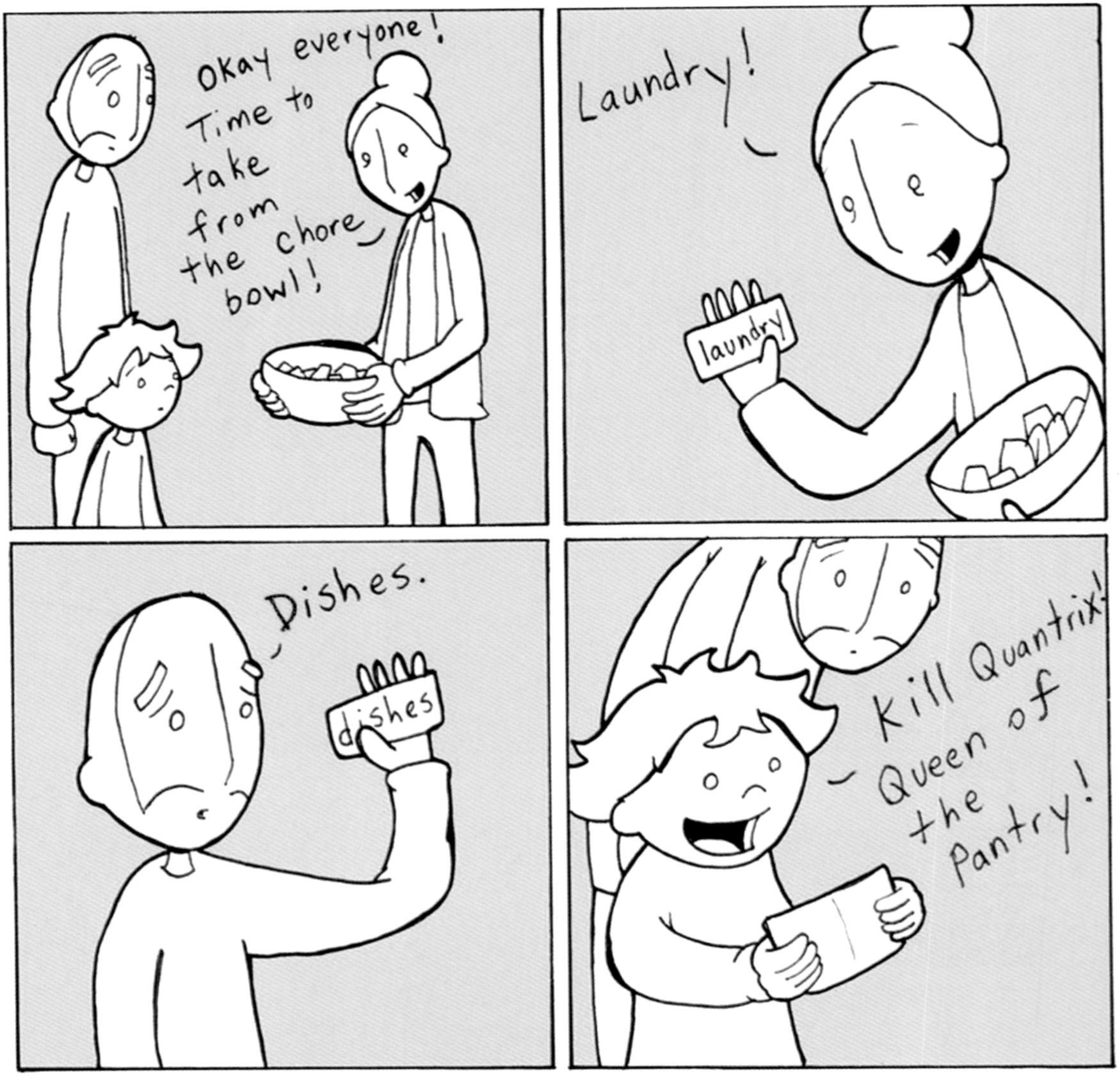
Okay everyone! Time to take from the chore bowl!
Laundry!
laundry
Dishes.
dishes
Kill Quantrix! Queen of the Pantry!

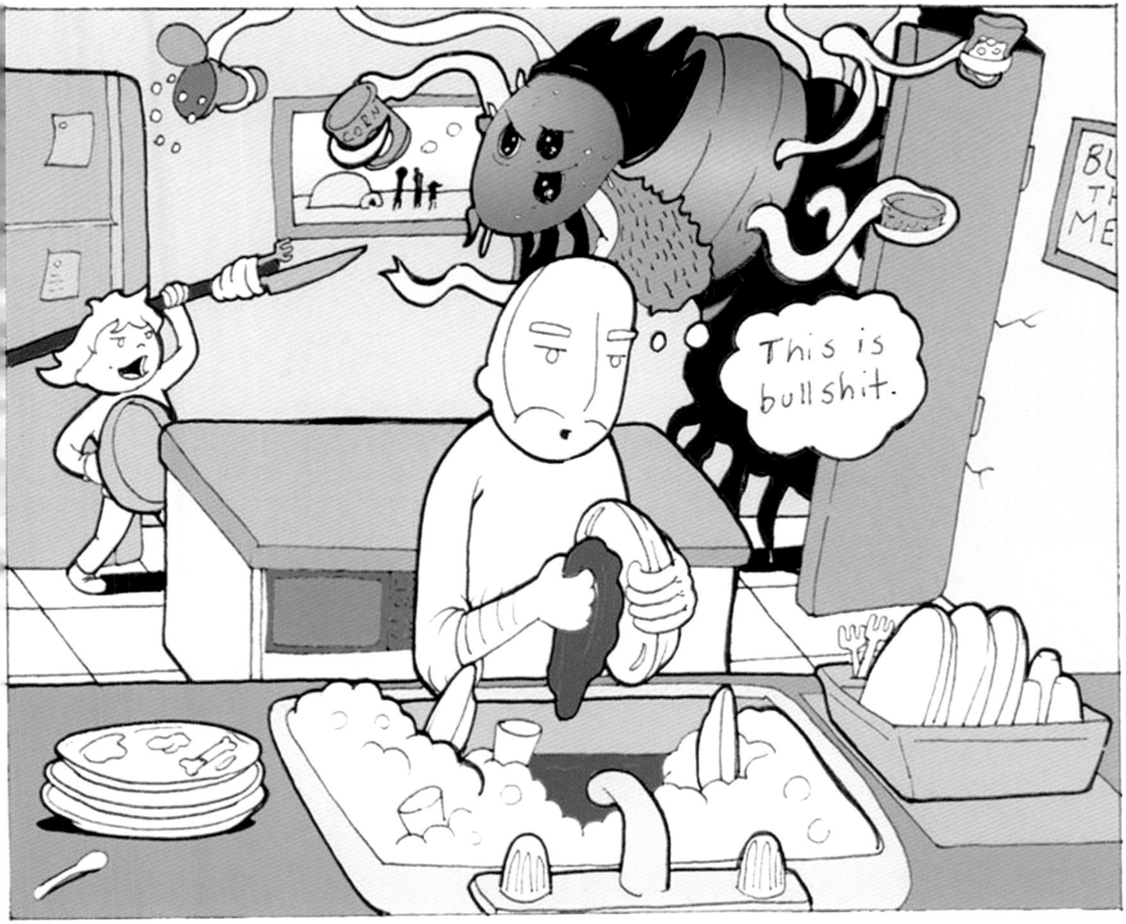
CORN
This is bullshit.

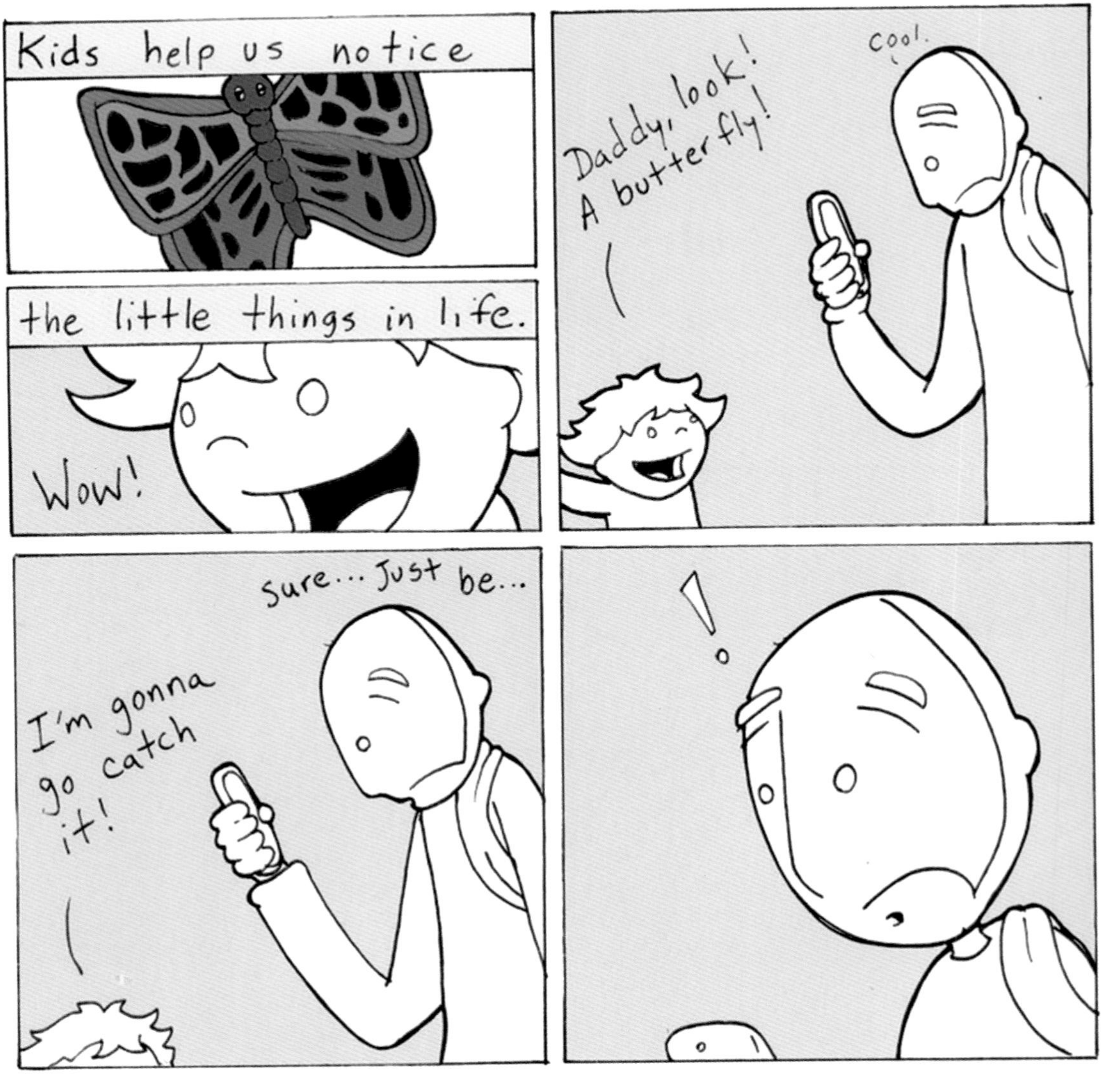
Kids help us notice
the little things in life.
Wow!
Daddy, look! A butterfly!
cool.
I'm gonna go catch it!
sure... Just be...
!

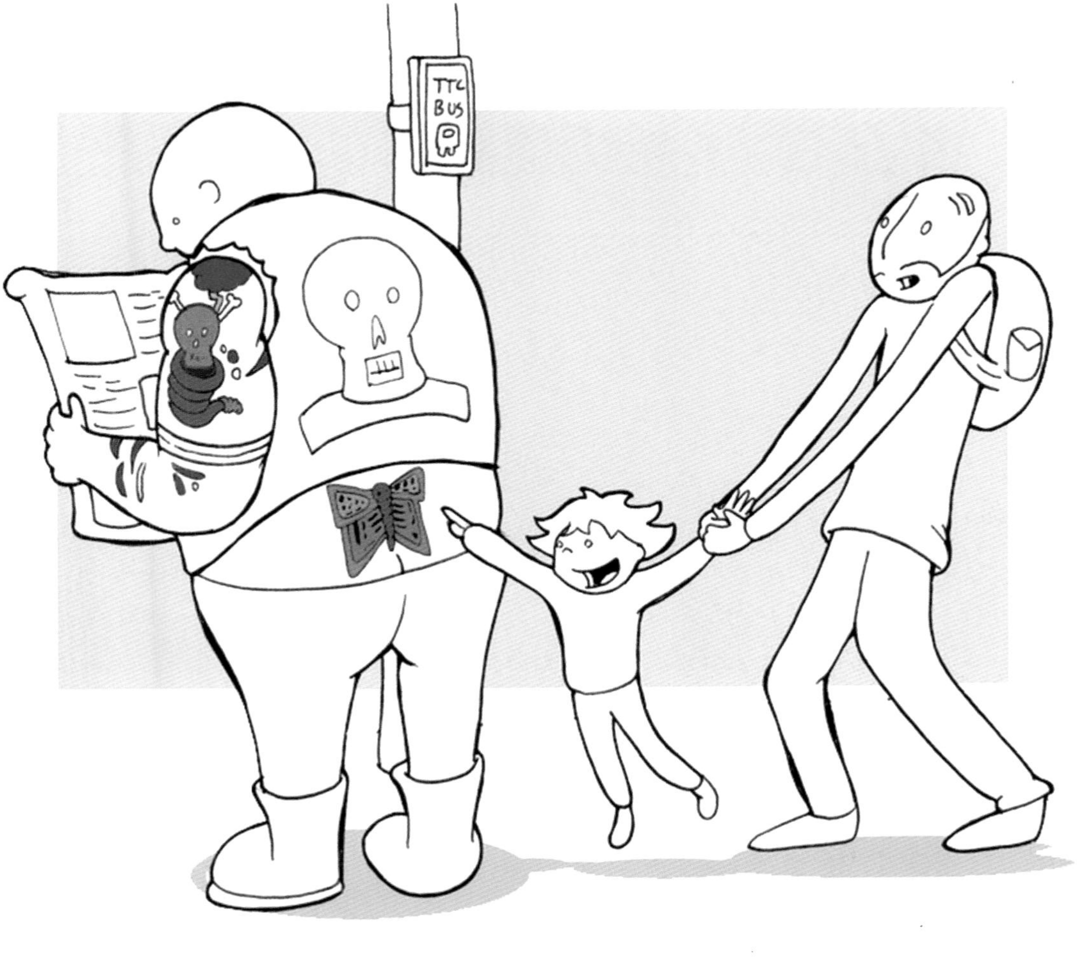
TTC
BUS

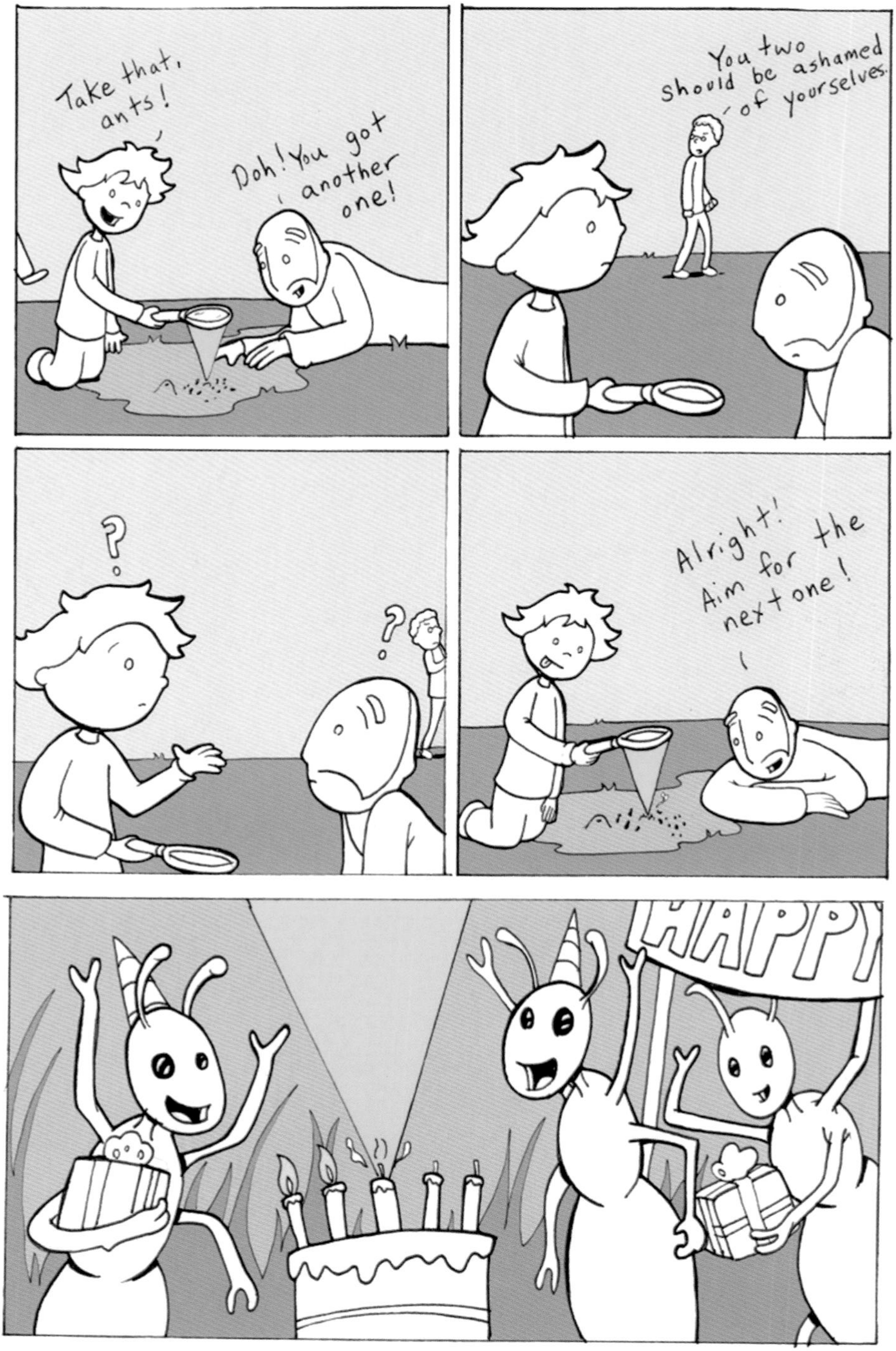
Take that, ants!
Doh! You got another one!
You two should be ashamed of yourselves.
?
?
Alright! Aim for the next one!
HAPPY

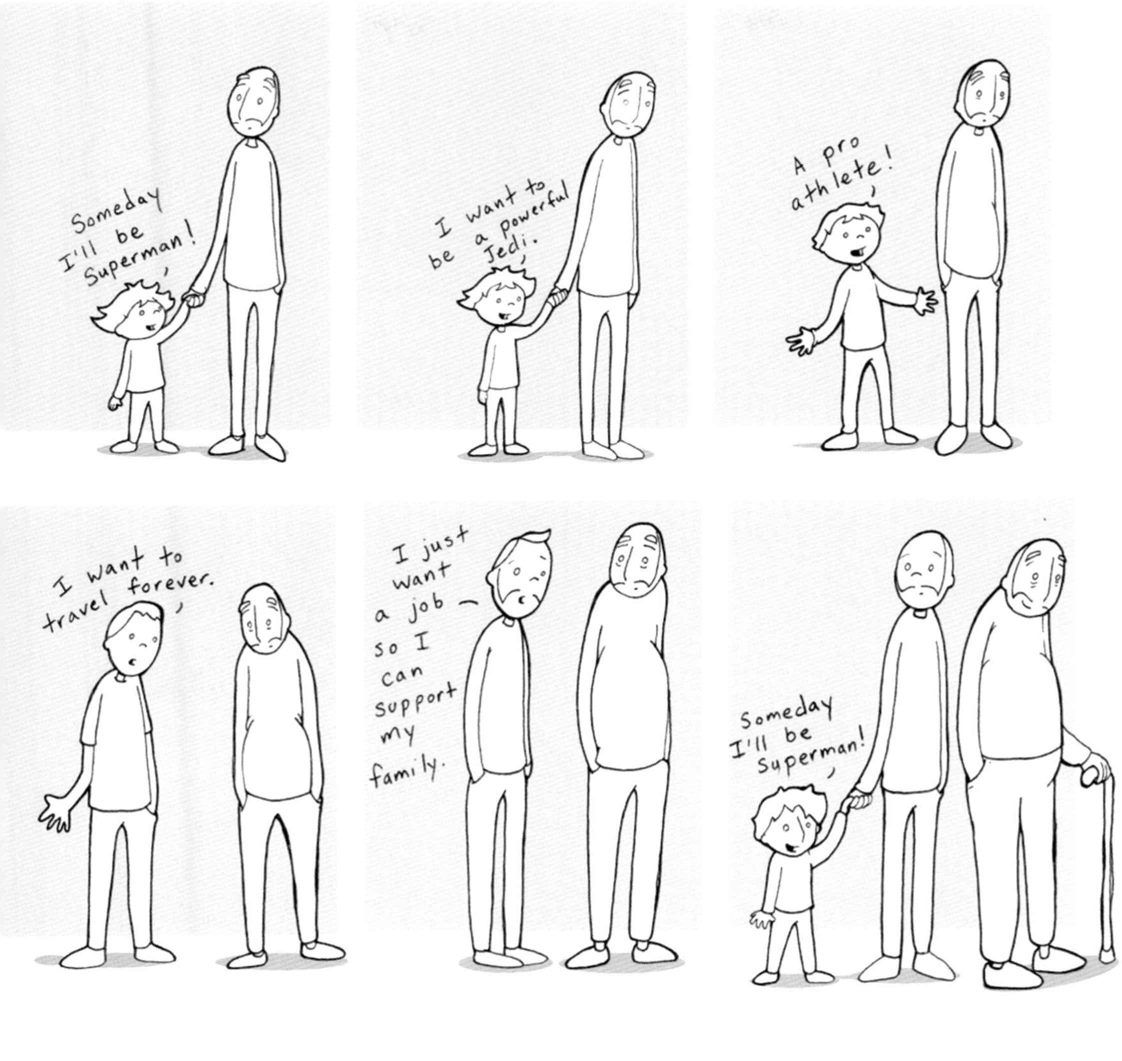
Someday I'll be Superman!
I want to be a powerful Jedi.
A pro athlete!
I want to travel forever.
I just want a job so I can support my family.
Someday I'll be Superman!

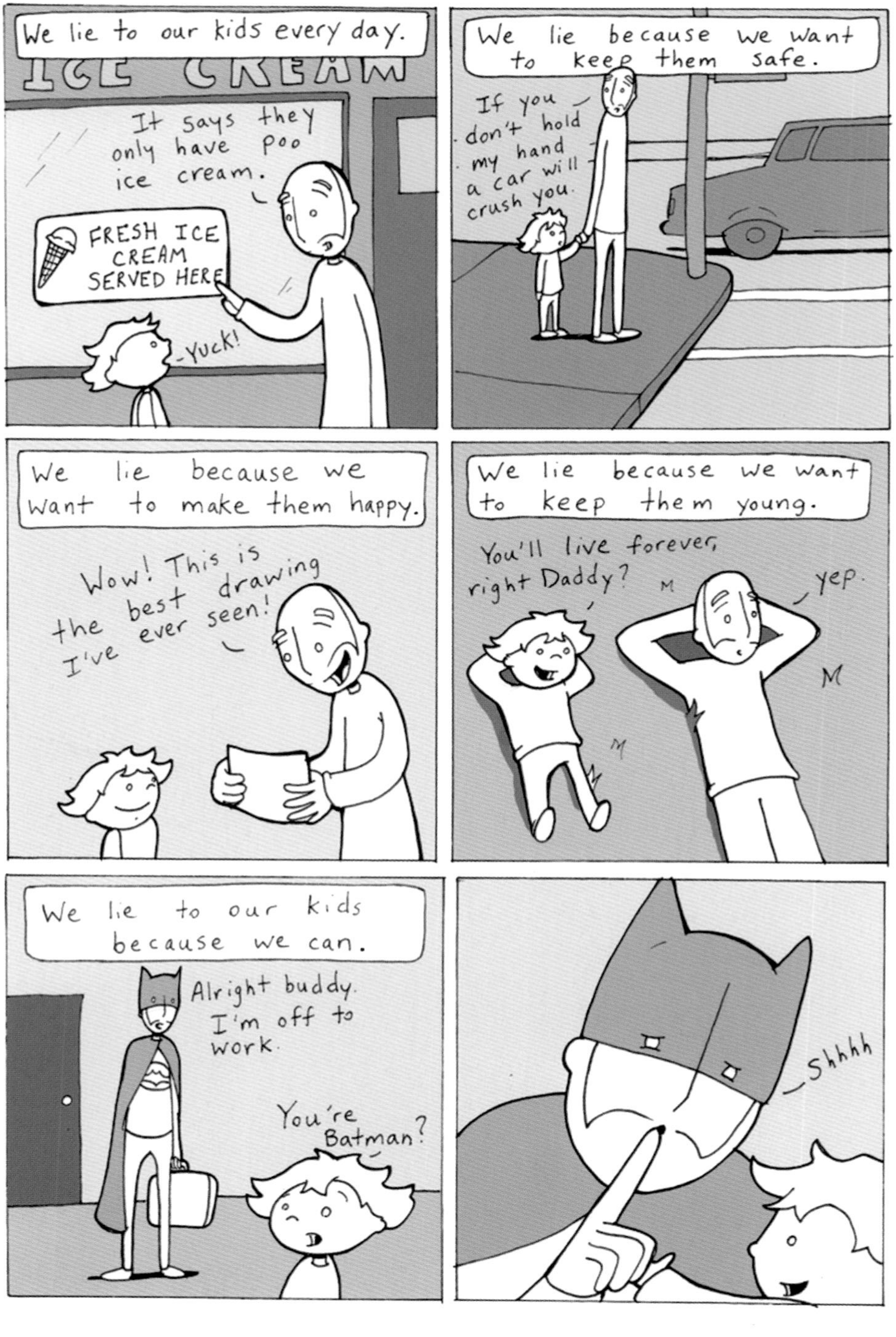
We lie to our kids every day.
ICE CREAM
It says they only have poo ice cream.
FRESH ICE CREAM SERVED HERE
YUCK!
We lie because we want to keep them safe.
If you don't hold my hand a car will crush you.
We lie because we want to make them happy.
Wow! This is the best drawing I've ever seen!
We lie because we want to keep them young.
You'll live forever, right Daddy?
yep.
We lie to our kids because we can.
Alright buddy. I'm off to work.
You're Batman?
Shhhh

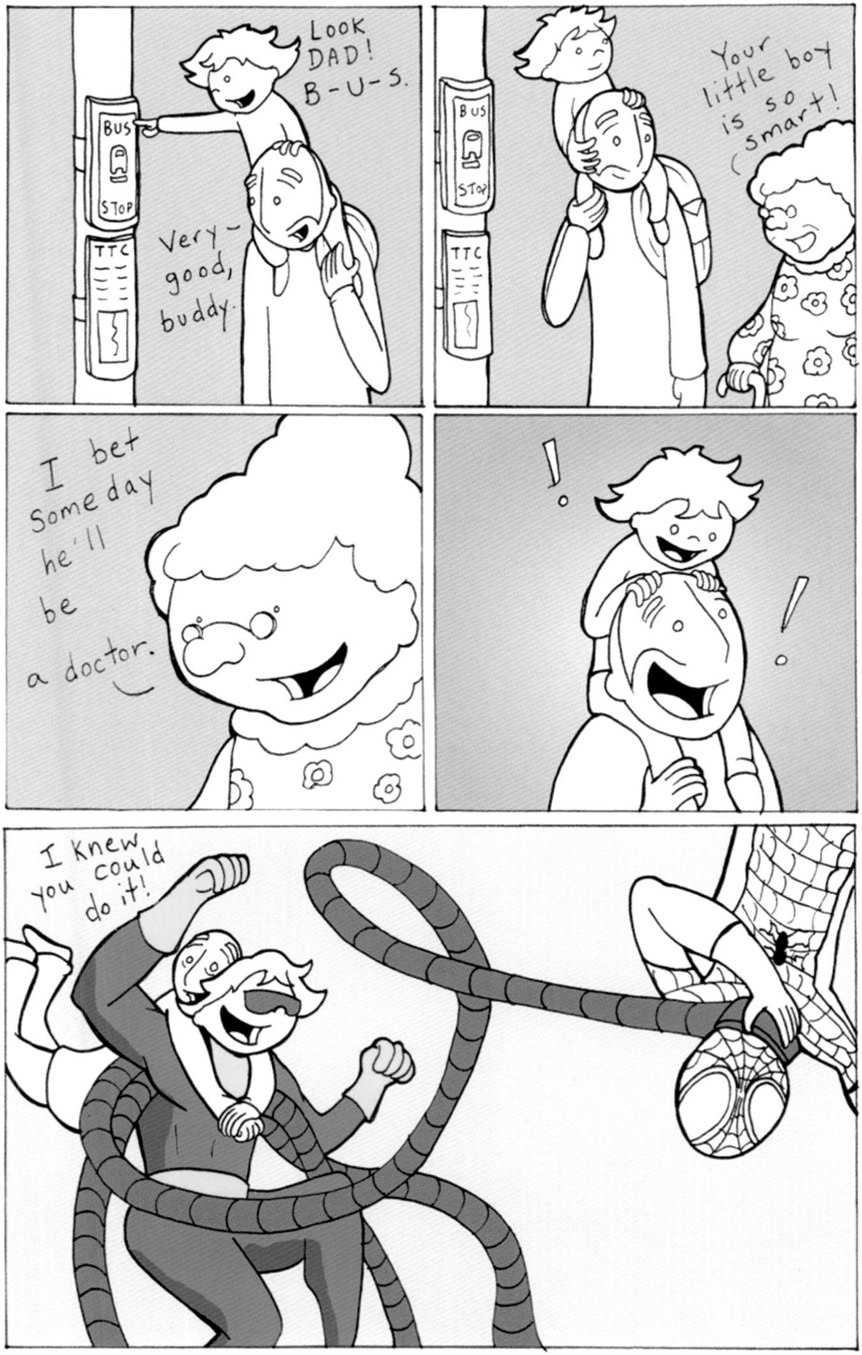
LOOK DAD! B-U-S.
BUS STOP
TTC
Very-good, buddy.
Your little boy is so smart!
I bet someday he'll be a doctor.
!
!
I knew you could do it!

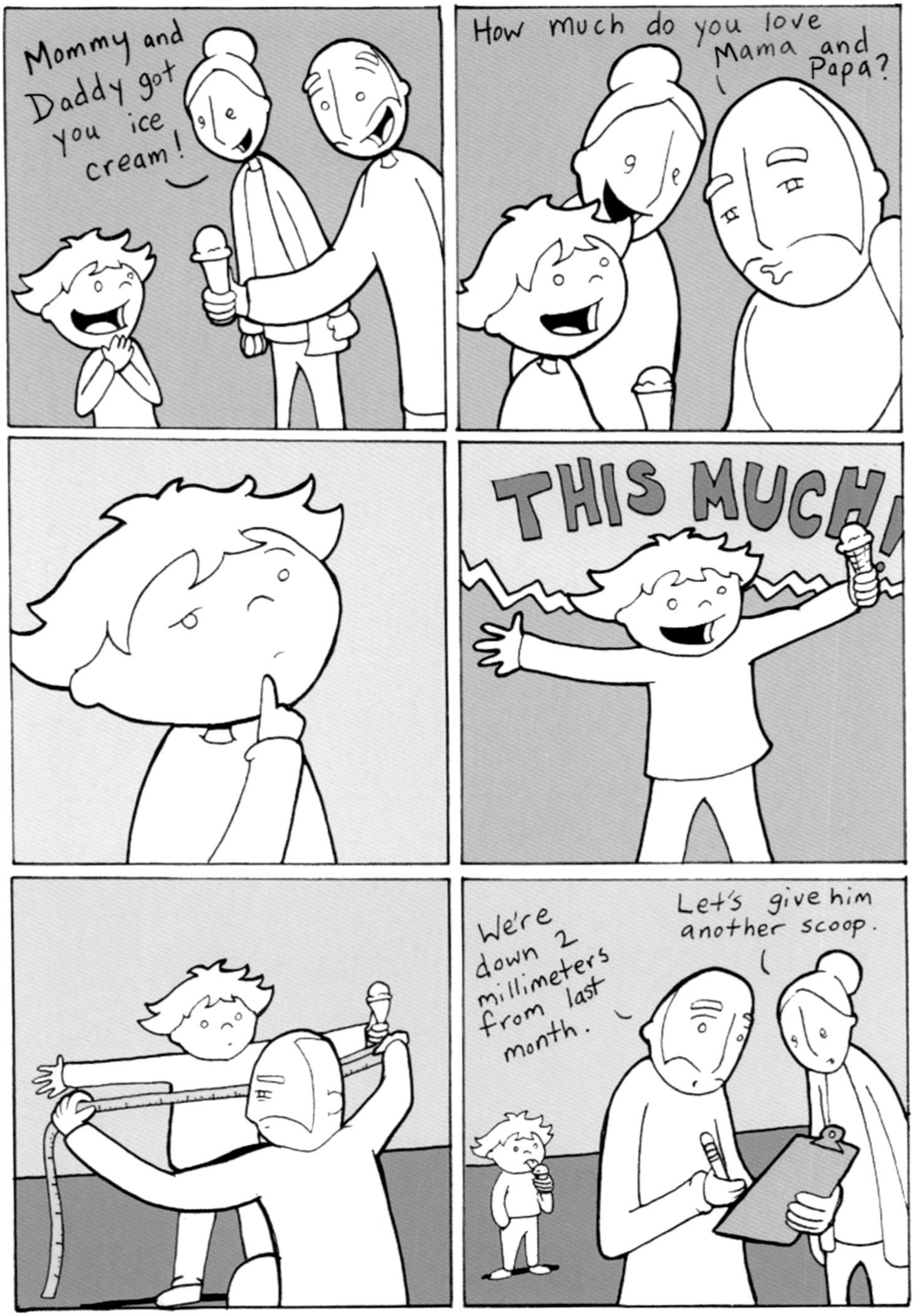
Mommy and Daddy got you ice cream!
How much do you love Mama and Papa?
THIS MUCH!
We're down 2 millimeters from last month.
Let's give him another scoop.

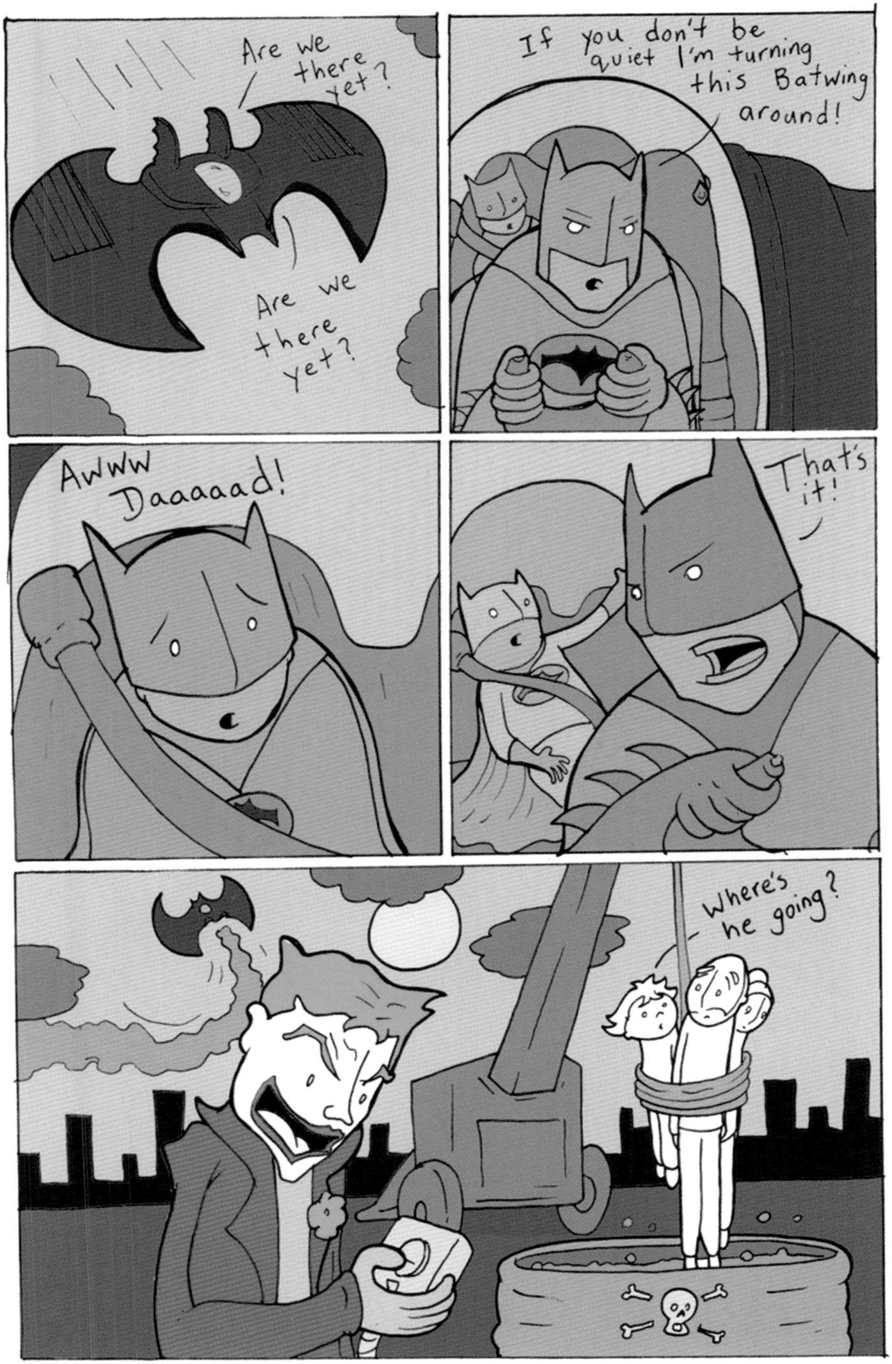
Are we there yet?
Are we there yet?
If you don't be quiet I'm turning this Batwing around!
Awww Daaaaad!
That's it!
Where's he going?

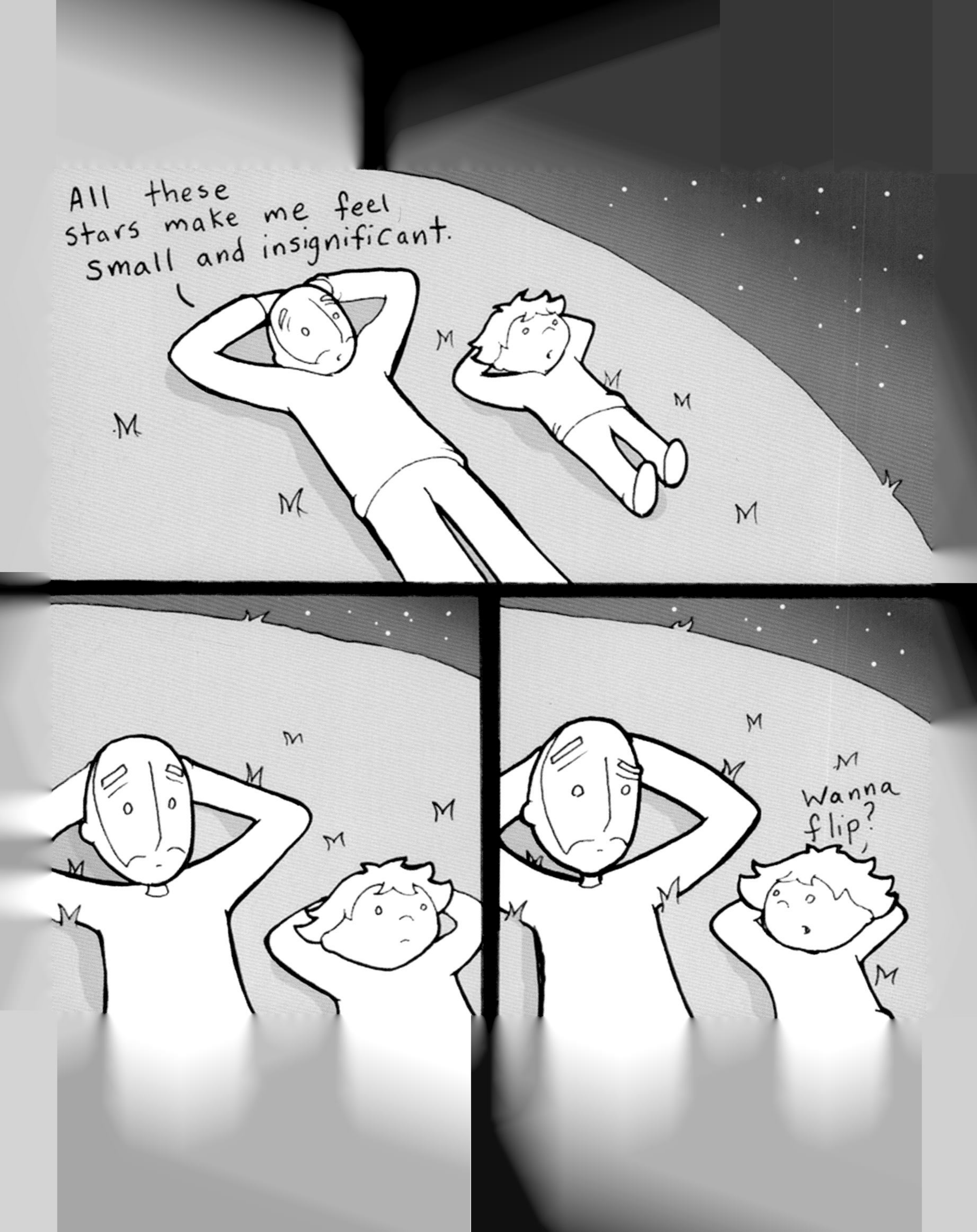
All these stars make me feel small and insignificant.
Wanna flip?

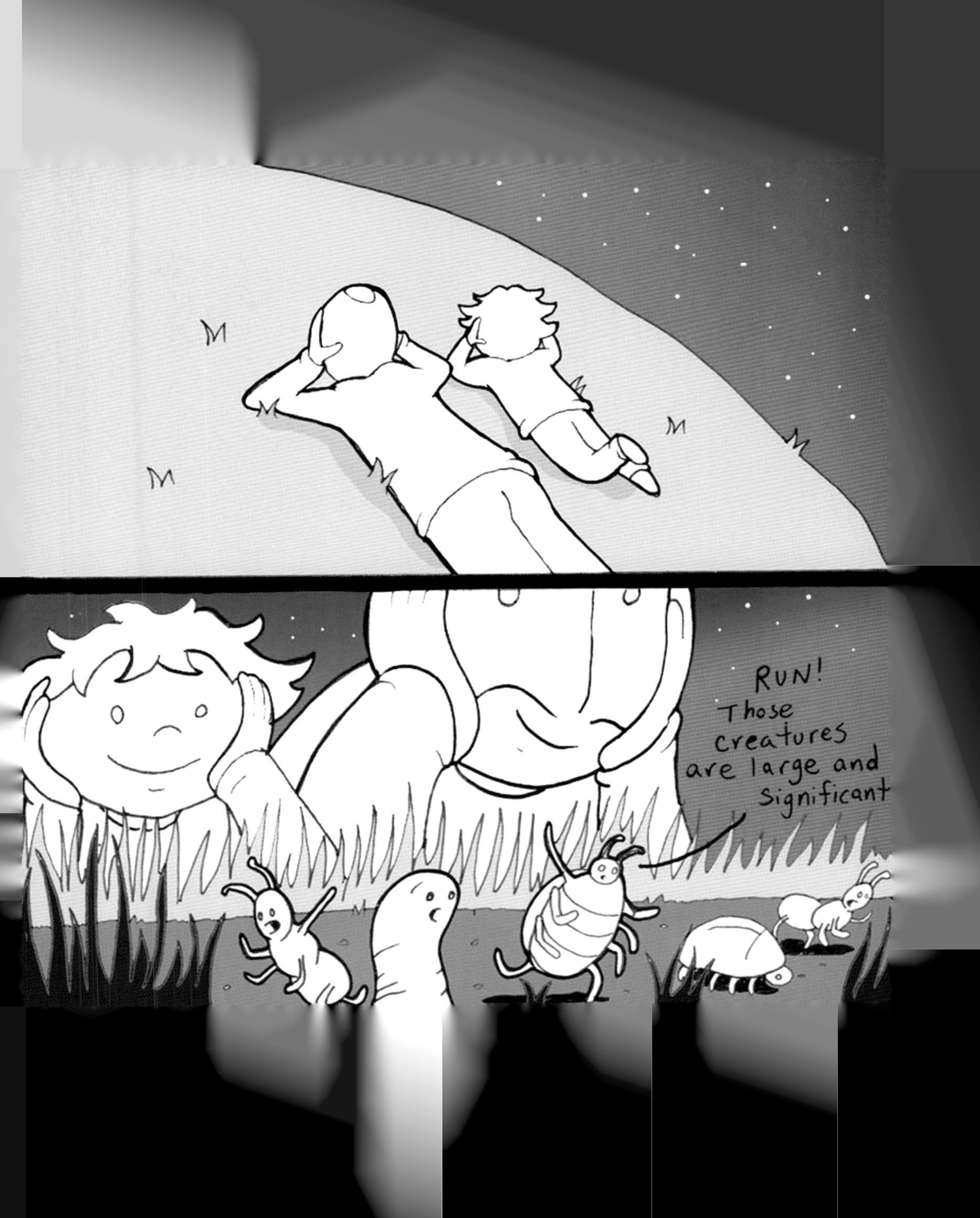
RUN!
Those creatures are large and significant

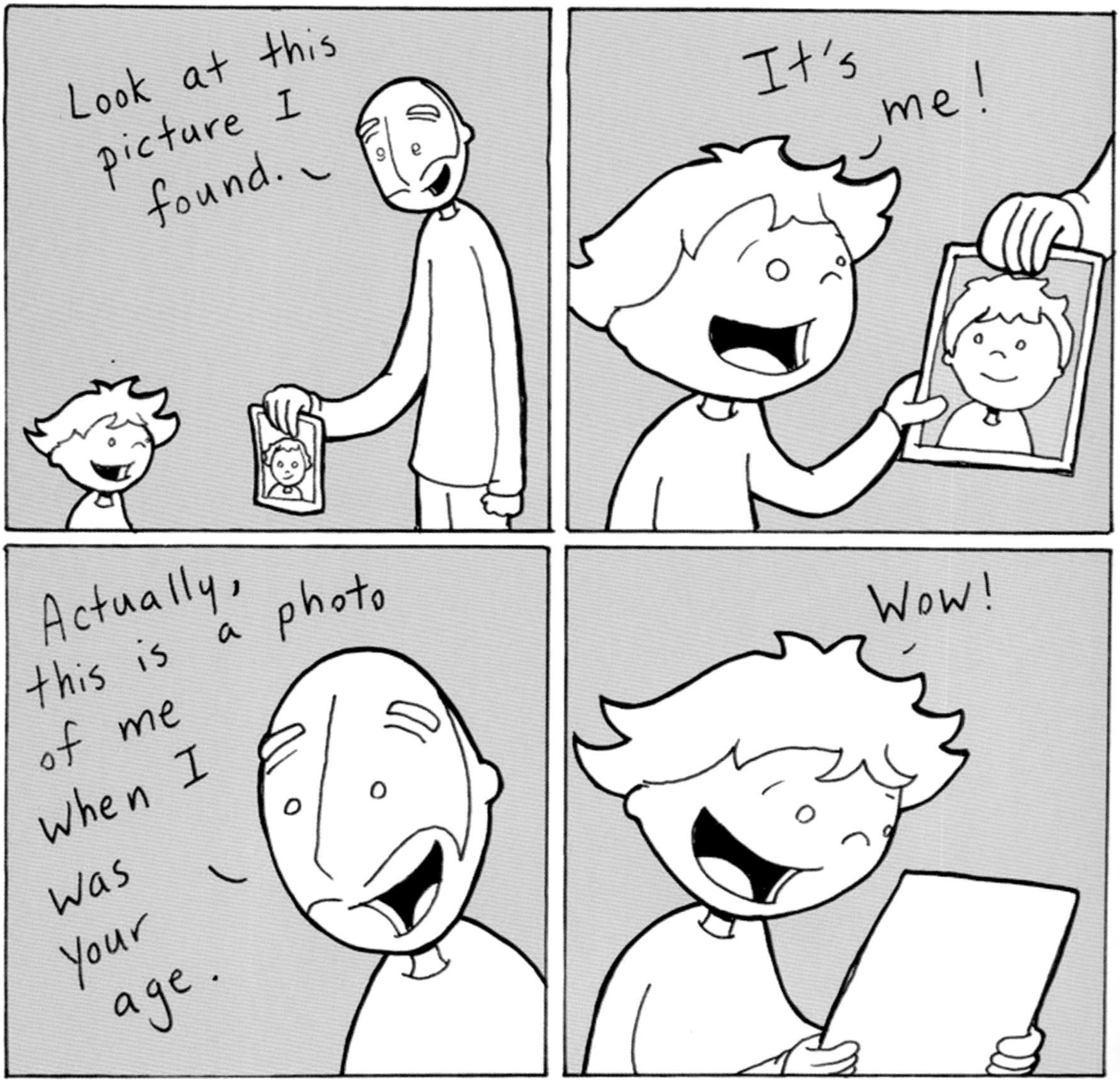
Look at this picture I found.
It's me!
Actually, this is a photo of me when I was your age.
Wow!

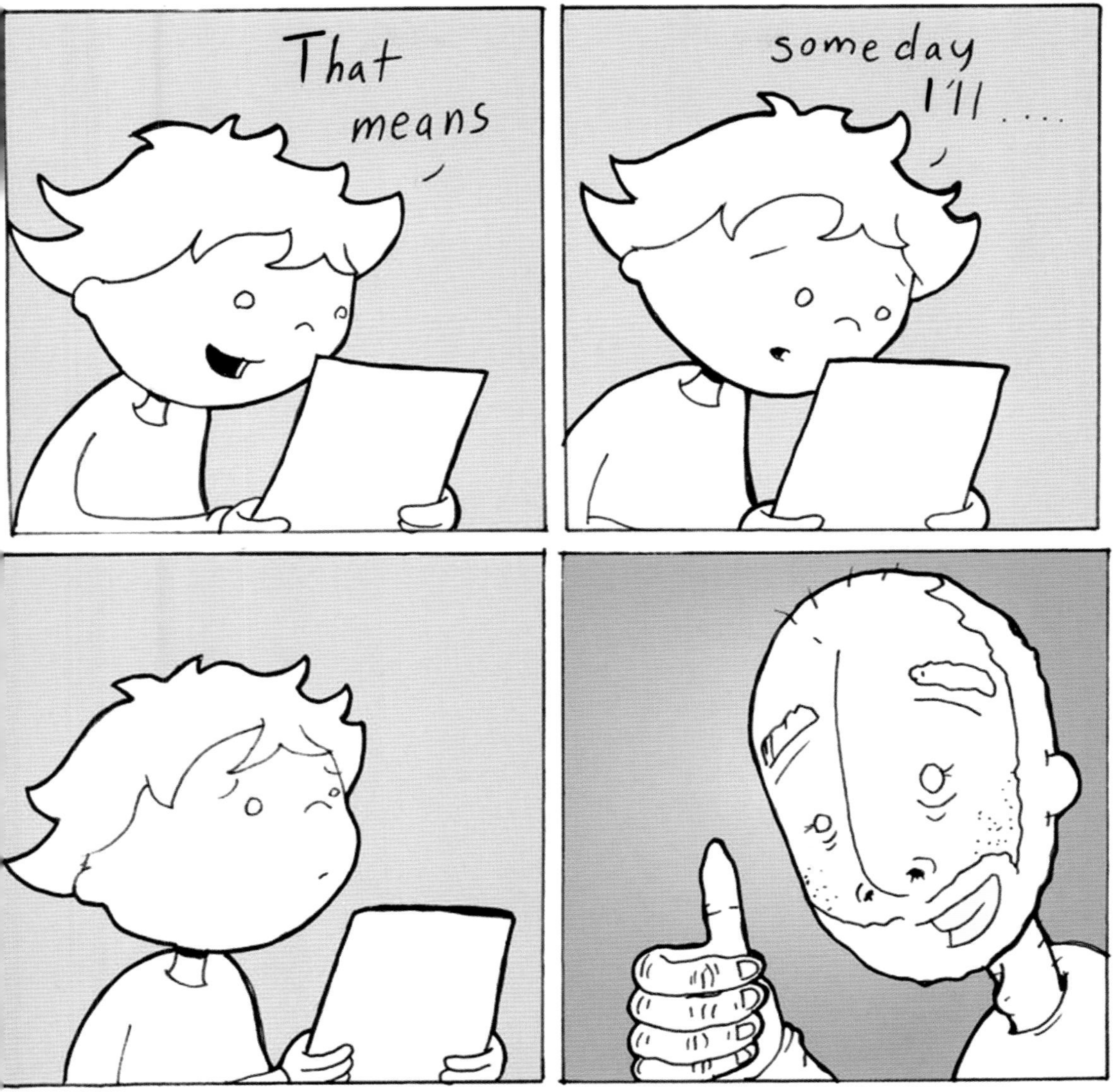
That means
someday I'll....

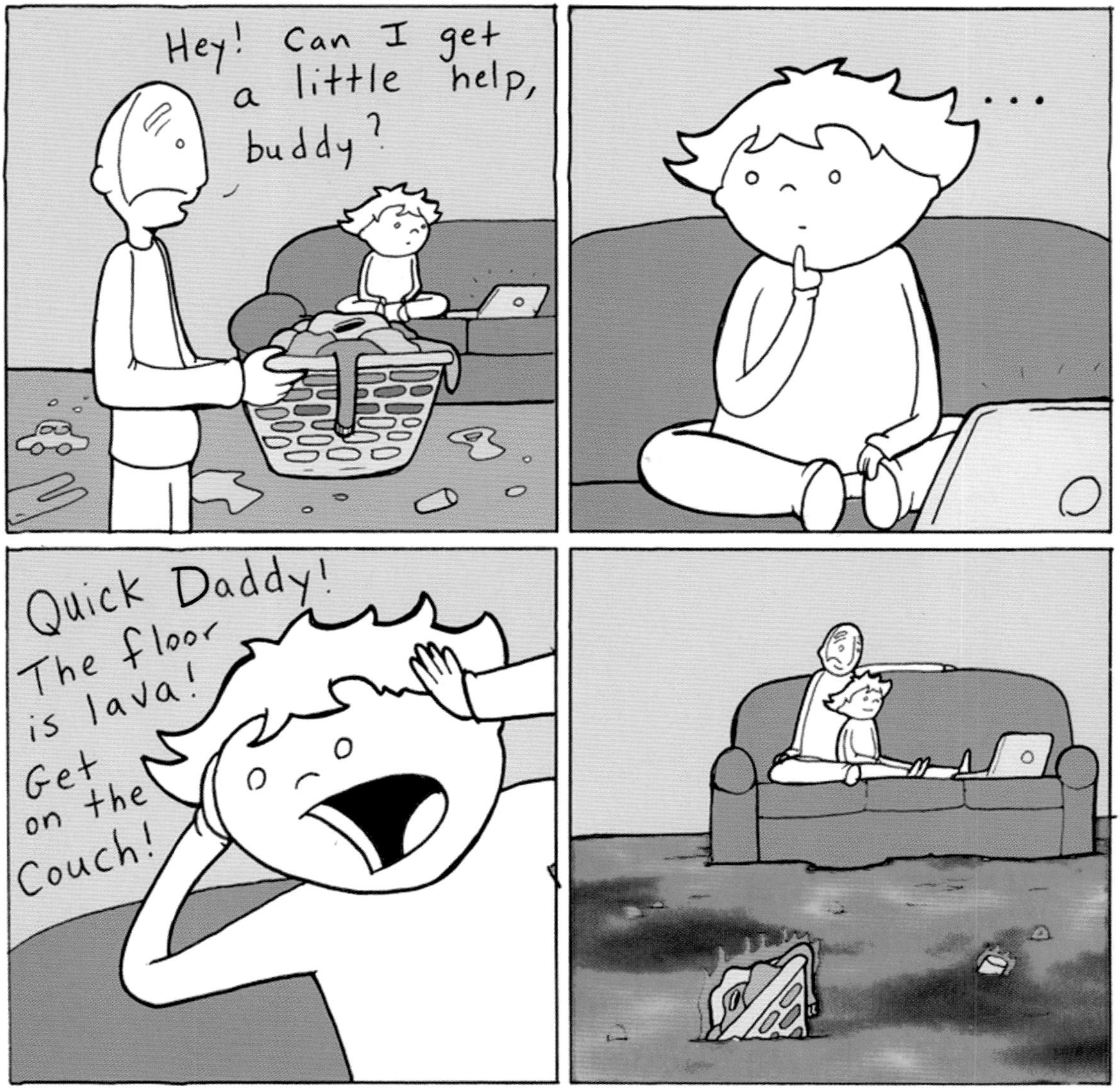
Hey! Can I get a little help, buddy?
...
Quick Daddy! The floor is lava! Get on the couch!

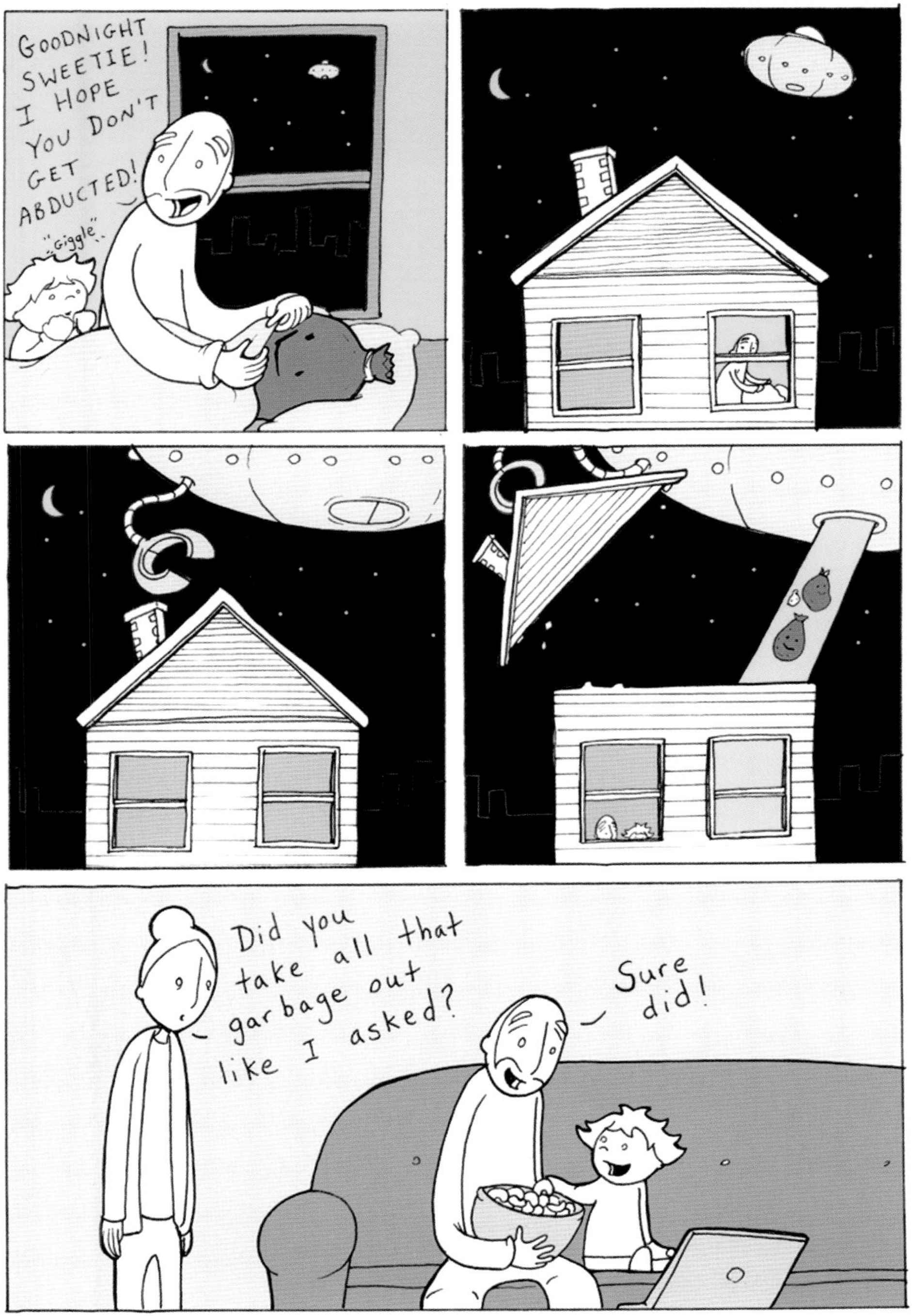
GOODNIGHT SWEETIE! I HOPE YOU DON'T GET ABDUCTED!
"giggle"
Did you take all that garbage out like I asked?
Sure did!

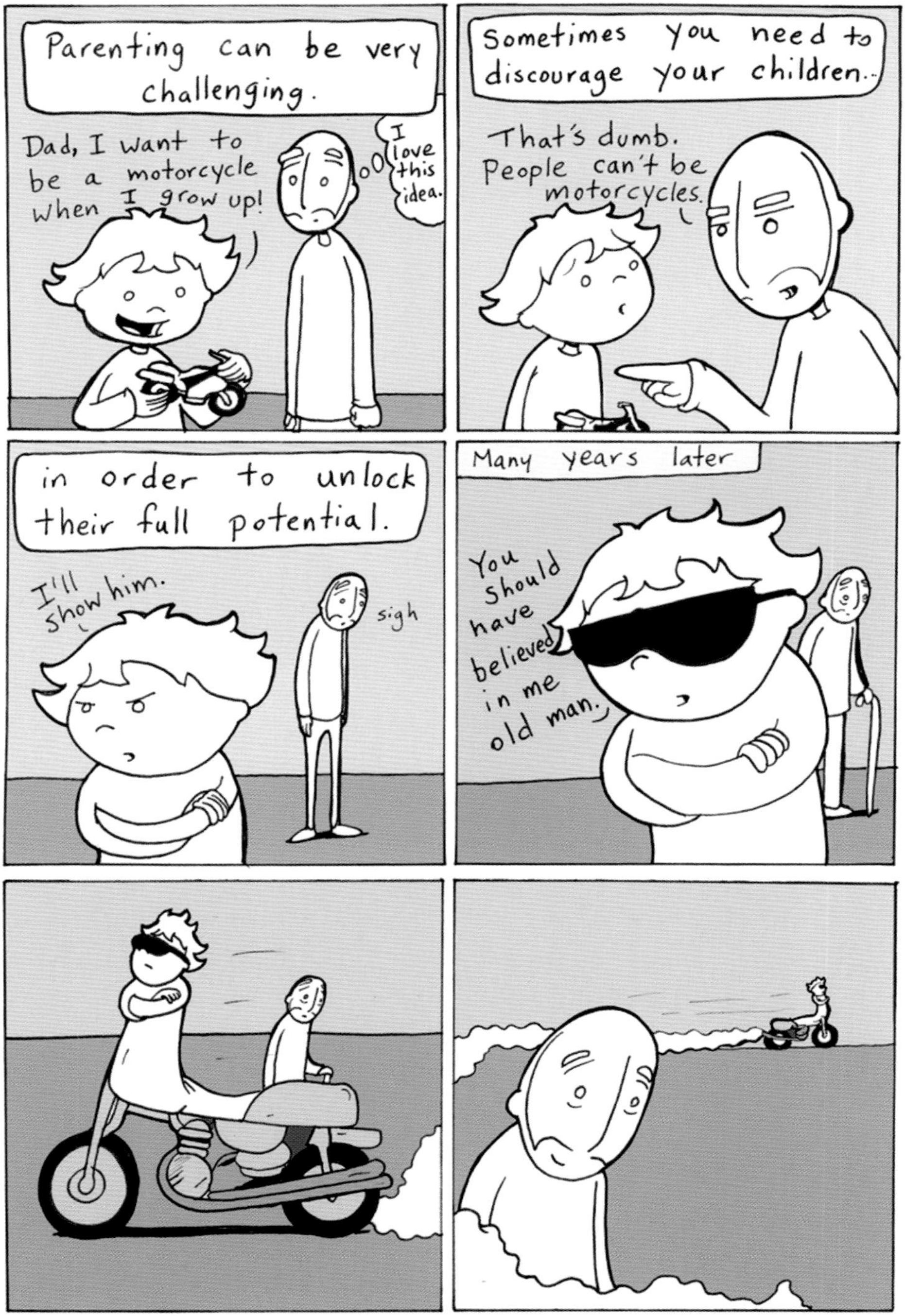
Parenting can be very challenging.
Dad, I want to be a motorcycle when I grow up!
I love this idea.
Sometimes you need to discourage your children...
That's dumb. People can't be motorcycles.
in order to unlock their full potential.
I'll show him.
sigh
Many years later
You should have believed in me old man.

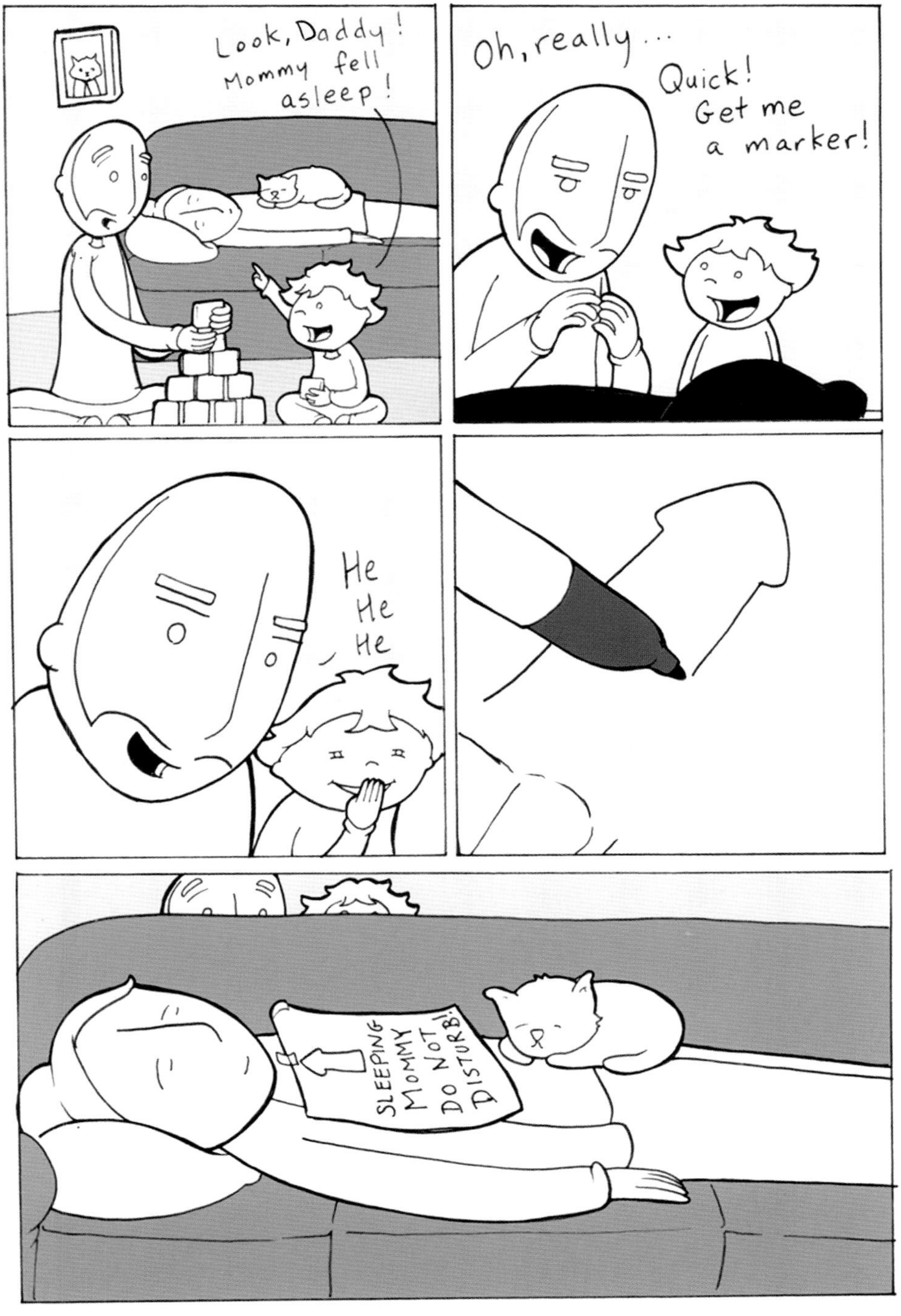
Look, Daddy! Mommy fell asleep!
Oh, really...
Quick! Get me a marker!
He He He
SLEEPING MOMMY DO NOT DISTURB!

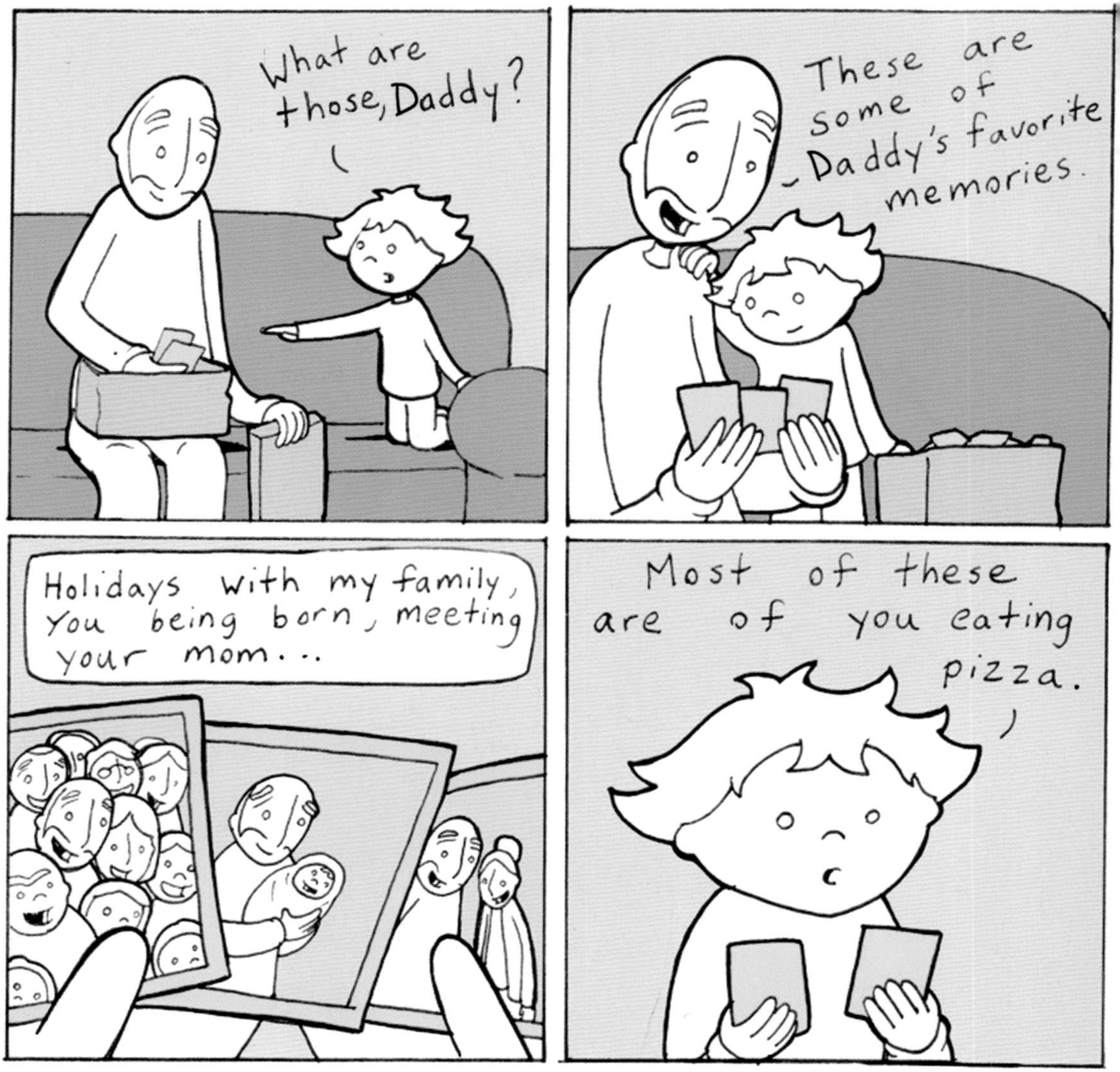
What are those, Daddy?
These are some of Daddy's favorite memories.
Holidays with my family, you being born, meeting your mom...
Most of these are of you eating pizza.

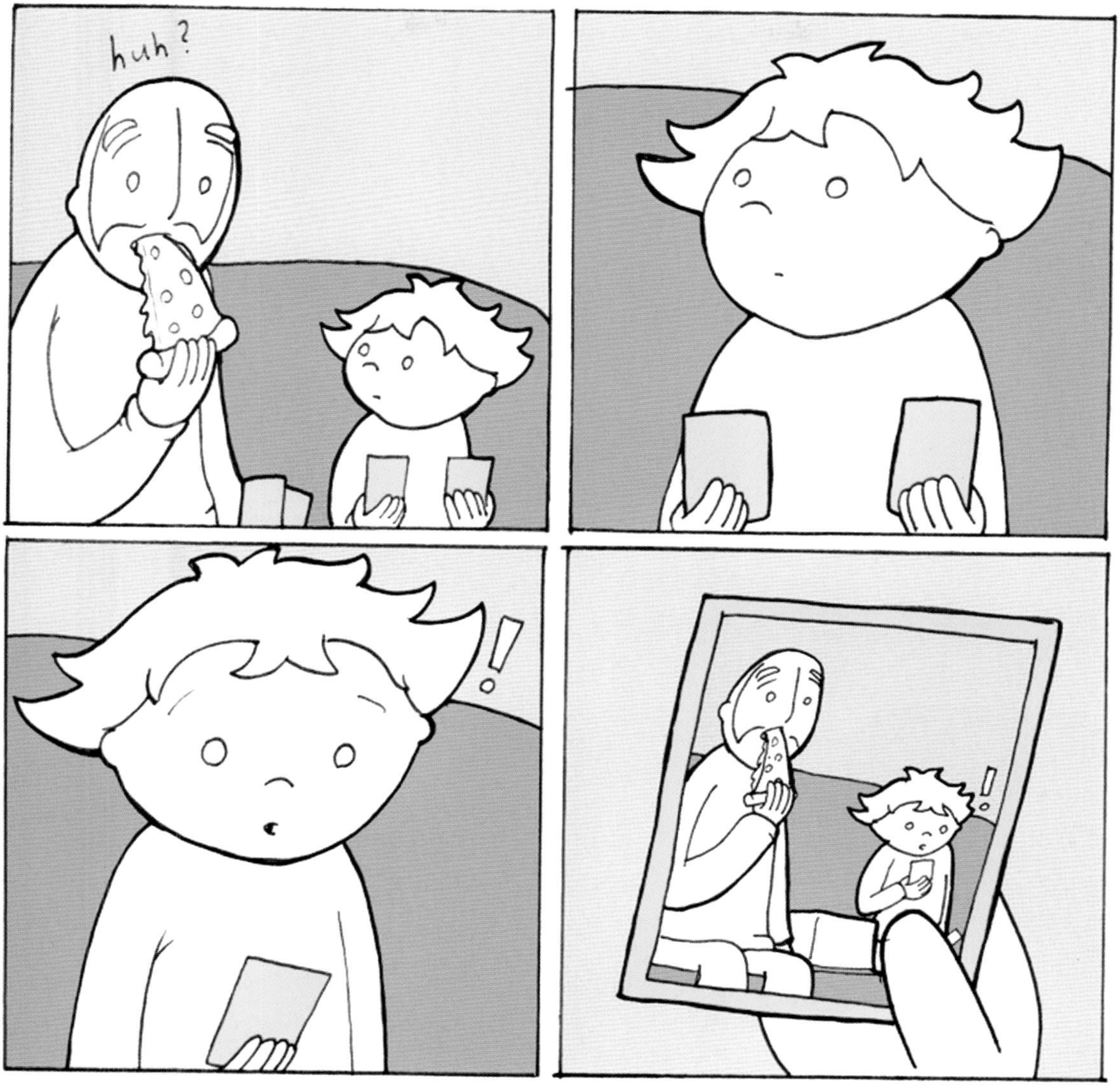
huh?
!

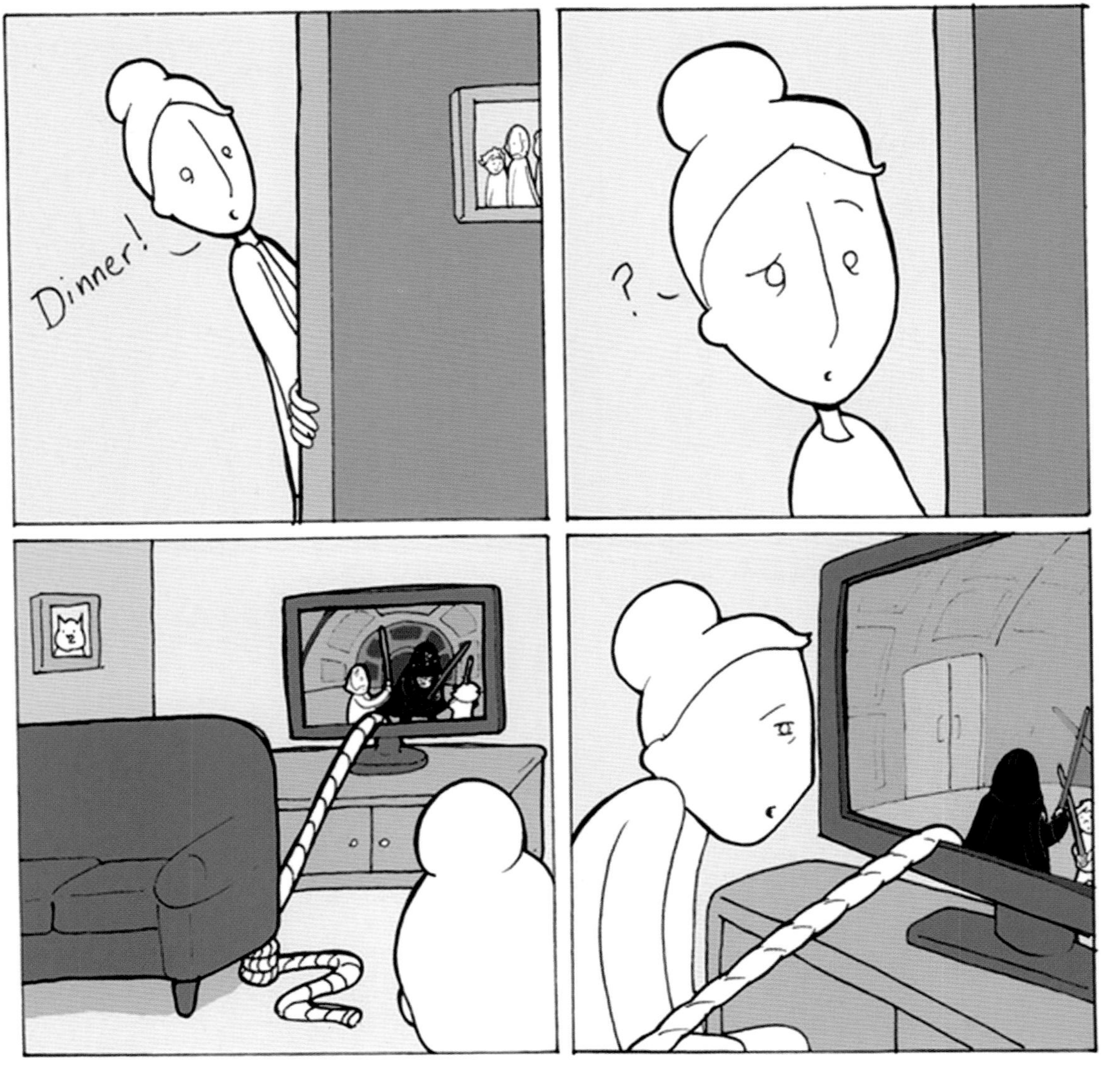
Dinner!
?

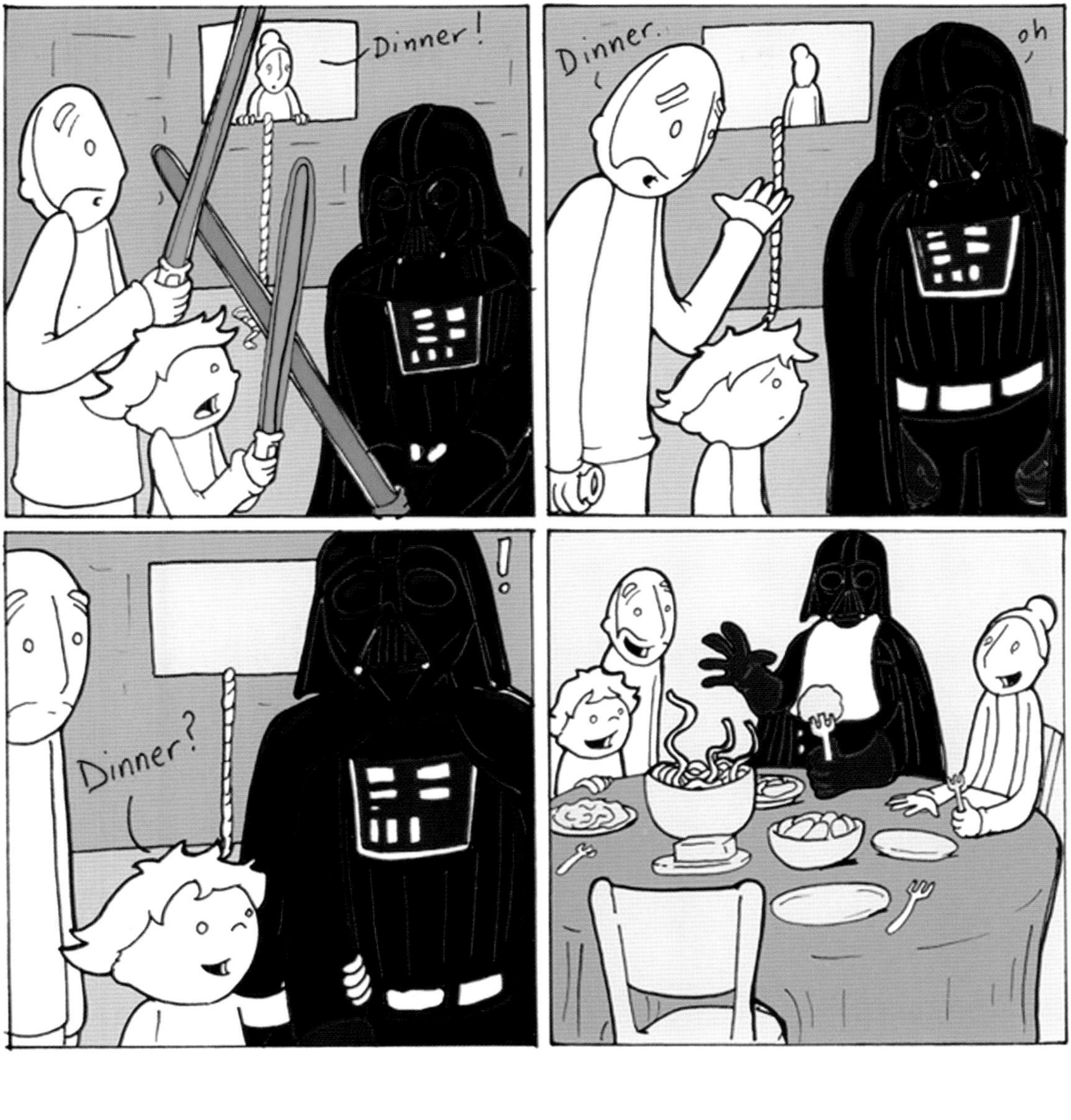
Dinner!
Dinner.
oh
!
Dinner?

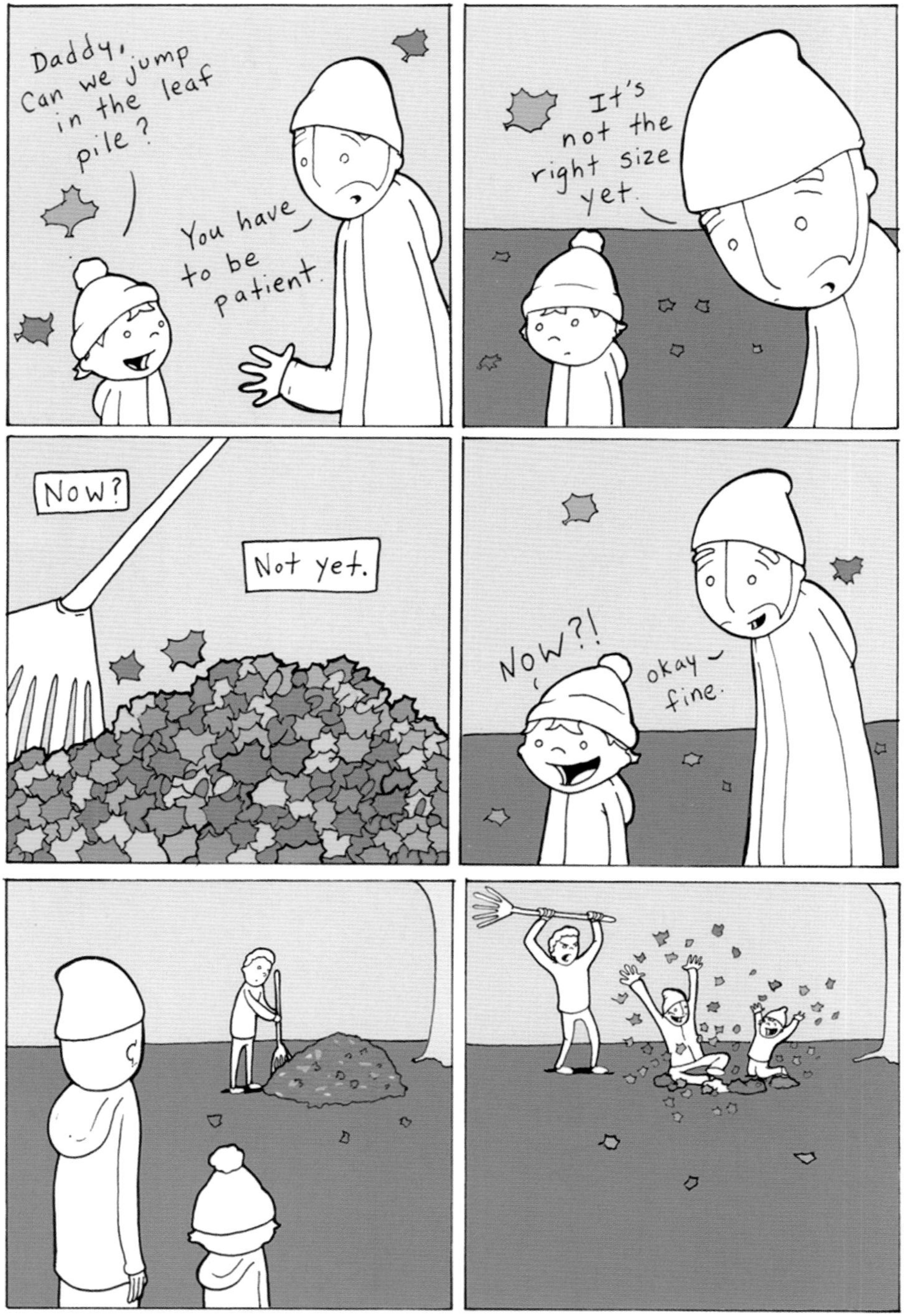
Daddy, Can we jump in the leaf pile?
You have to be patient.
It's not the right size yet.
Now?
Not yet.
Now?!
okay fine.

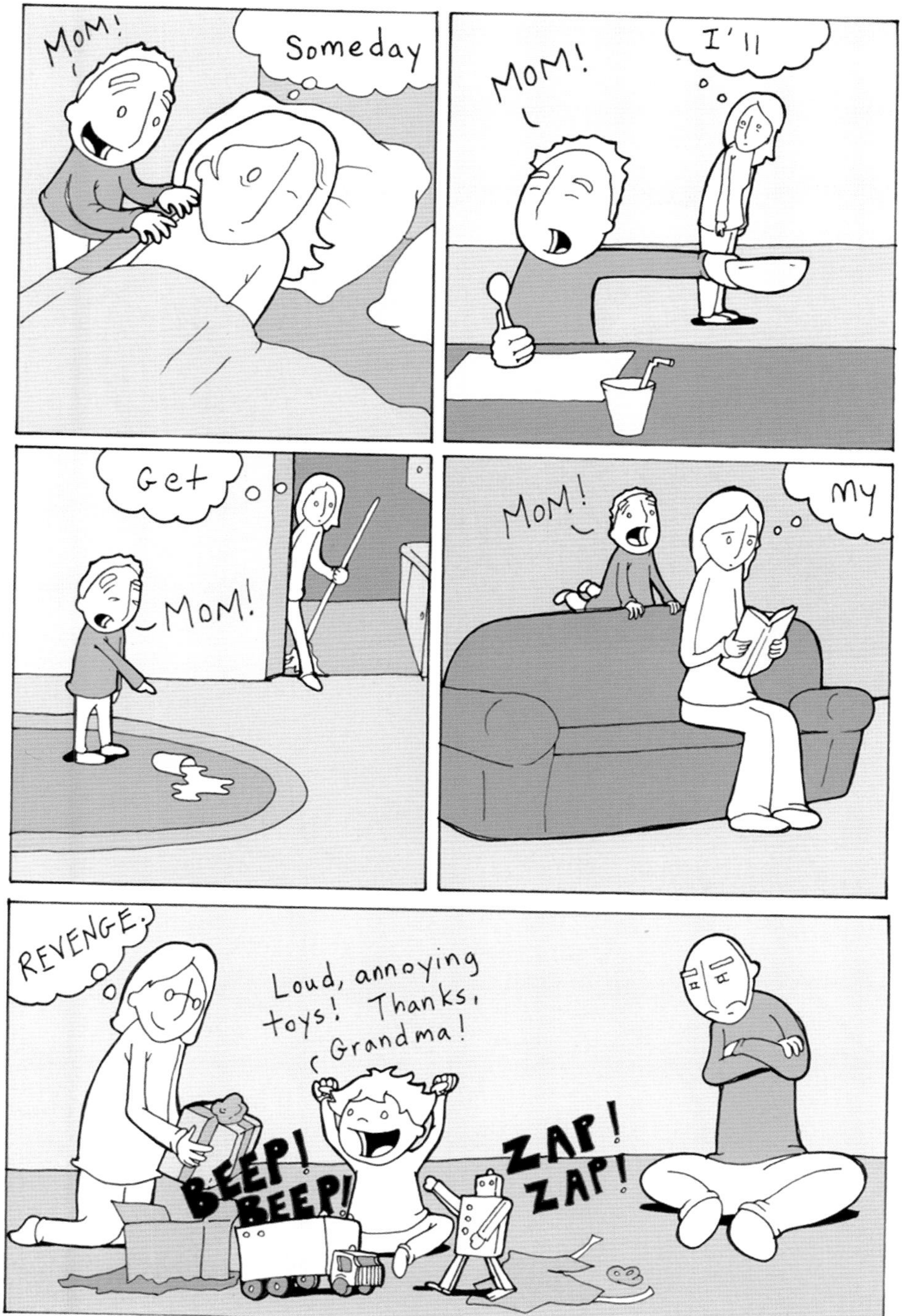
MOM!
Someday
MOM!
I'll
Get
MOM!
MOM!
my
REVENGE.
Loud, annoying toys! Thanks, Grandma!
BEEP! BEEP!
ZAP! ZAP!

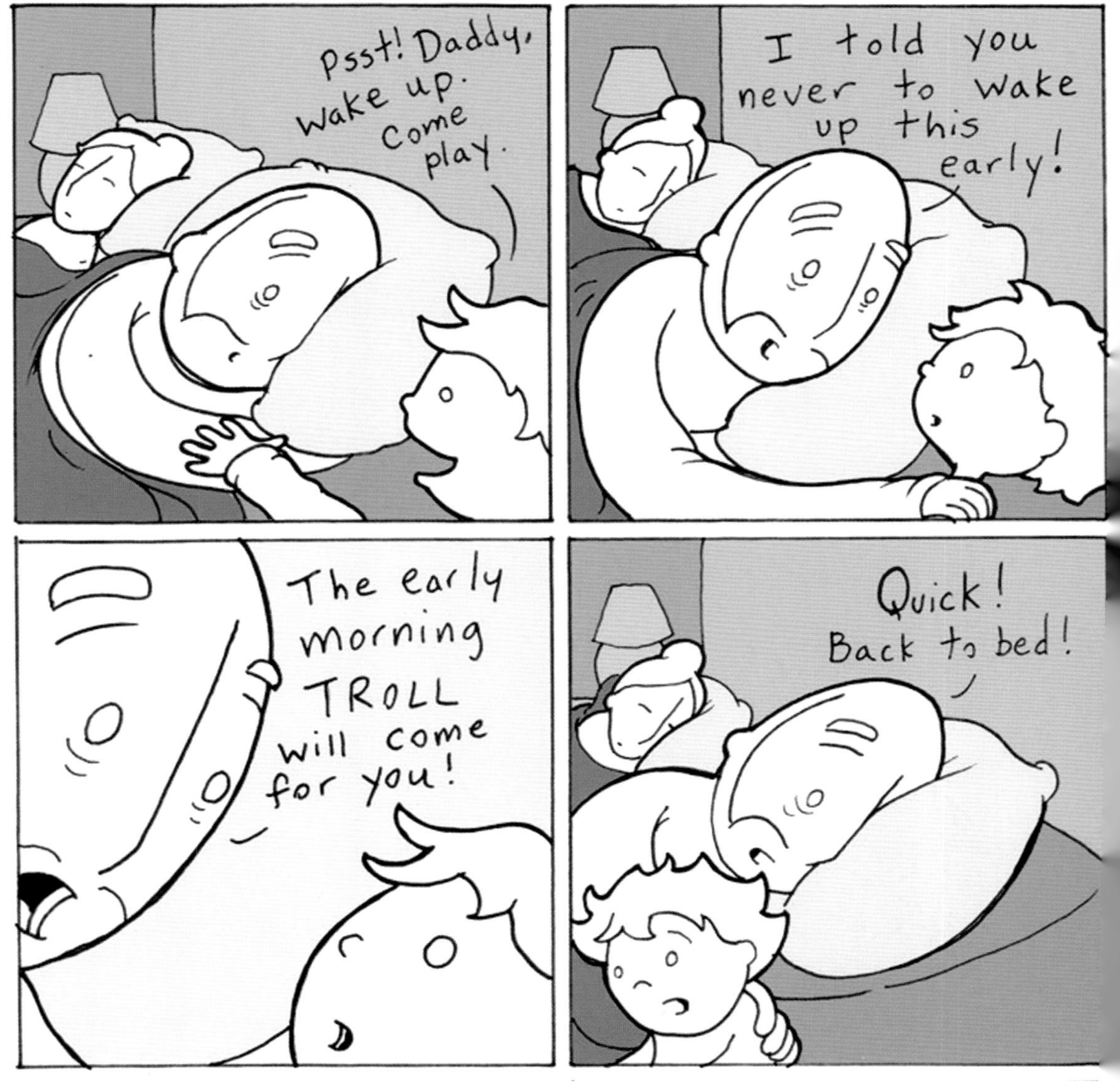
Psst! Daddy, wake up. Come play.
I told you never to wake up this early!
The early morning TROLL will come for you!
Quick! Back to bed!

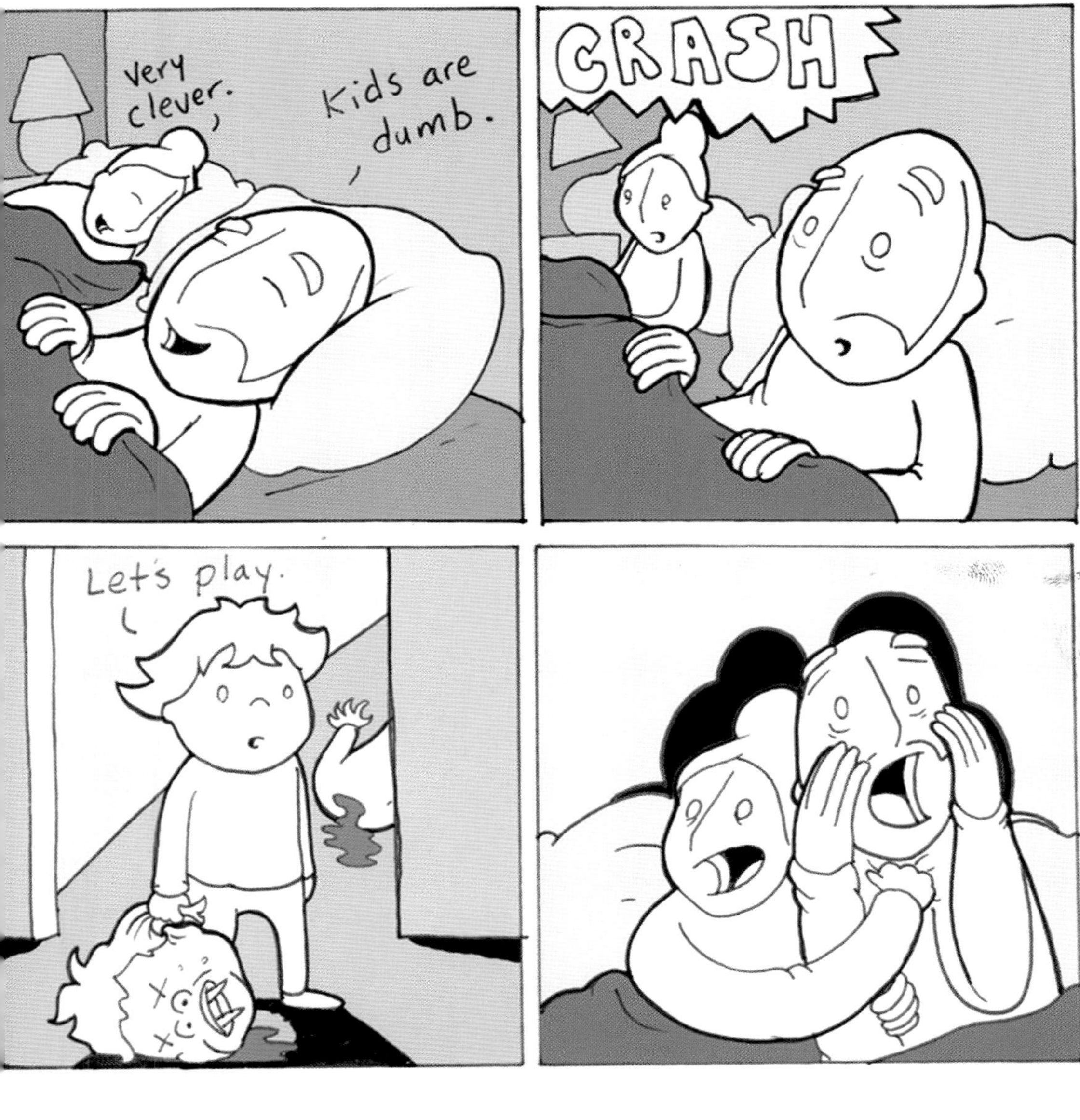
Very clever.
Kids are dumb.
CRASH
Let's play.

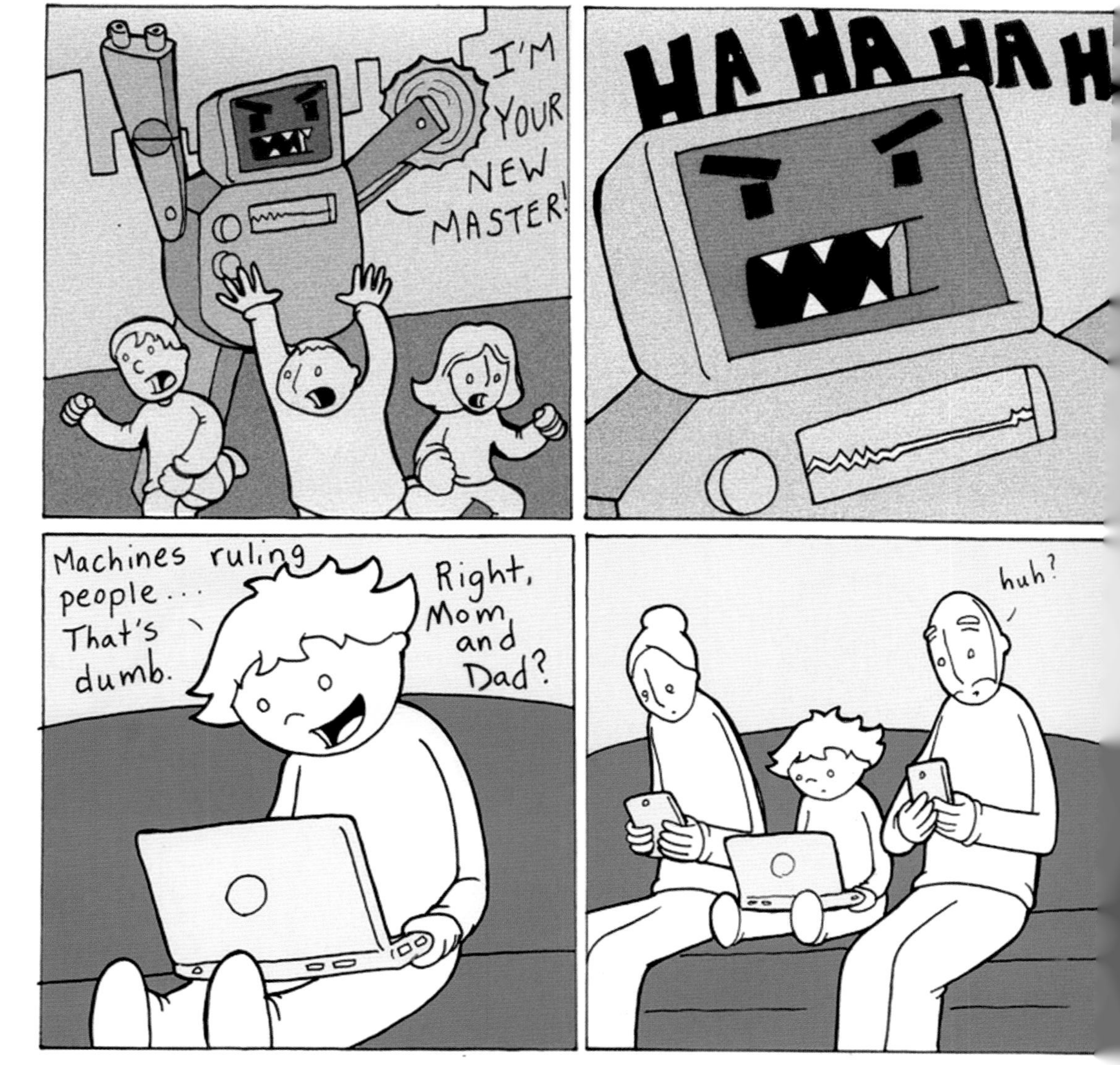
I'M YOUR NEW MASTER!
HA HA HA HA H
Machines ruling people... That's dumb.
Right, Mom and Dad?
huh?

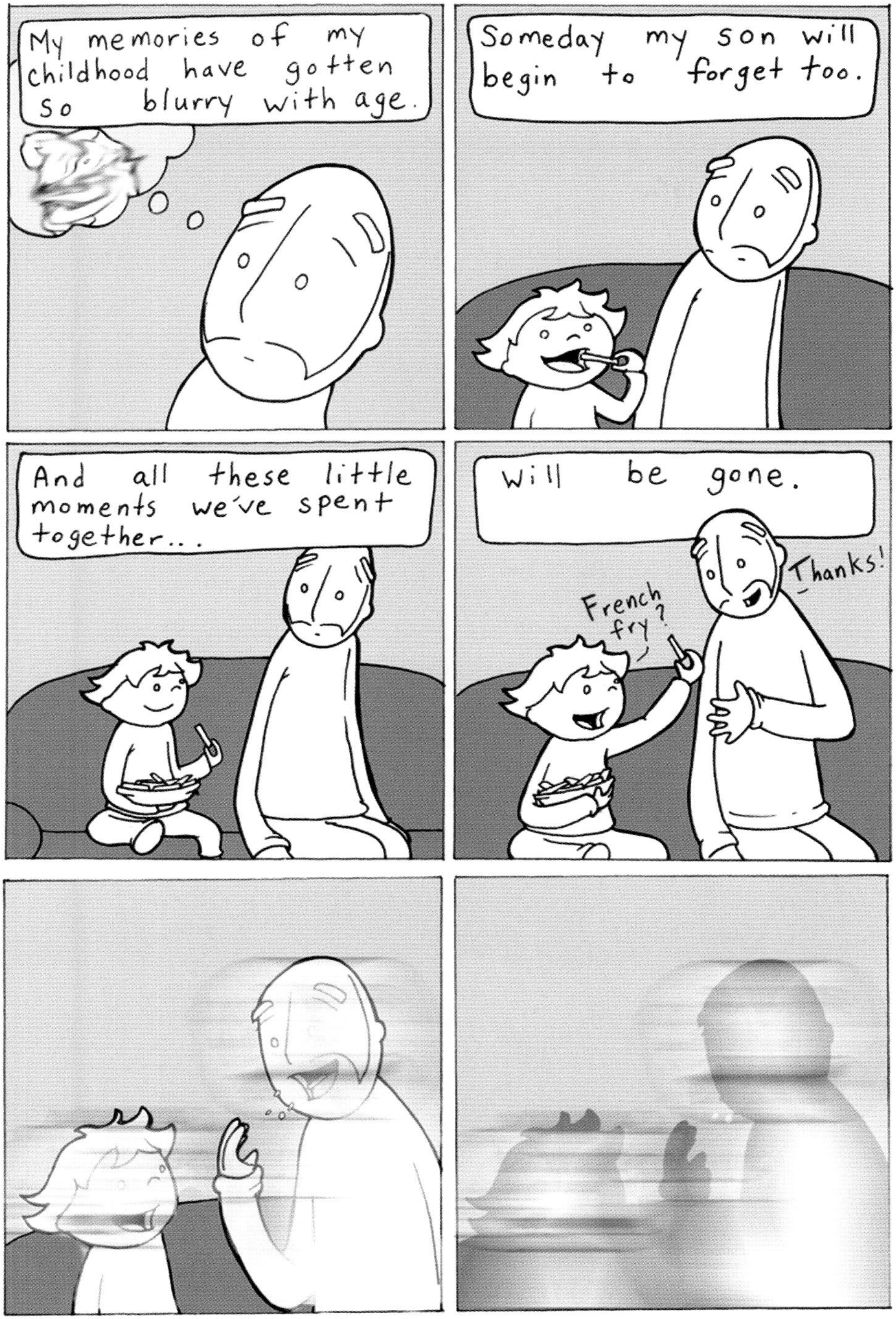
My memories of my childhood have gotten so blurry with age.
Someday my son will begin to forget too.
And all these little moments we've spent together...
Will be gone.
French fry?
Thanks!

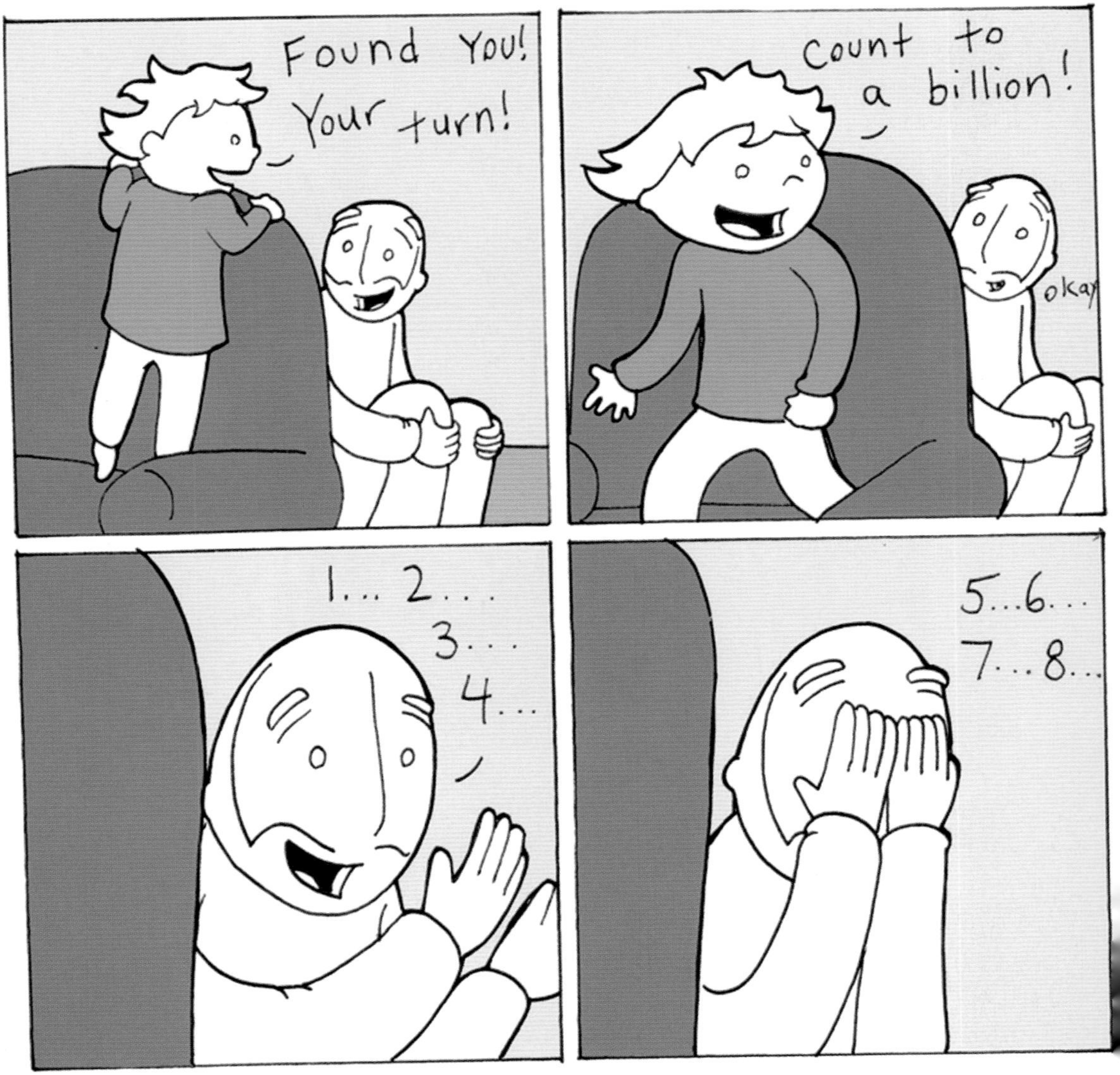
Found You! Your turn!
Count to a billion!
okay
1... 2....
3....
4....
5...6...
7...8...

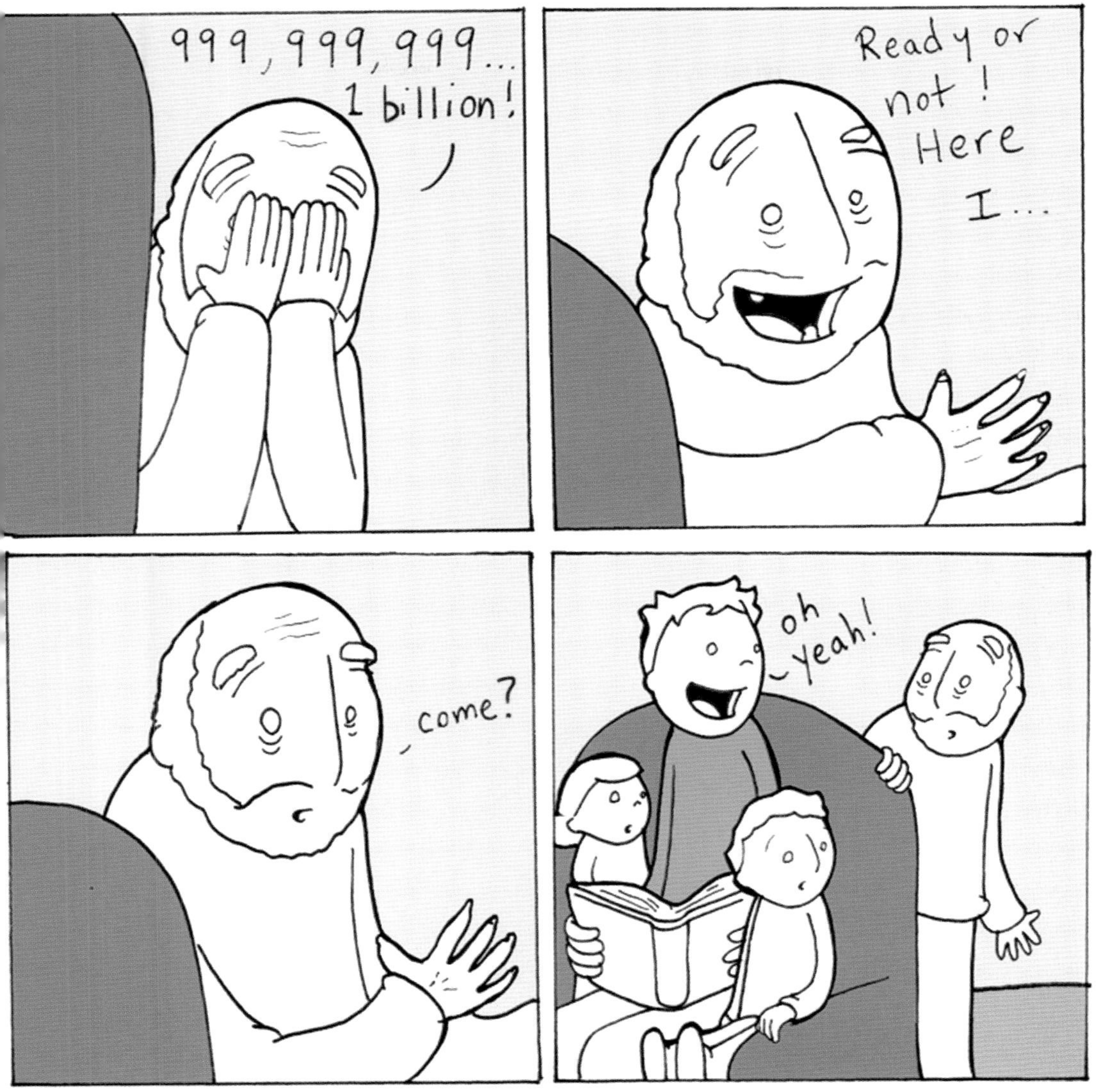
999,999,999... 1 billion!
Ready or not! Here I...
come?
oh yeah!

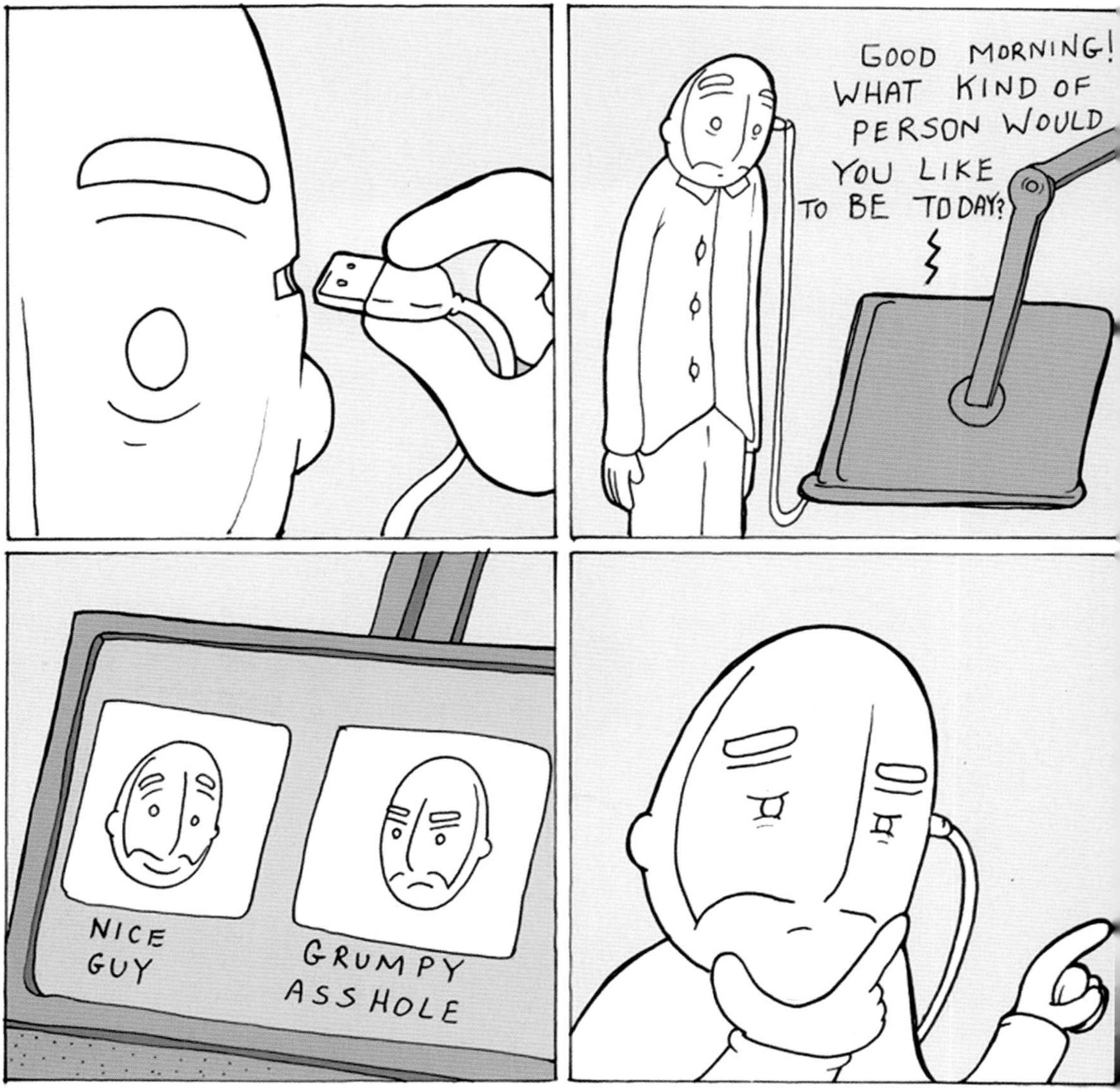
GOOD MORNING! WHAT KIND OF PERSON WOULD YOU LIKE TO BE TODAY?
NICE GUY
GRUMPY ASSHOLE

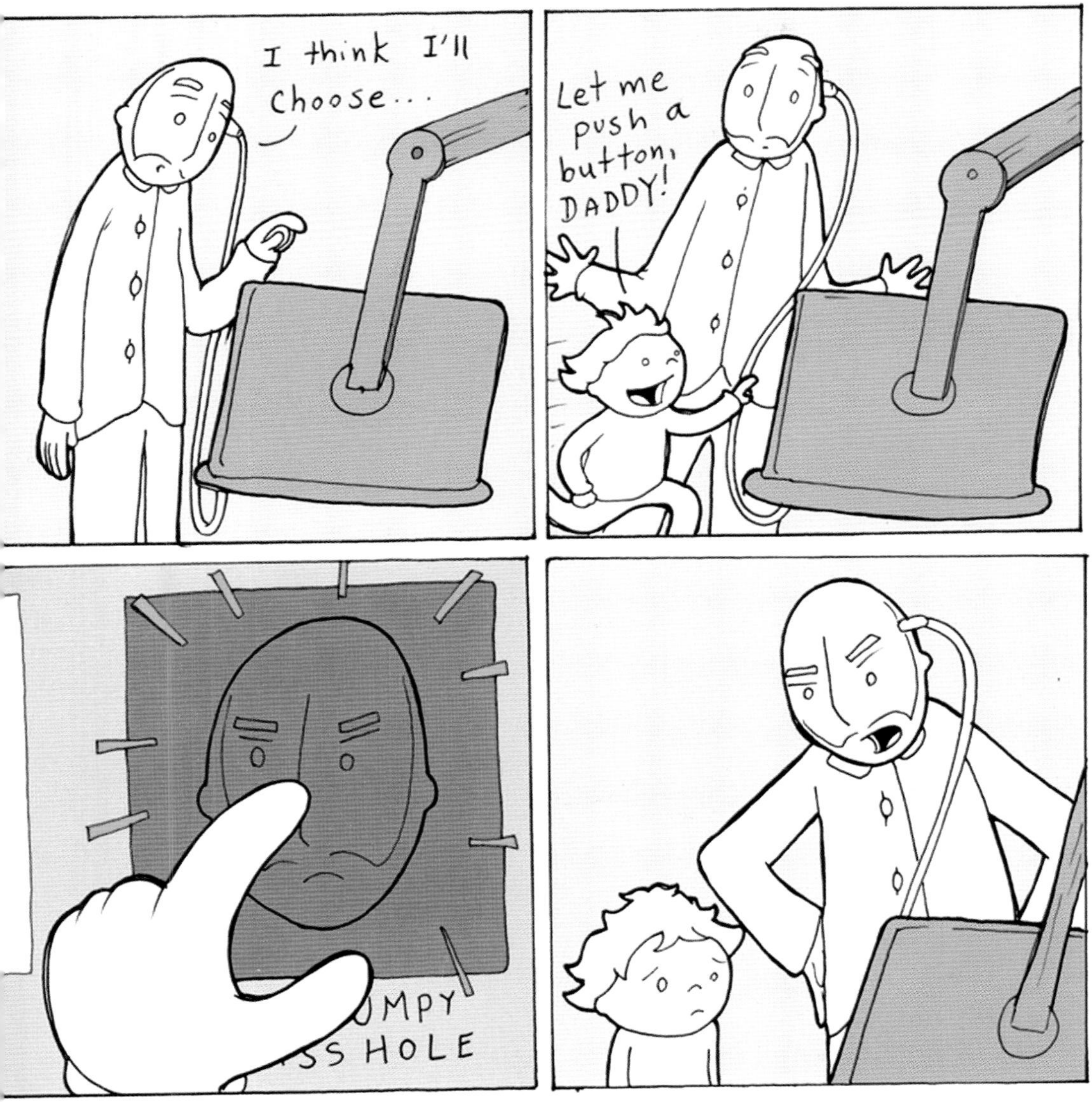
I think I'll choose...
Let me push a button, DADDY!
UMPY
SS HOLE

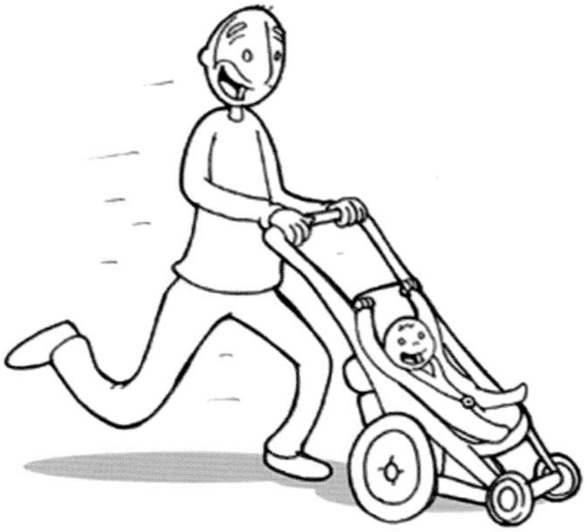

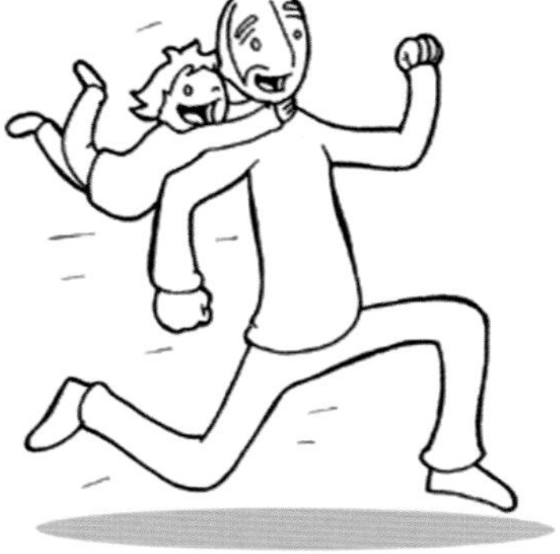

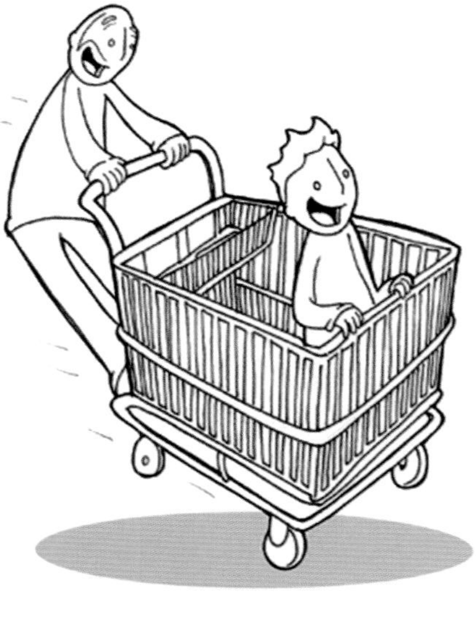

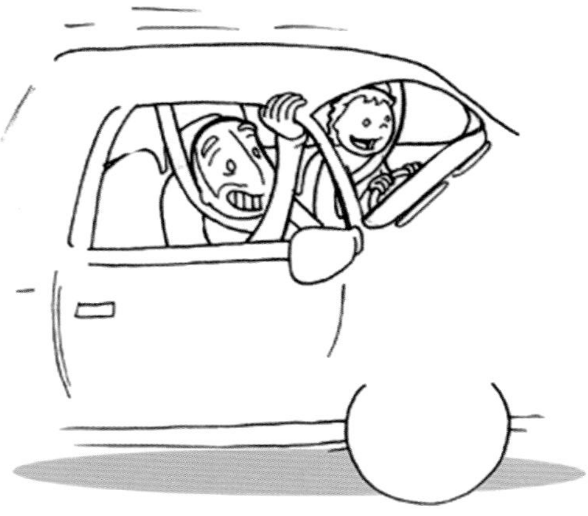

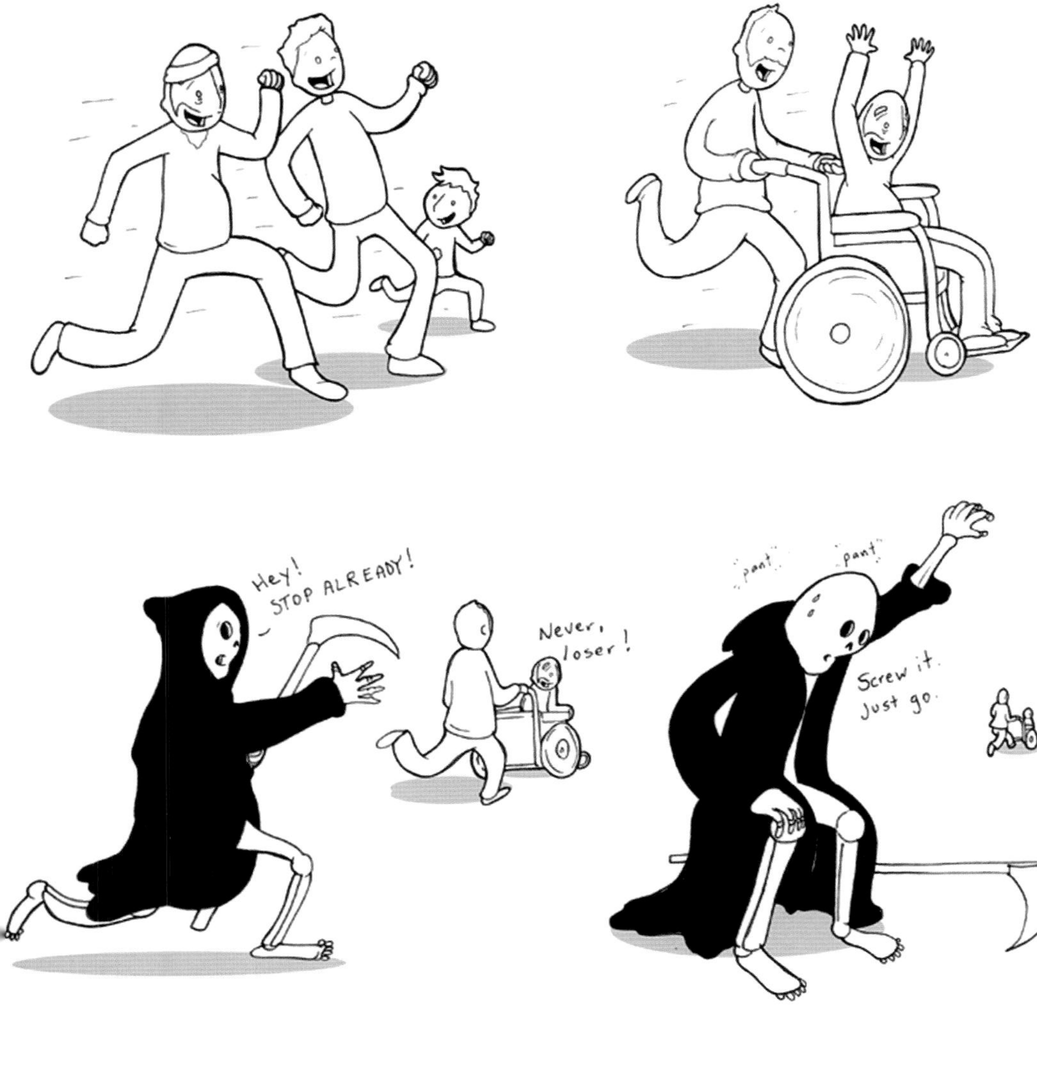
Hey! STOP ALREADY!
Never, loser!
pant
pant
Screw it. Just go.

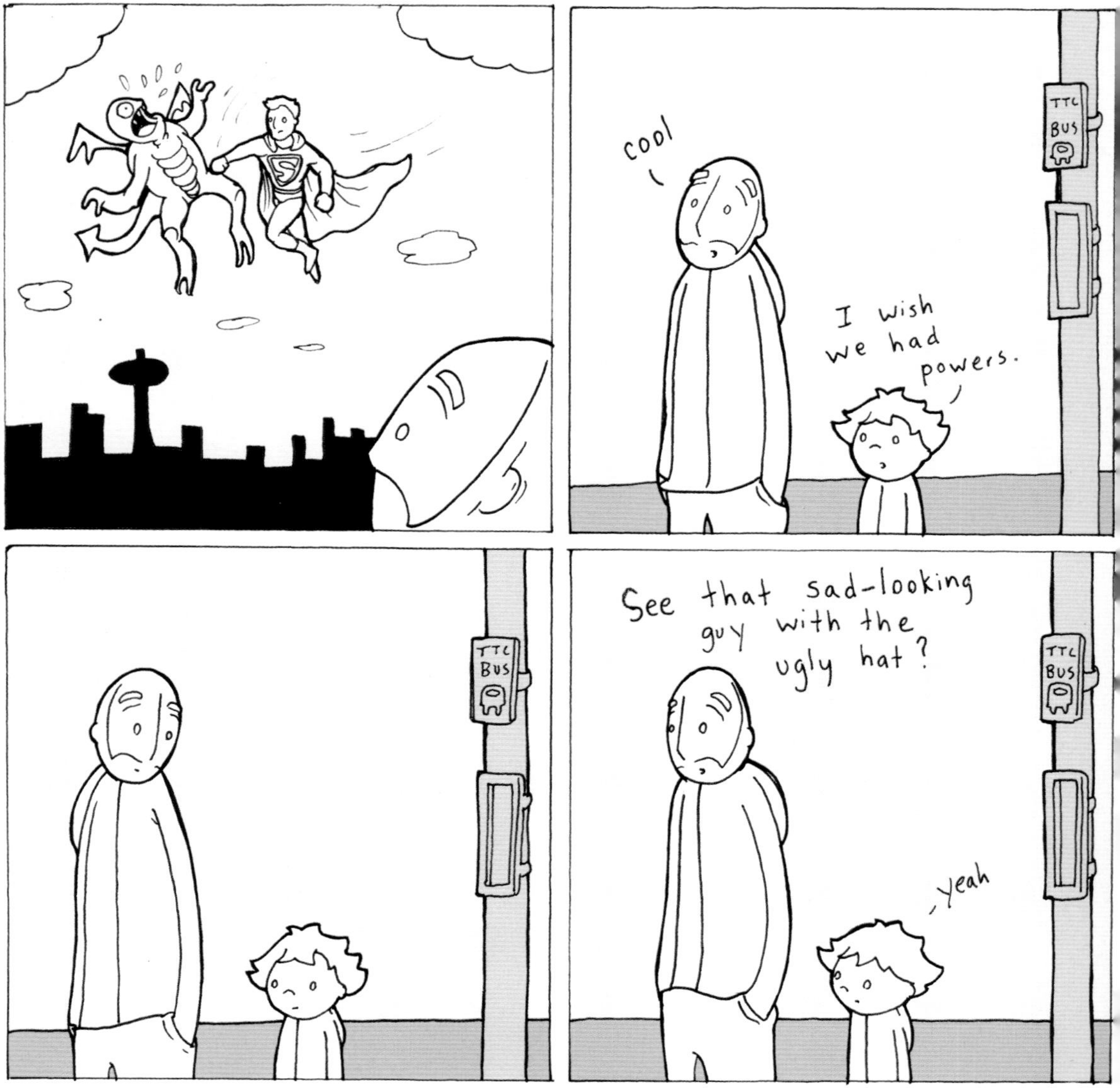
cool
I wish we had powers.
TTC BUS
TTC BUS
See that sad-looking guy with the ugly hat?
TTC BUS
yeah

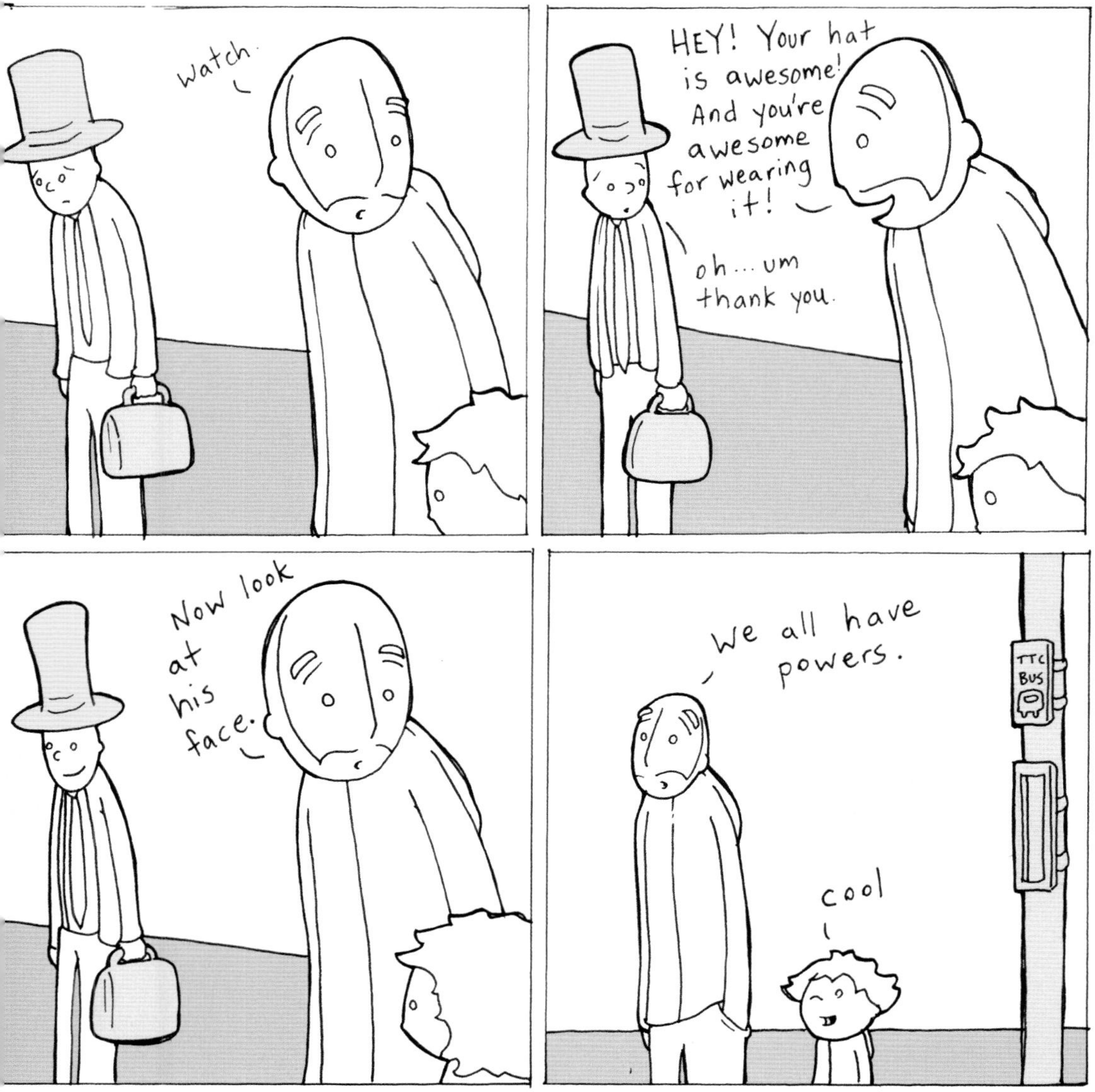
watch.
HEY! Your hat is awesome! And you're awesome for wearing it!
oh... um thank you.
Now look at his face.
We all have powers.
TTC BUS
cool

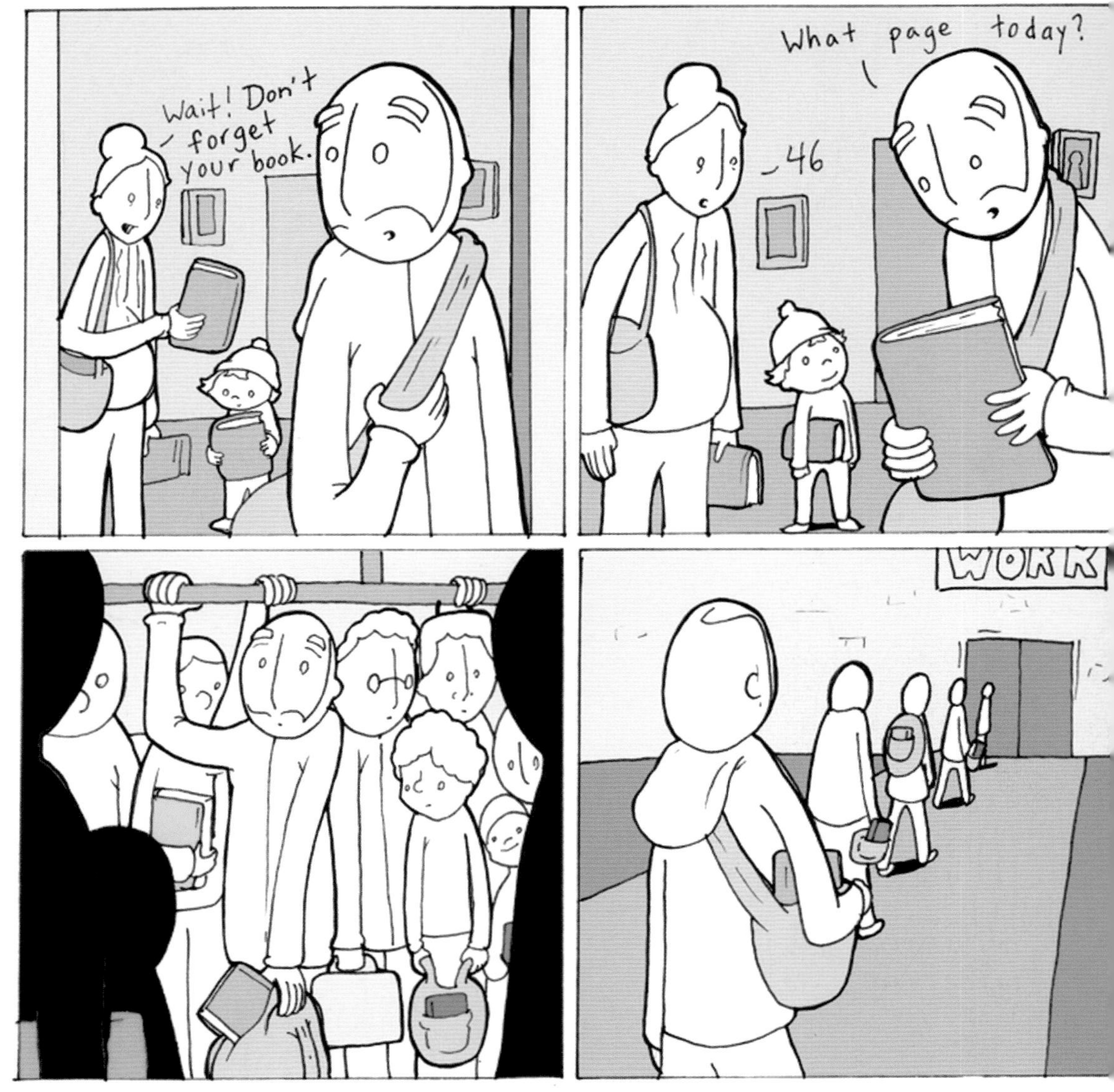

Wait! Don't forget your book.
What page today?
46
WORK

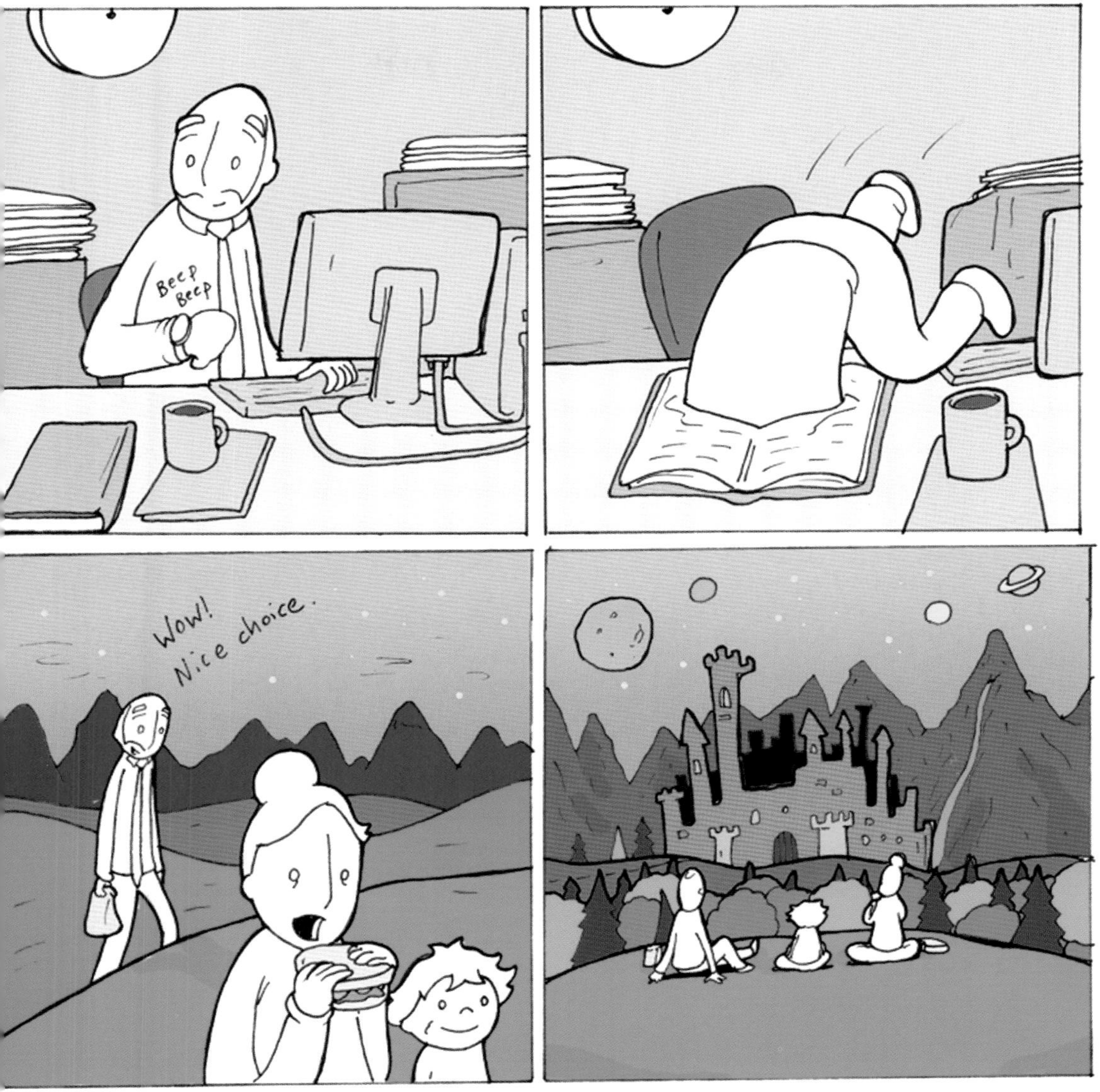
Beep Beep
Wow! Nice choice.

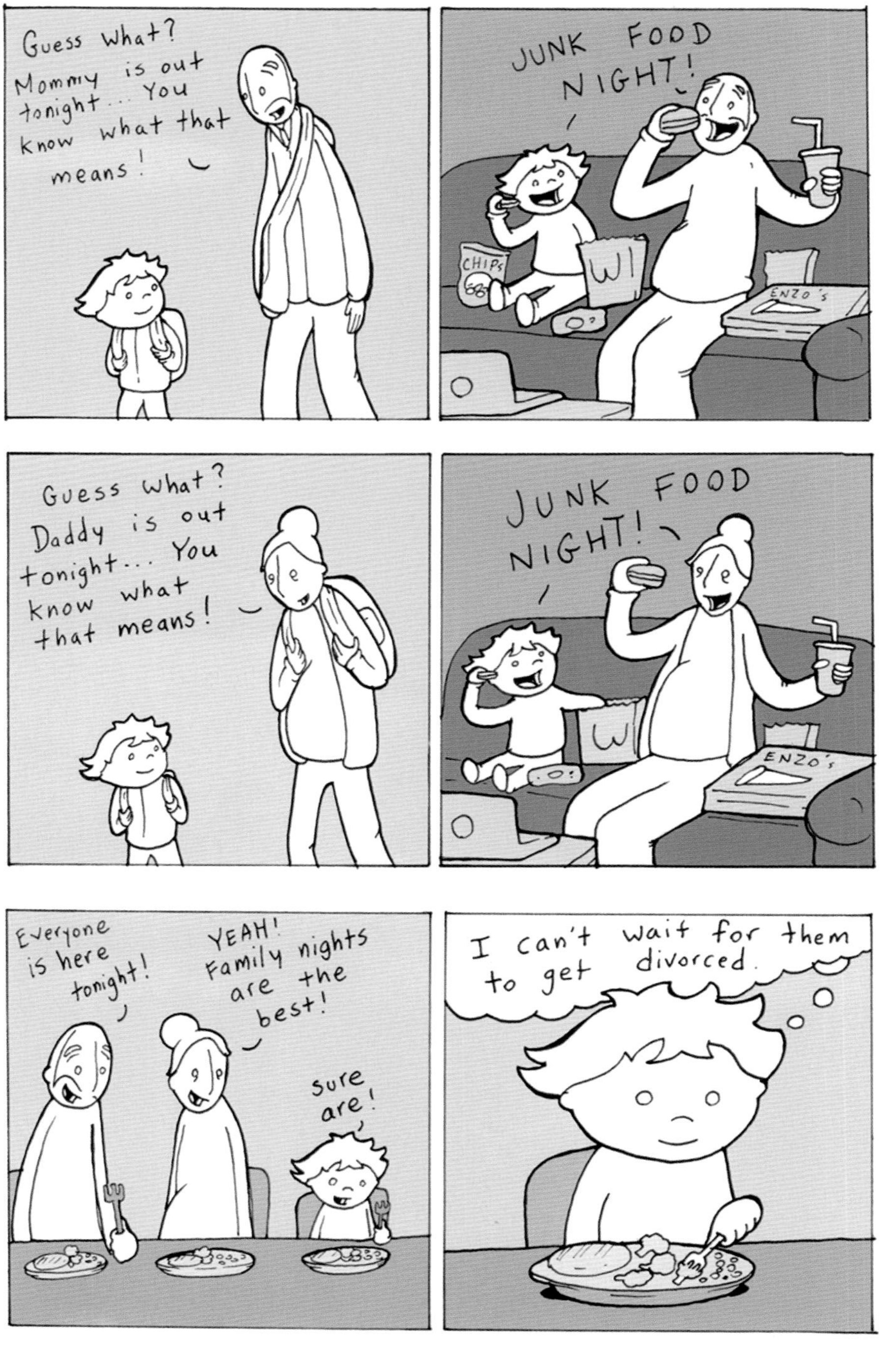
Guess what? Mommy is out tonight... You know what that means!
JUNK FOOD NIGHT!
CHIPS
ENZO's
Guess what? Daddy is out tonight... You know what that means!
JUNK FOOD NIGHT!
ENZO's
Everyone is here tonight!
YEAH! Family nights are the best!
Sure are!
I can't wait for them to get divorced.

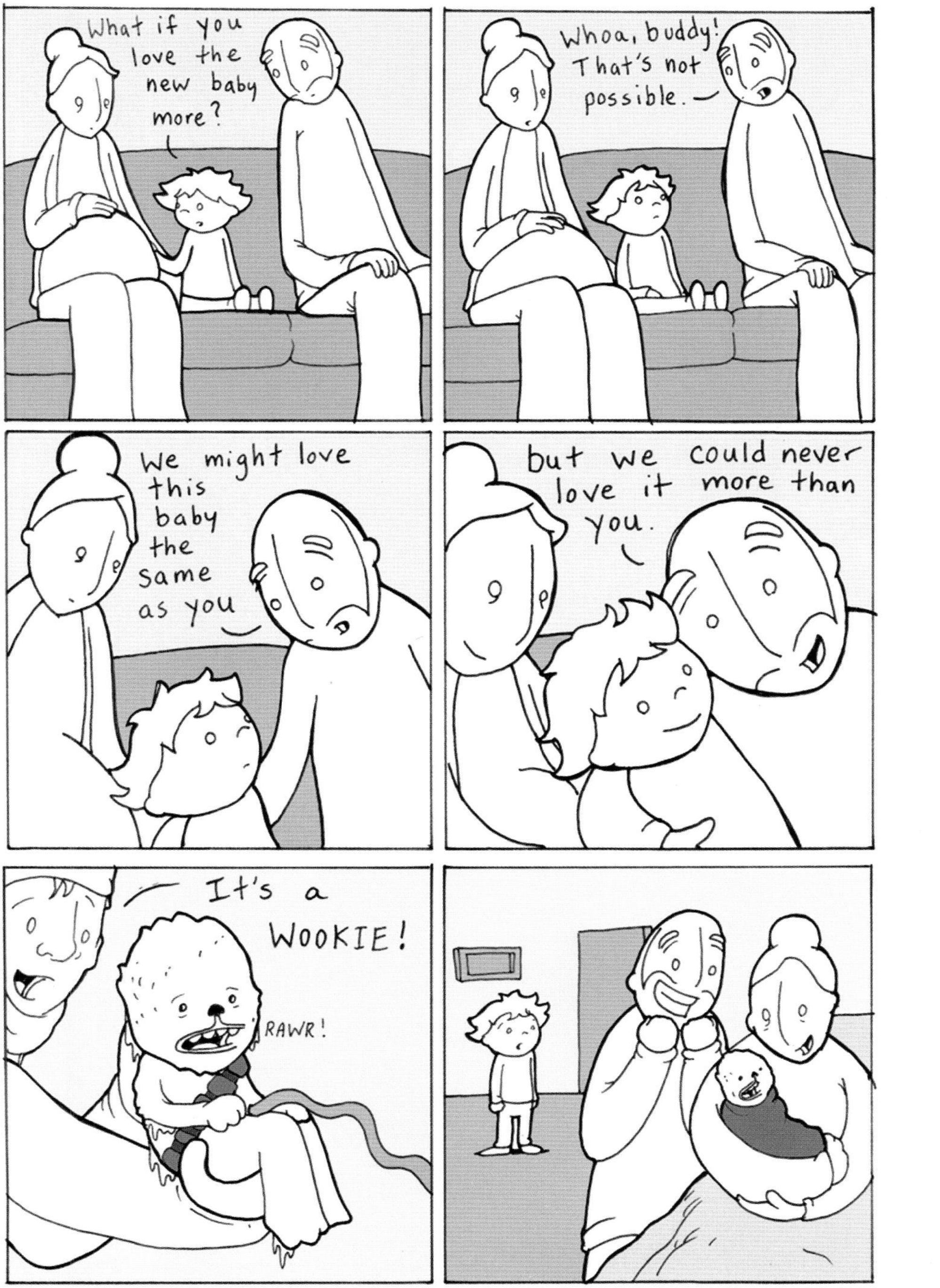
What if you love the new baby more?
Whoa, buddy! That's not possible.
We might love this baby the same as you
but we could never love it more than you.
It's a WOOKIE!
RAWR!

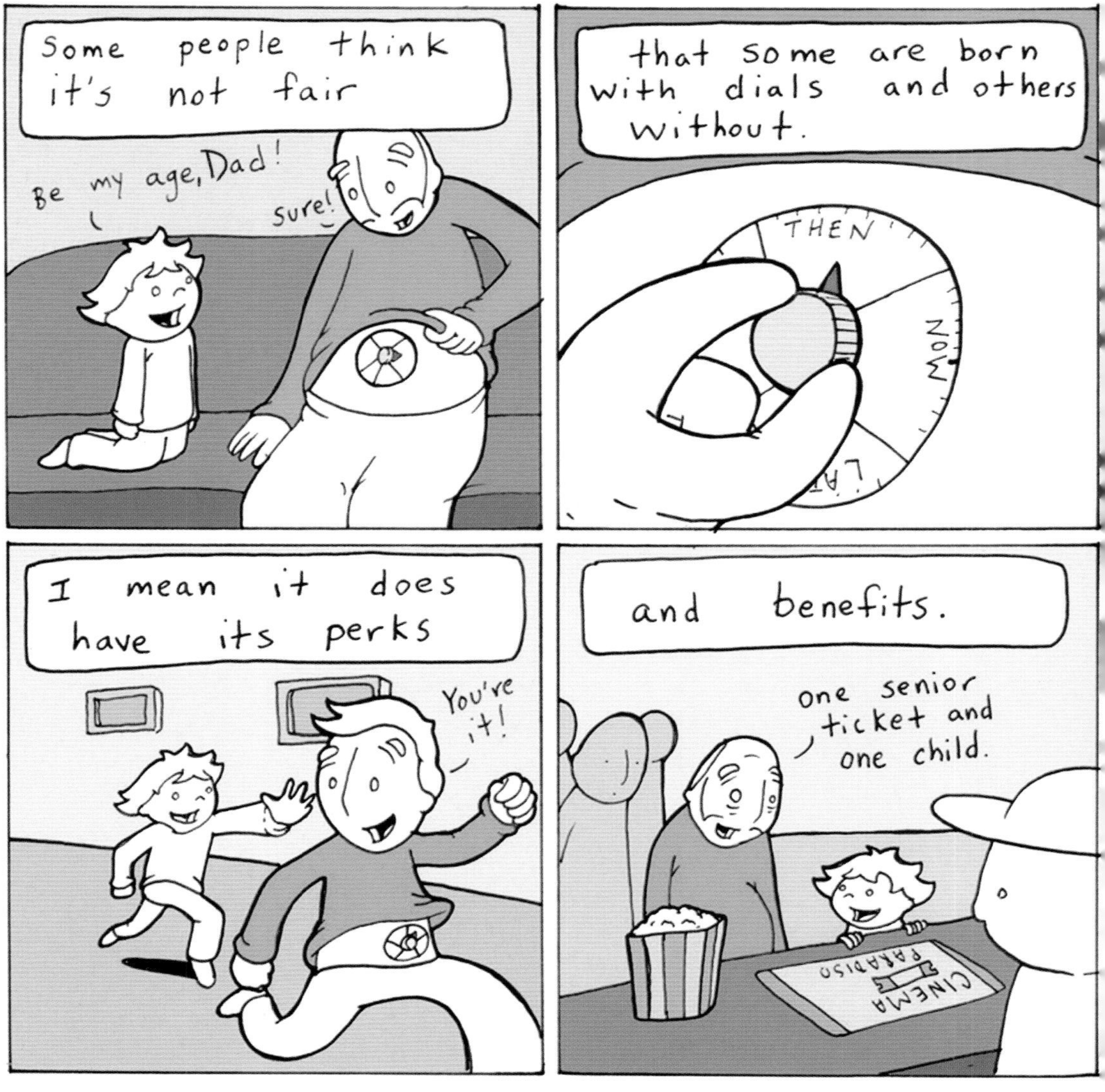
Some people think it's not fair
Be my age, Dad!
Sure!
that some are born with dials and others without.
THEN
NOW
I mean it does have its perks
You're it!
and benefits.
one senior ticket and one child.
CINEMA PARADISO

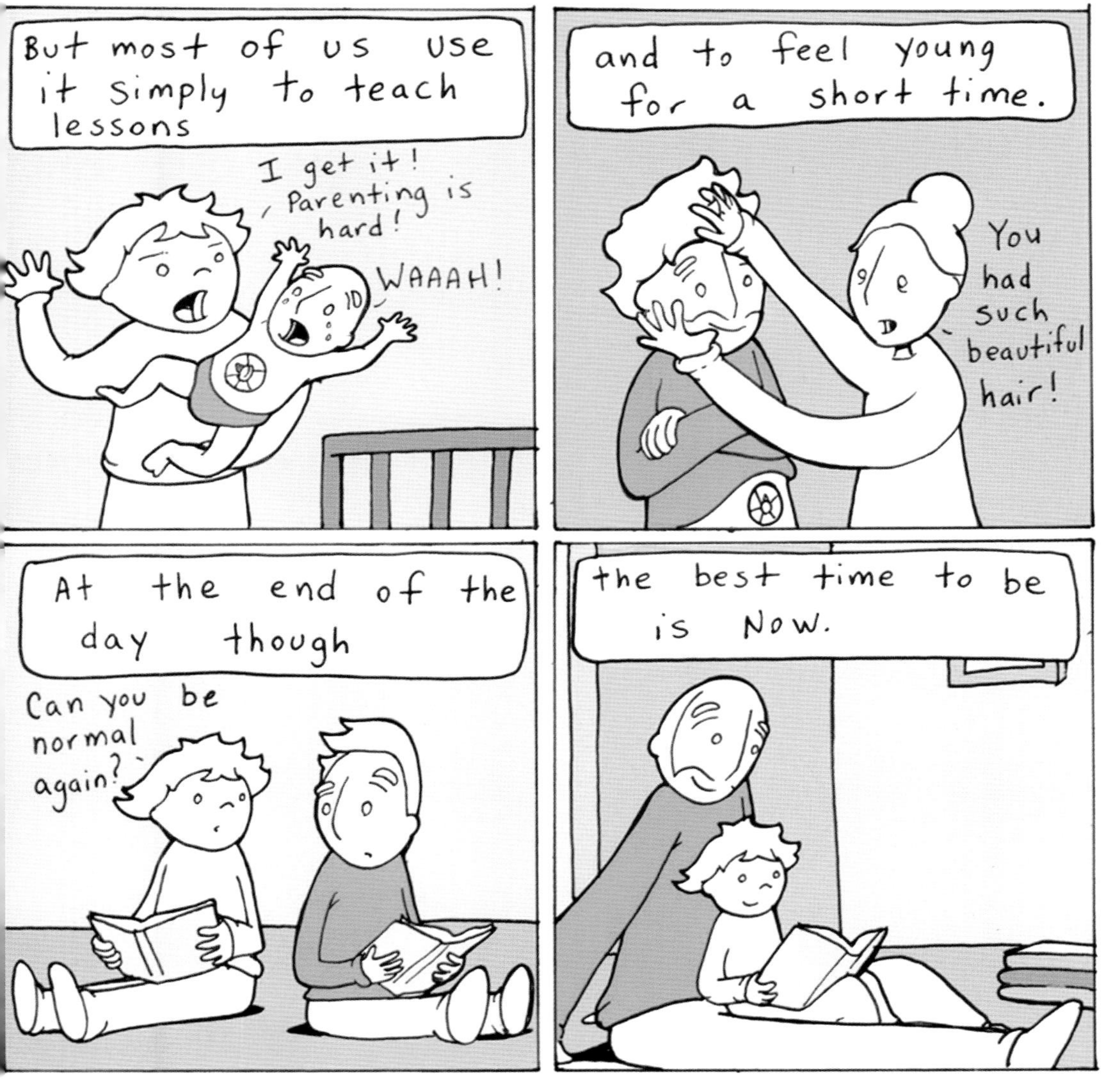
But most of us use it simply to teach lessons
I get it! Parenting is hard!
WAAAH!
and to feel young for a short time.
You had such beautiful hair!
At the end of the day though
Can you be normal again?
the best time to be is NOW.

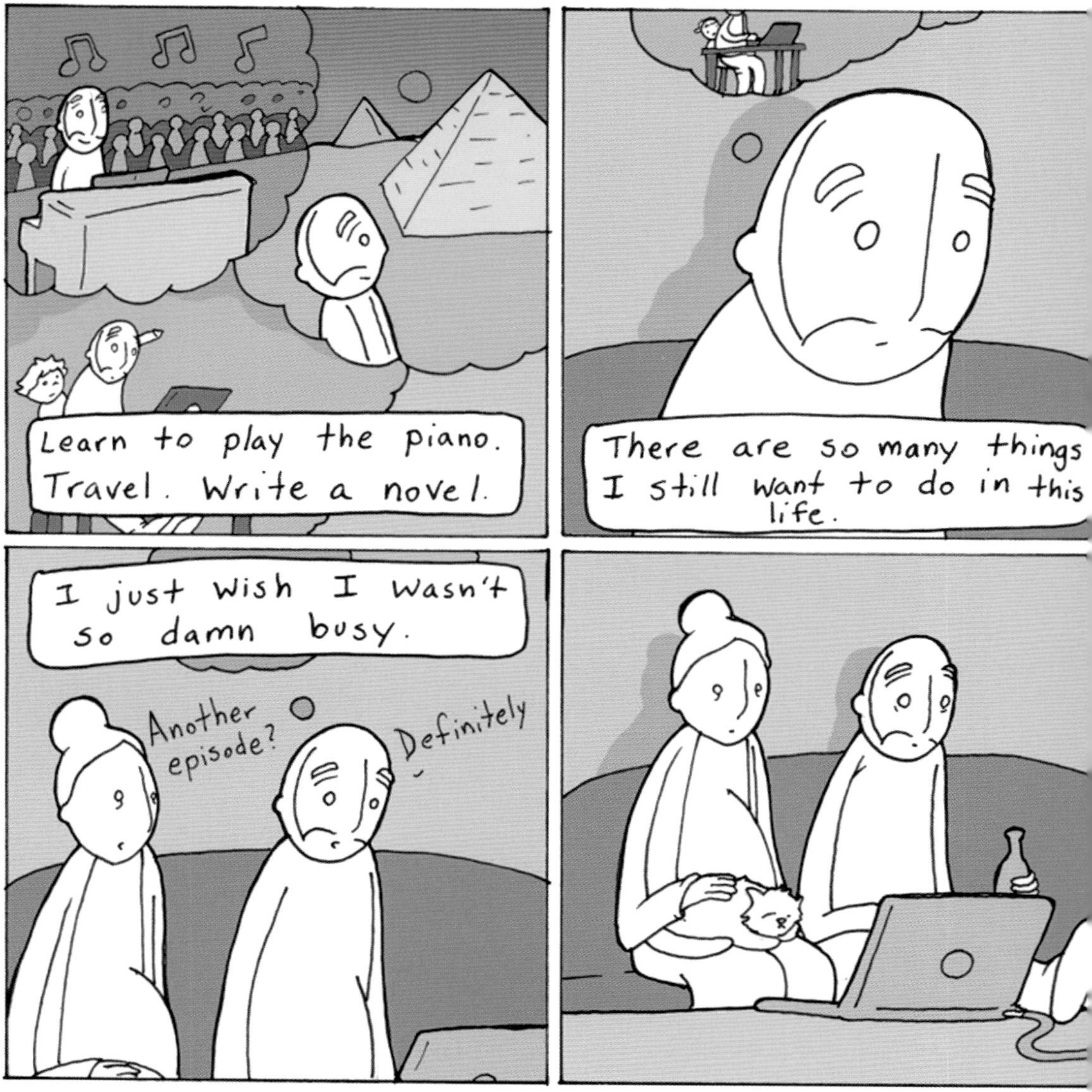
Learn to play the piano. Travel. Write a novel.
There are so many things I still want to do in this life.
I just wish I wasn't so damn busy.
Another episode?
Definitely

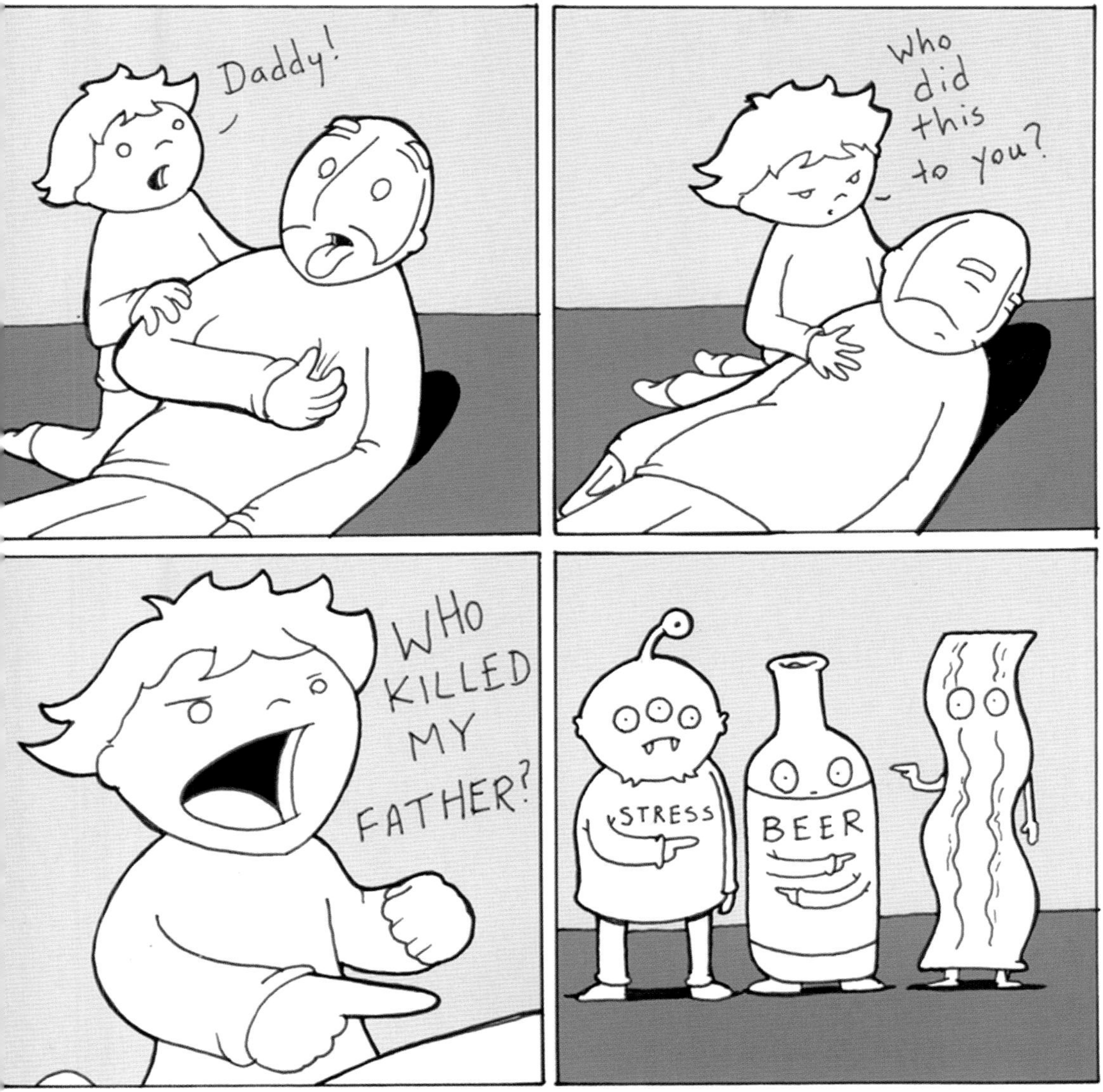
Daddy!
who did this to you?
WHO KILLED MY FATHER?
STRESS
BEER

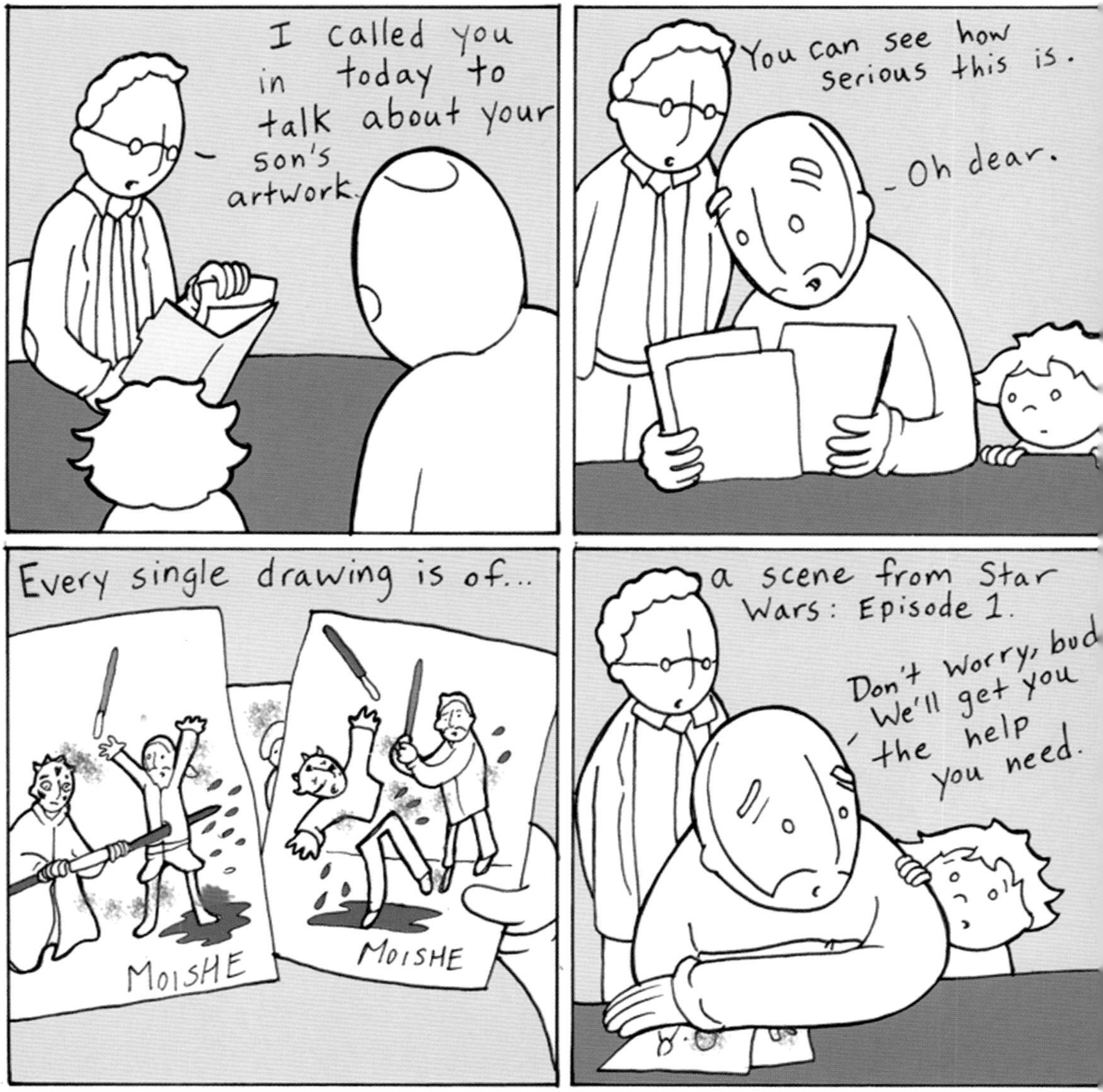
I called you in today to talk about your son's artwork.
You can see how serious this is.
Oh dear.
Every single drawing is of...
MOISHE
MOISHE
a scene from Star Wars: Episode 1.
Don't worry, bud. We'll get you the help you need.

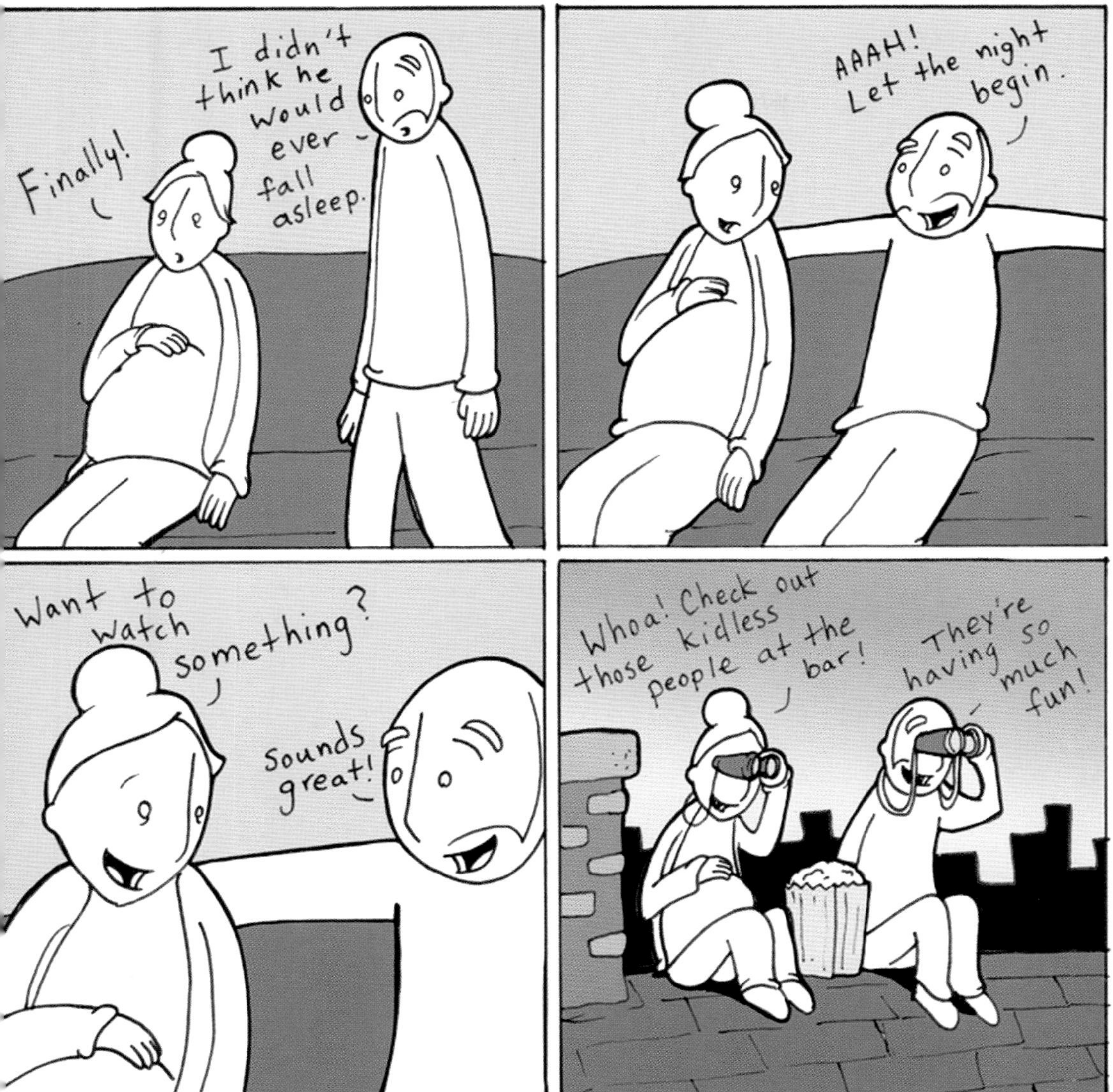
Finally!
I didn't think he would ever fall asleep.
AAAH! Let the night begin.
Want to watch something?
Sounds great!
Whoa! Check out those kidless people at the bar!
They're having so much fun!

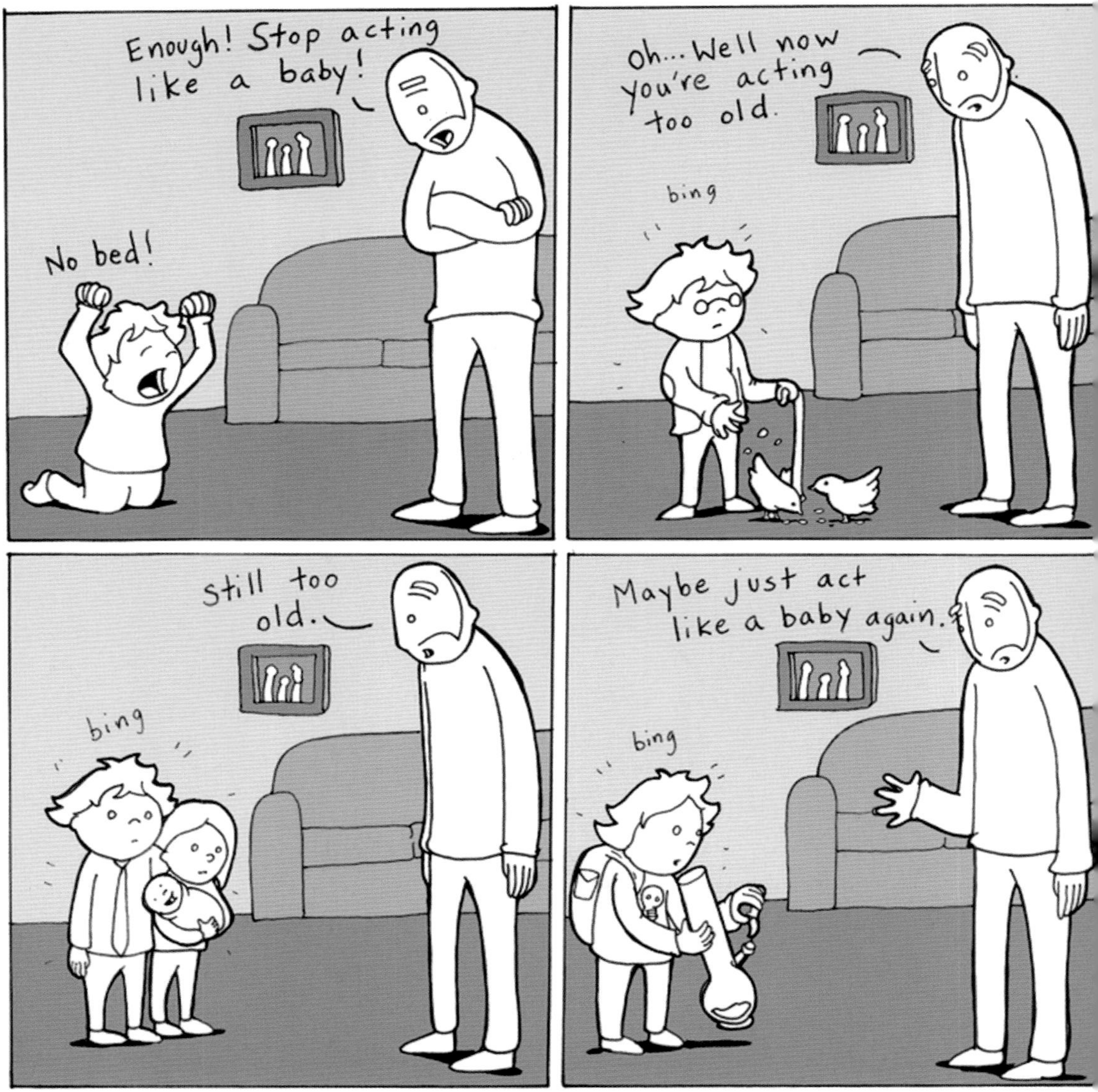
Enough! Stop acting like a baby!
No bed!
Oh... Well now you're acting too old.
bing
Still too old.
bing
Maybe just act like a baby again.
bing

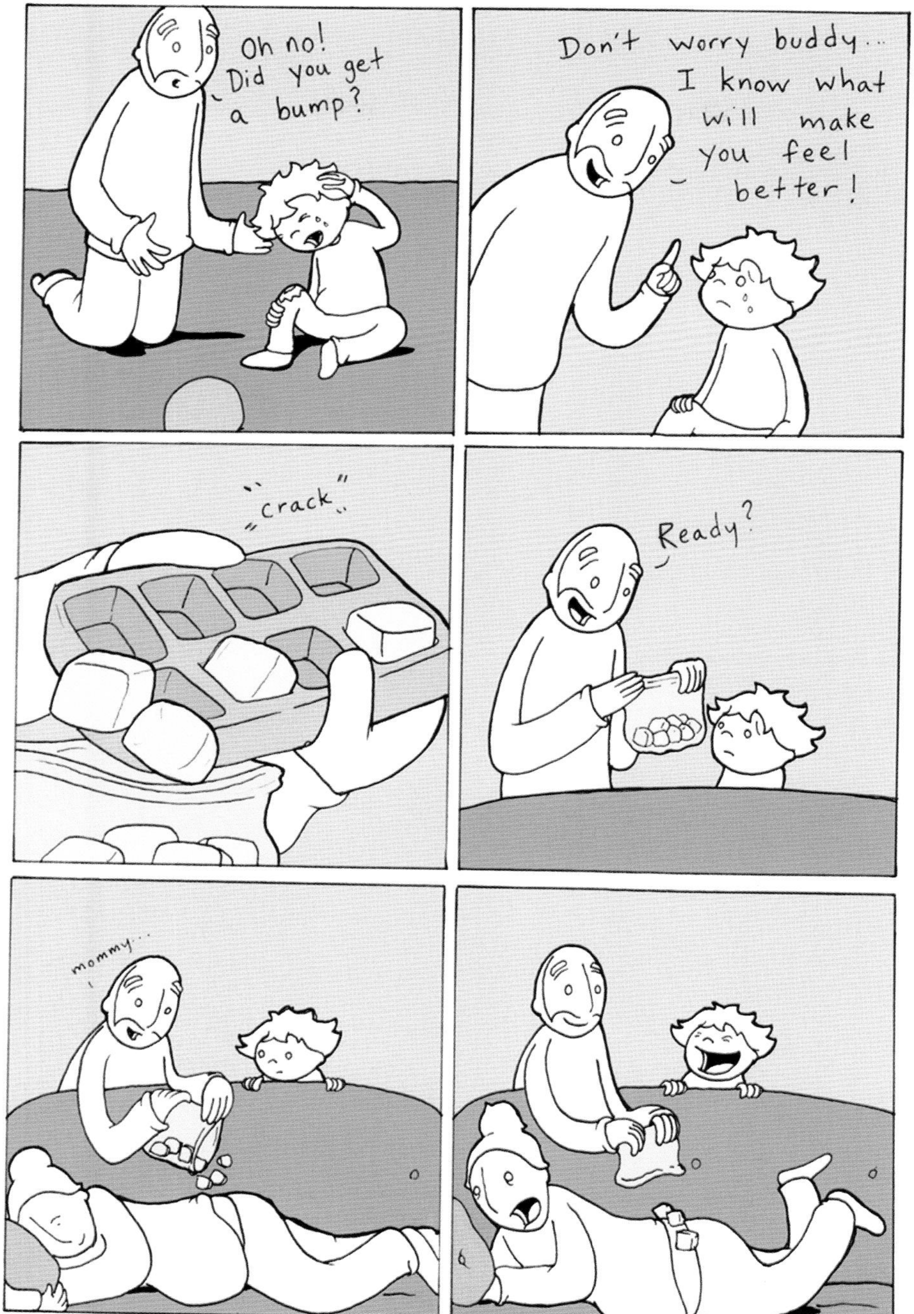
Oh no! Did you get a bump?
Don't worry buddy... I know what will make you feel better!
crack
Ready?
mommy...

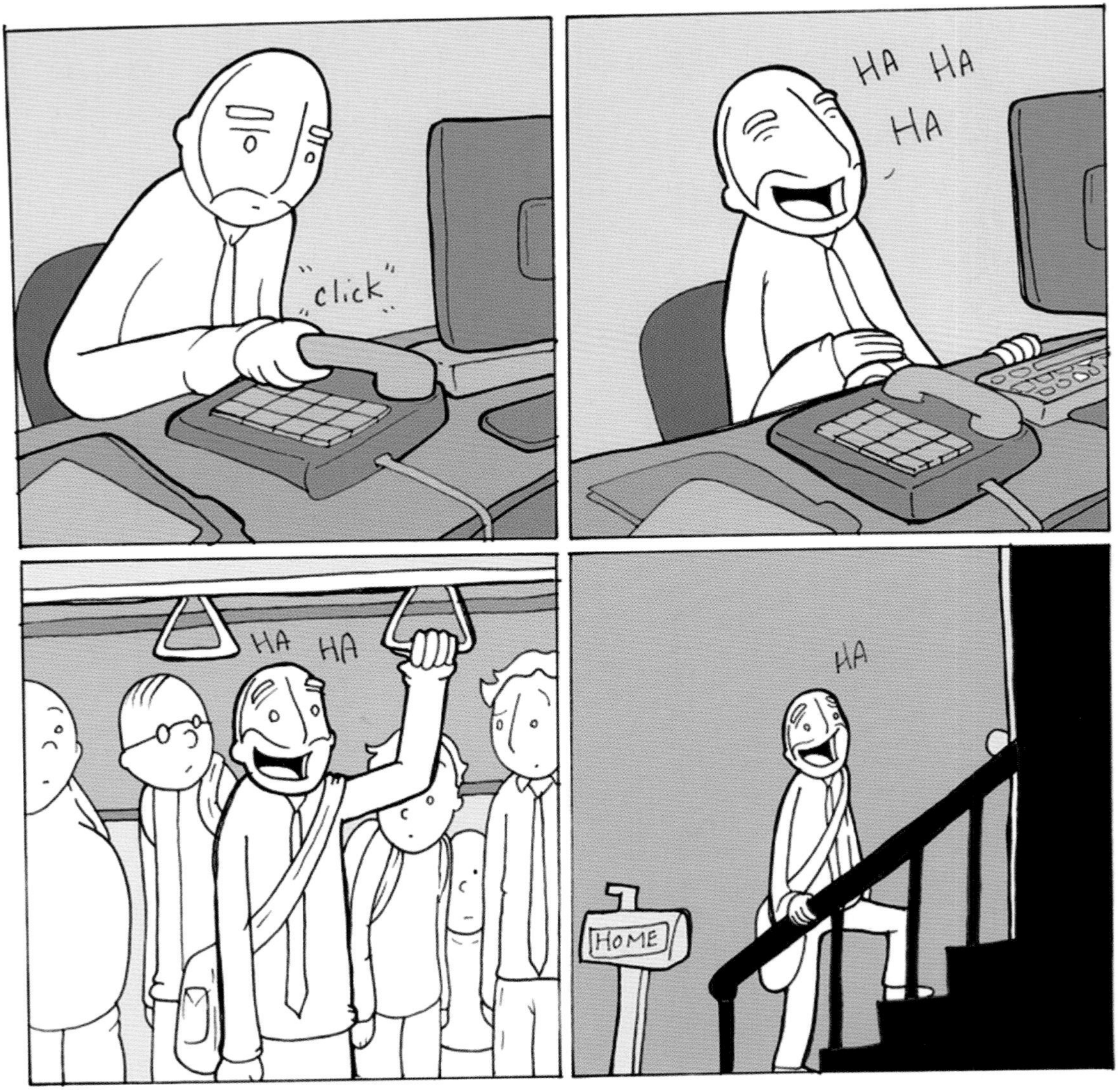
"click"
HA HA
HA
HA HA
HA
HOME

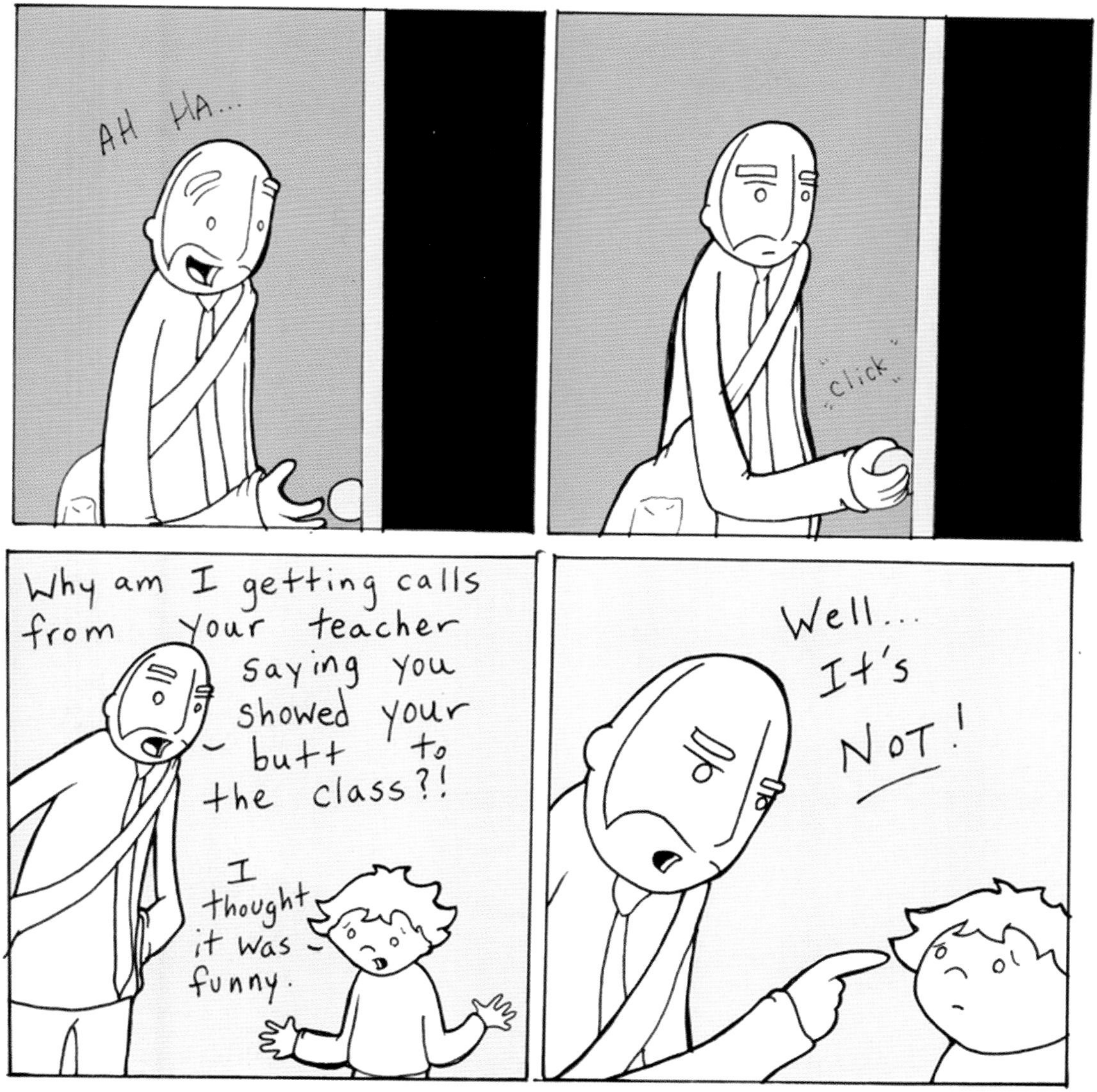
AH HA...
click
Why am I getting calls from your teacher saying you showed your butt to the class?!
I thought it was funny.
Well... It's NOT!

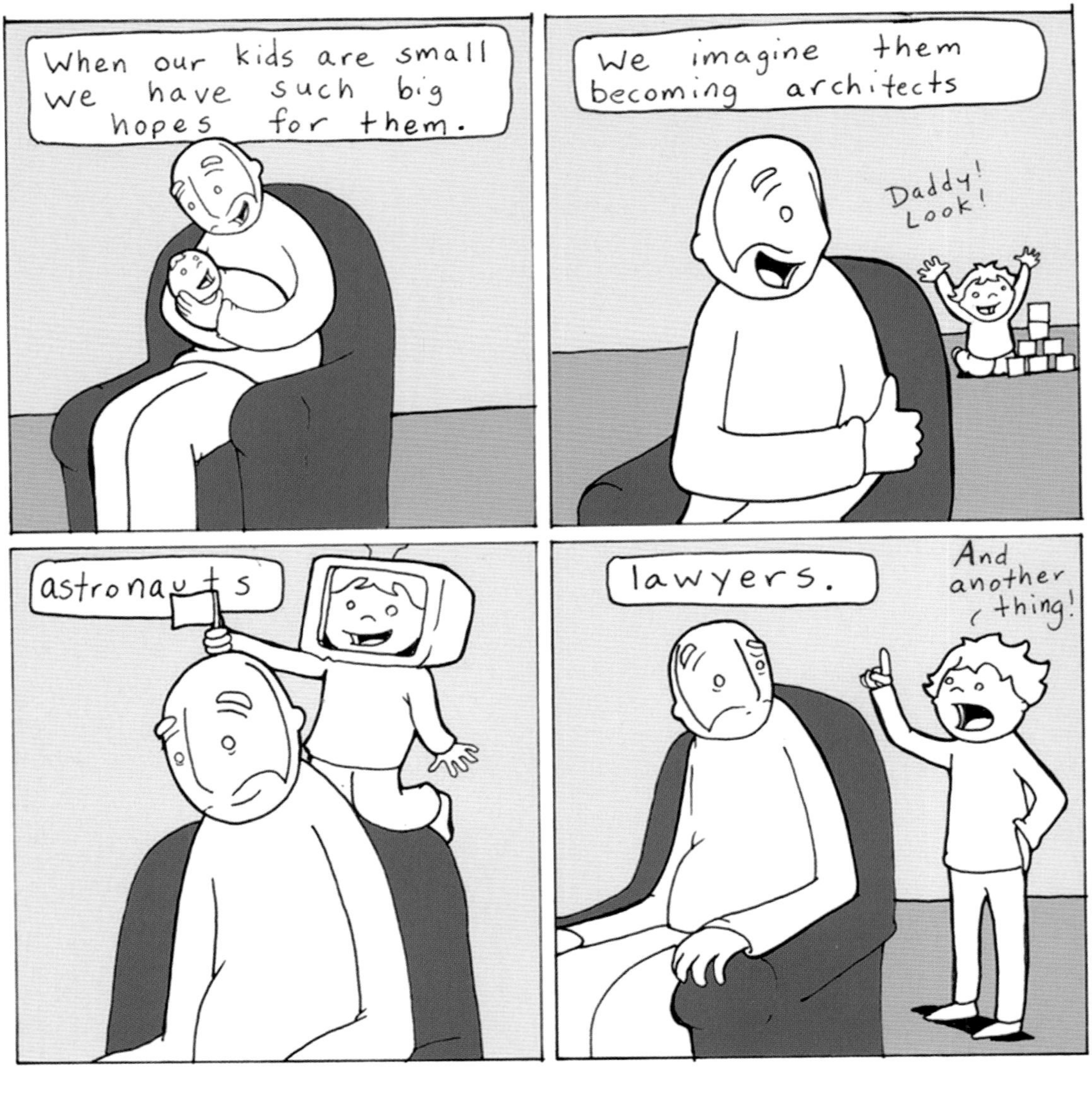
When our kids are small we have such big hopes for them.
We imagine them becoming architects
Daddy! Look!
astronauts
lawyers.
And another thing!

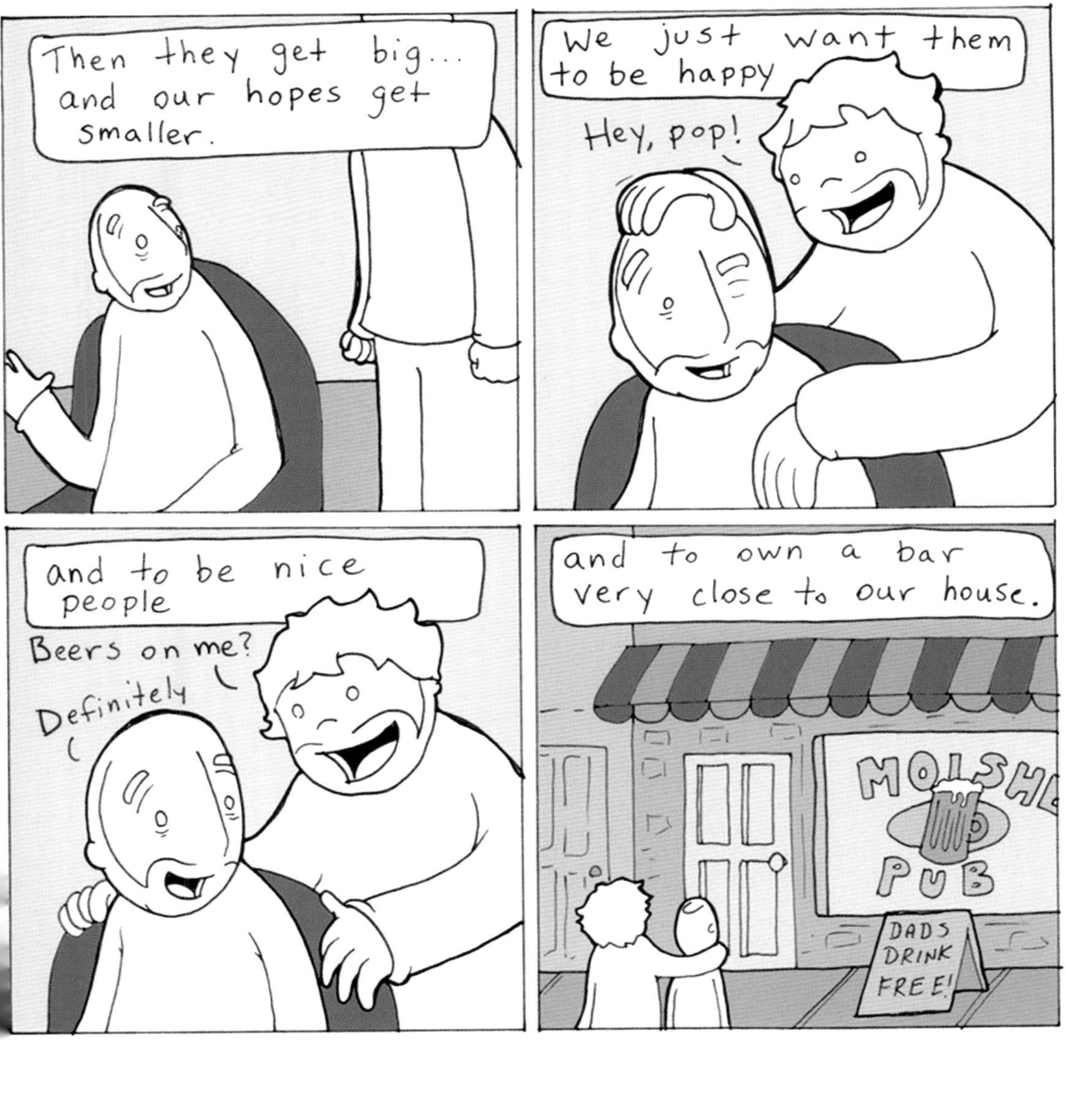
Then they get big... and our hopes get smaller.
We just want them to be happy
Hey, pop!
and to be nice people
Beers on me?
Definitely
and to own a bar very close to our house.
MOLSH
PUB
DADS DRINK FREE!

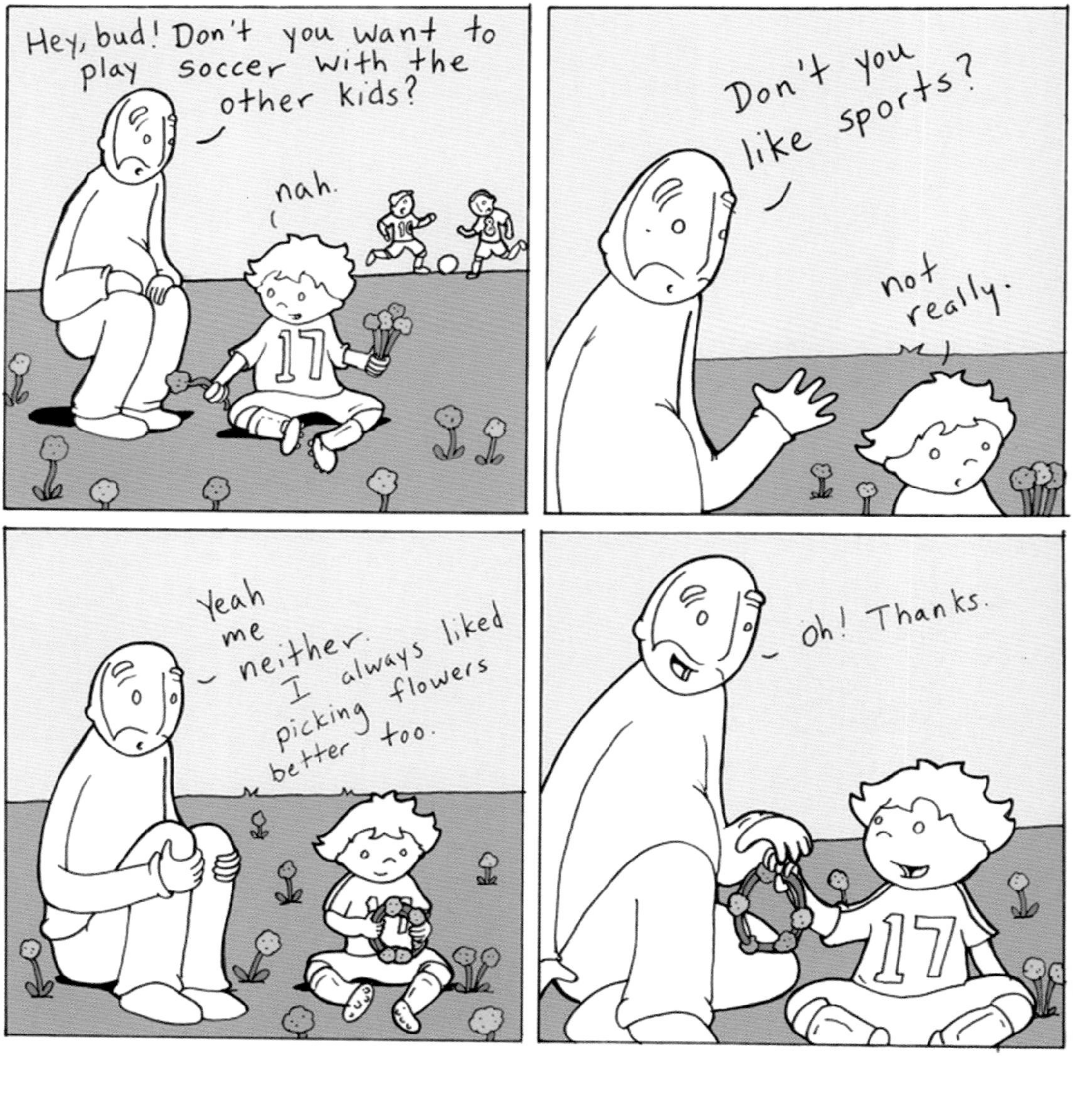
Hey, bud! Don't you want to play soccer with the other kids?
nah.
Don't you like sports?
not really.
Yeah me neither. I always liked picking flowers better too.
Oh! Thanks.

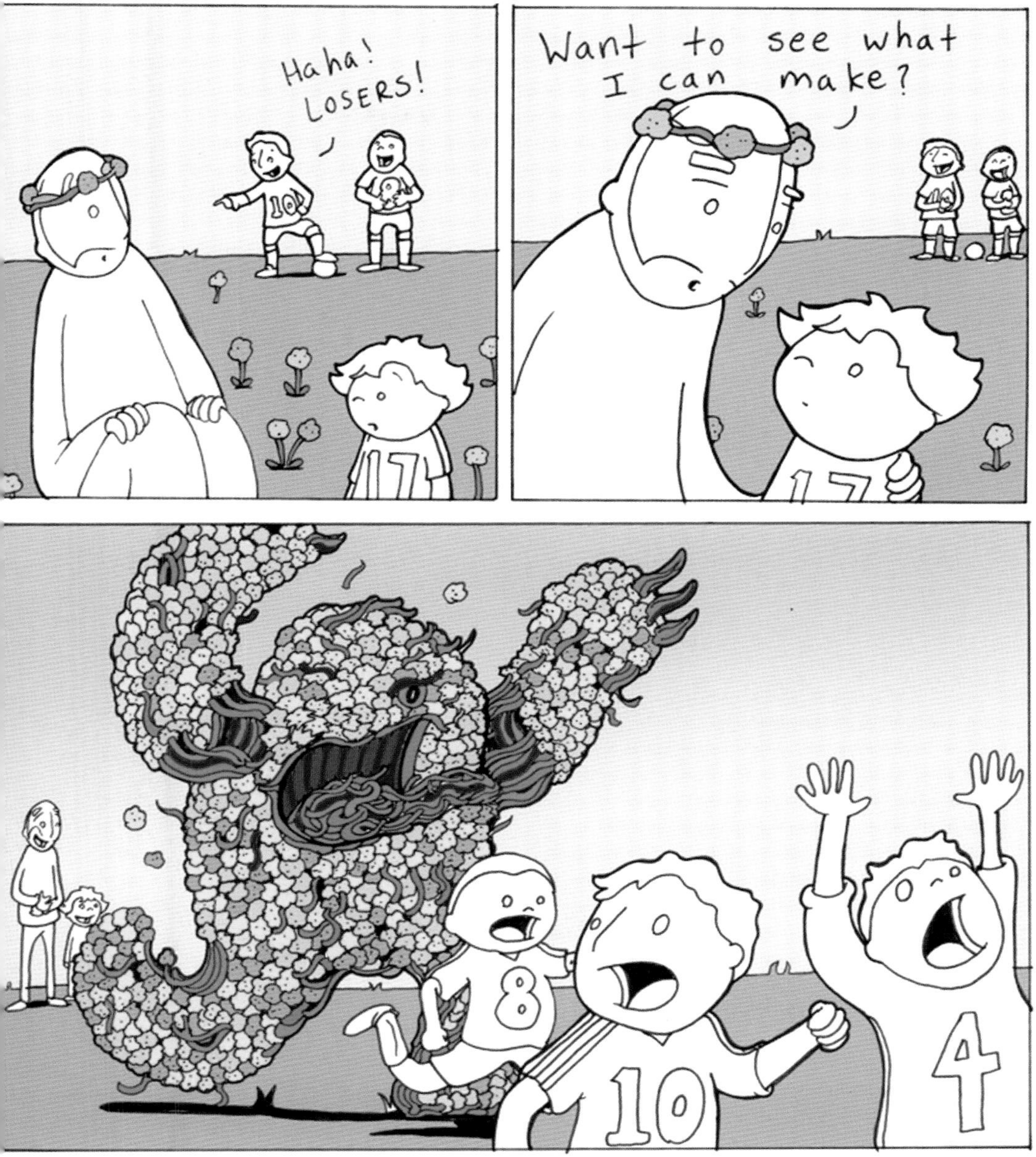
Haha! LOSERS!
Want to see what I can make?

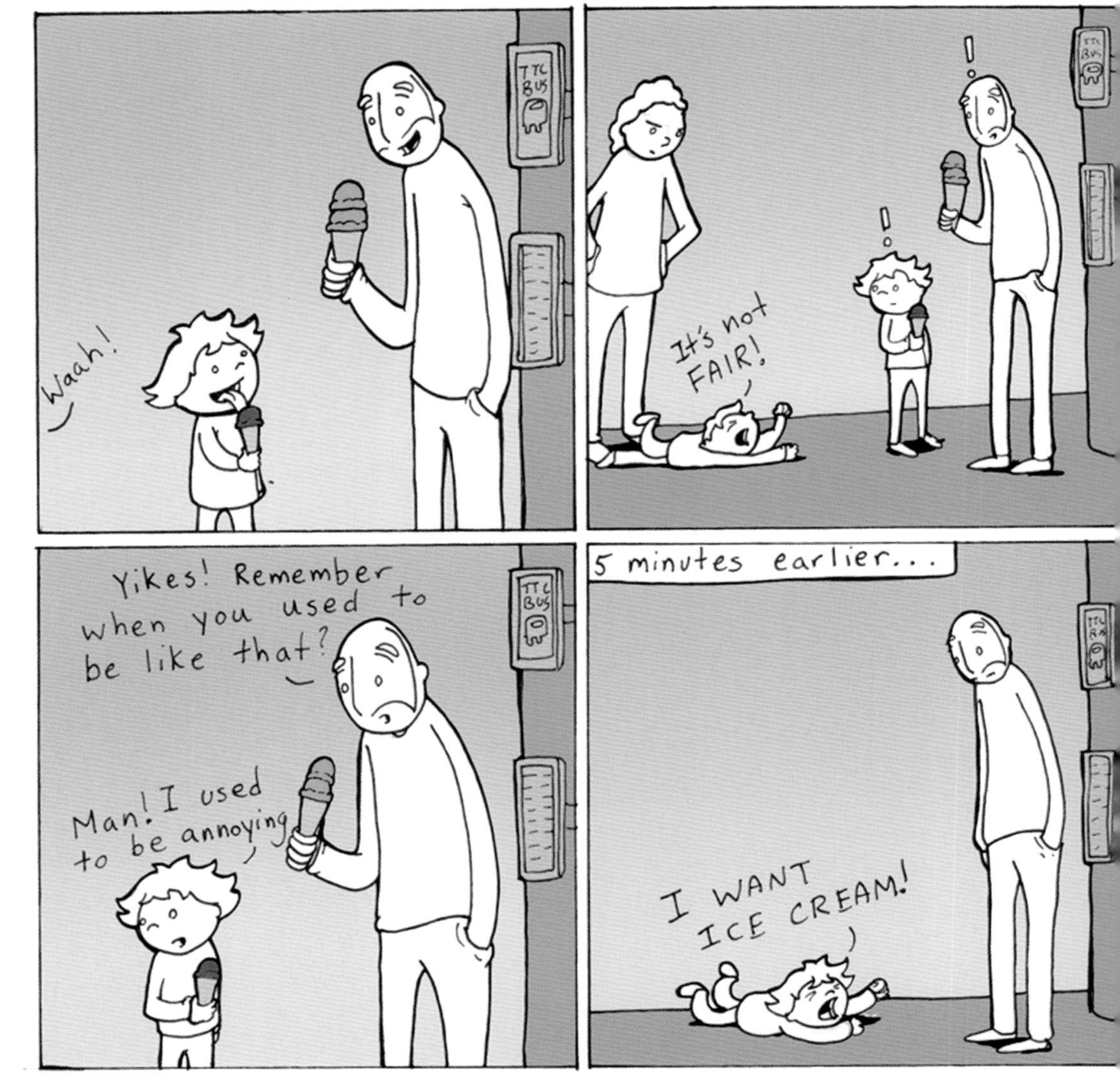
TTC BUS
Waah!
It's not FAIR!
Yikes! Remember when you used to be like that?
TTC BUS
Man! I used to be annoying
5 minutes earlier...
I WANT ICE CREAM!

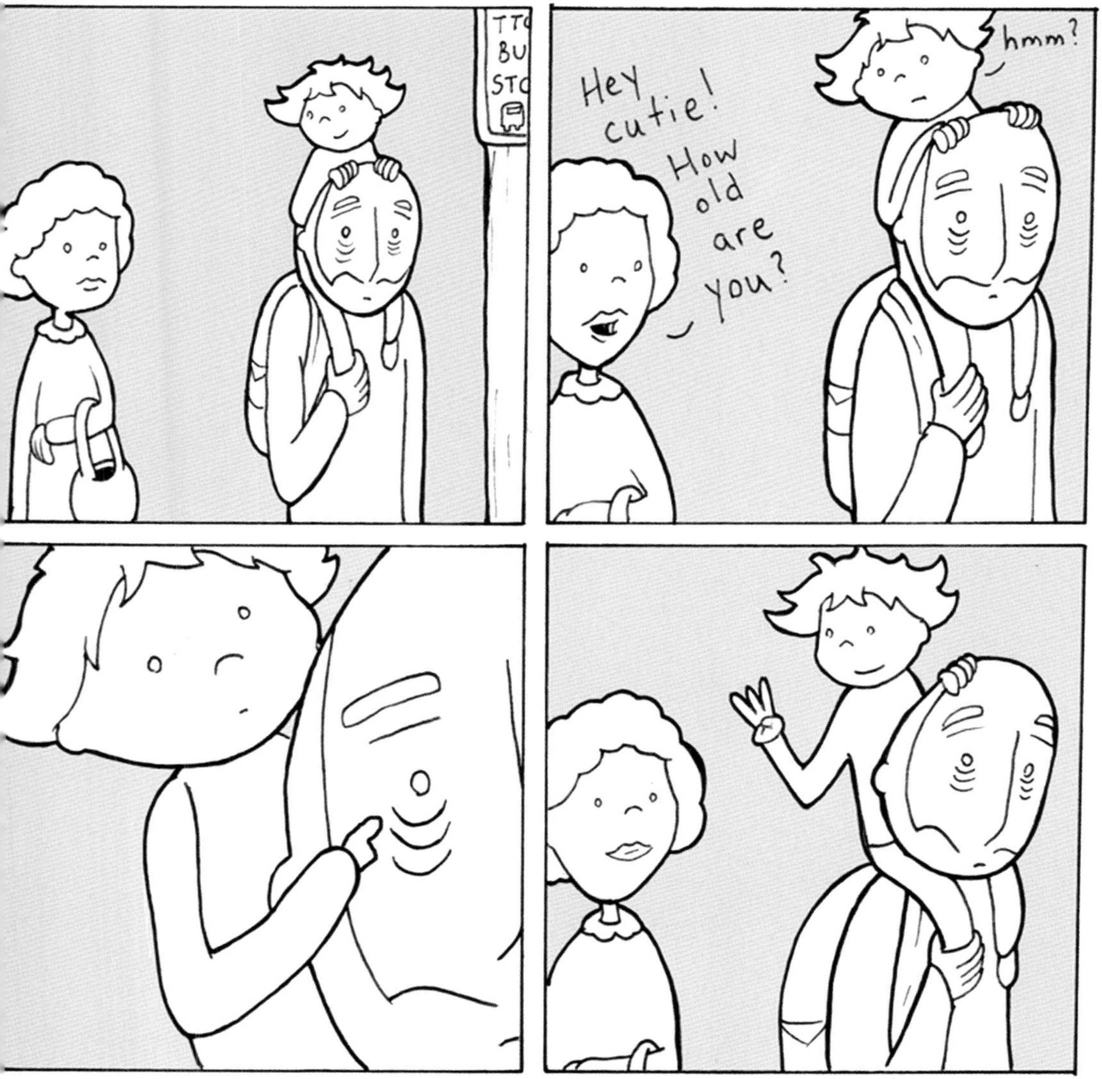
TTC
BU
STO
Hey cutie! How old are you?
hmm?

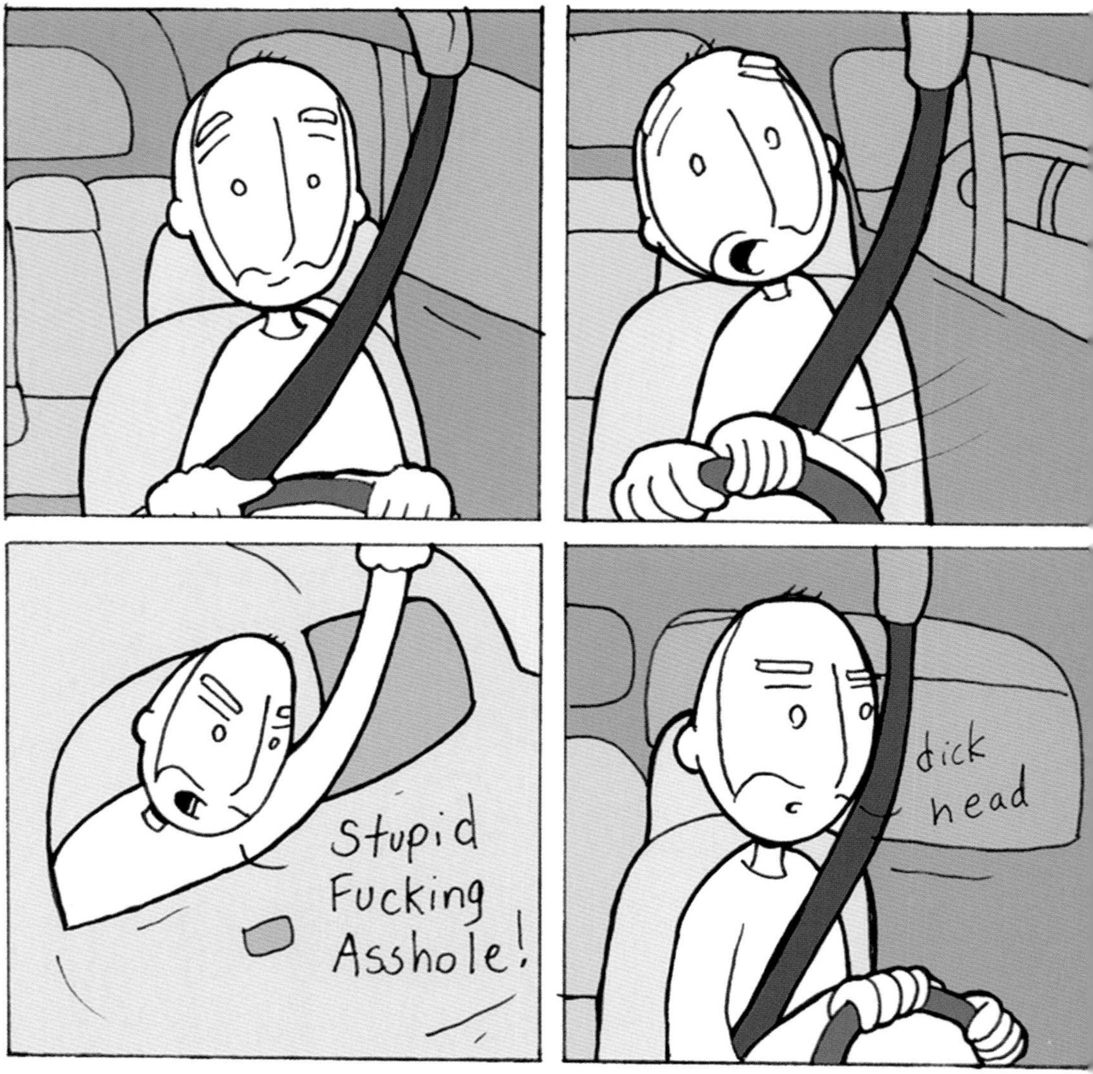
Stupid Fucking Asshole!
dick head

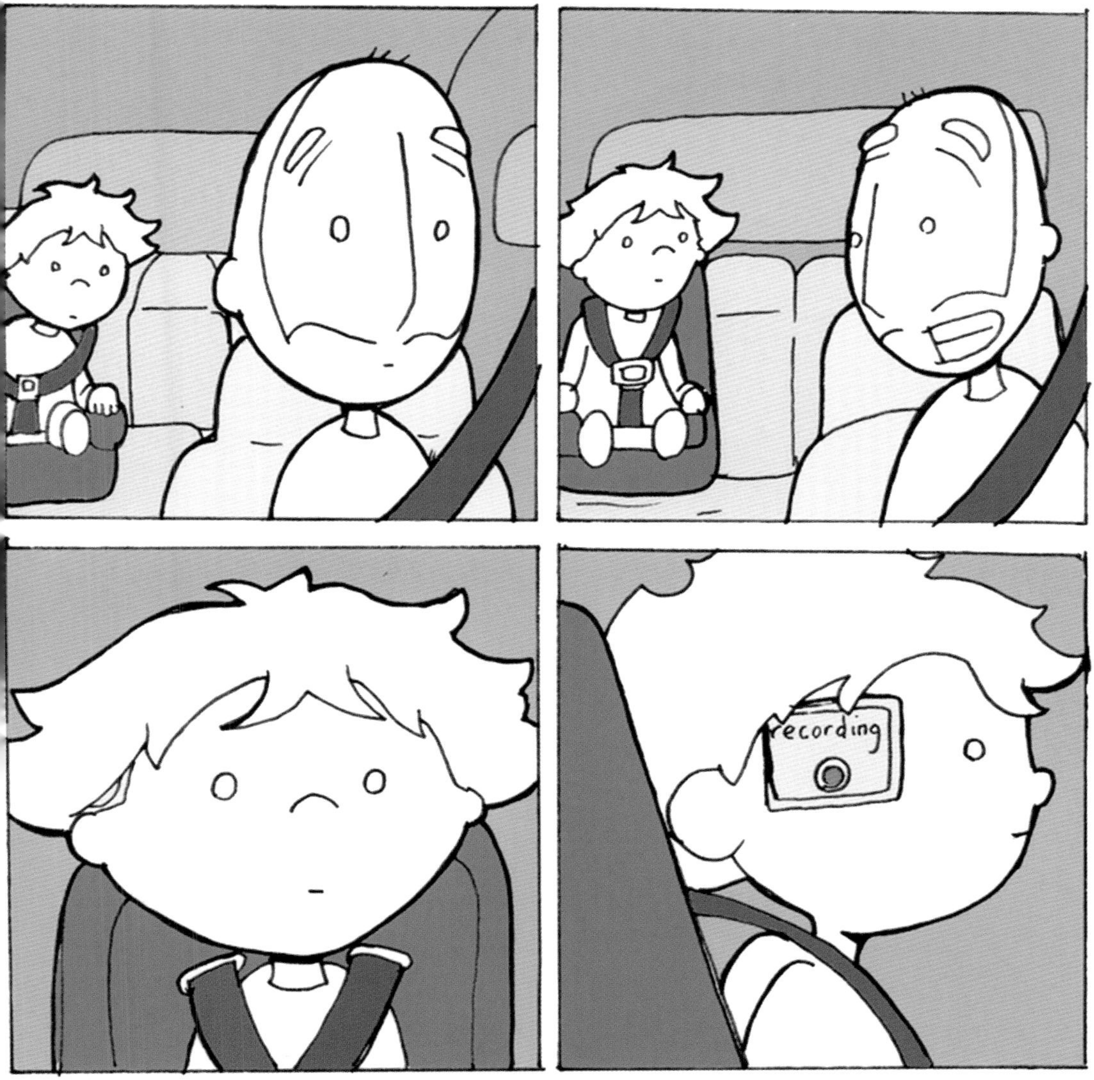
recording

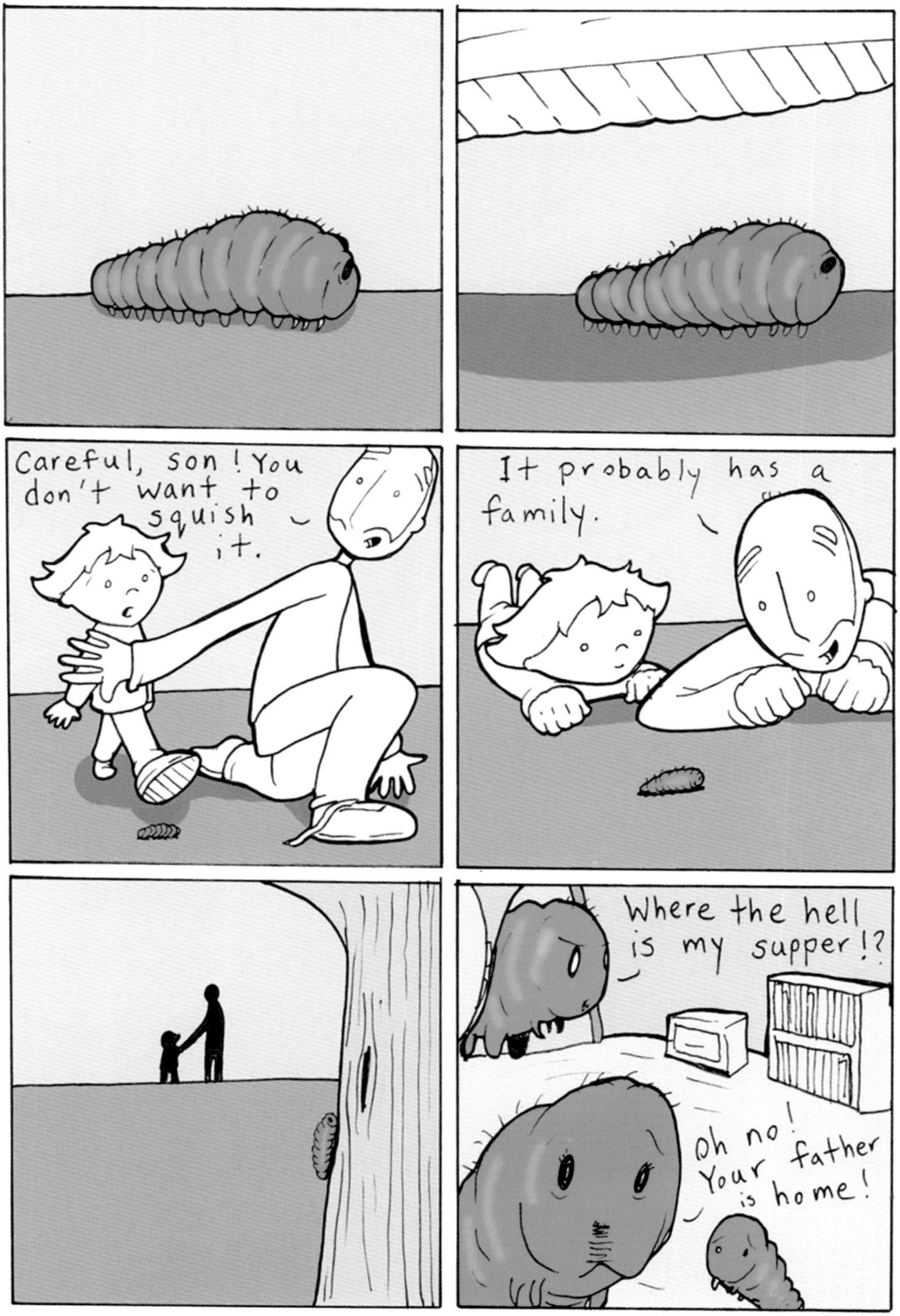
Careful, son! You don't want to squish it.
It probably has a family.
Where the hell is my supper!?
Oh no! Your father is home!

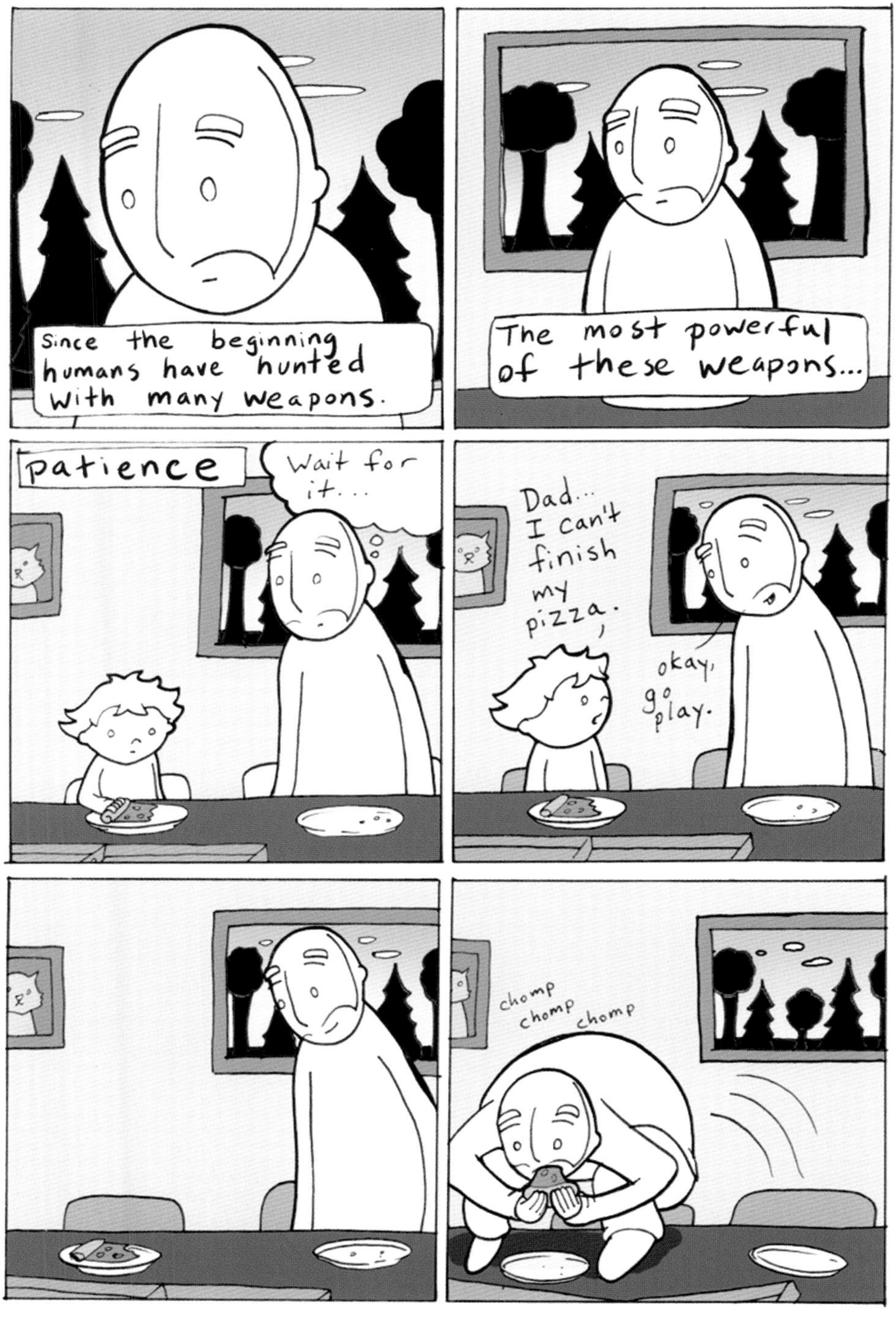
Since the beginning humans have hunted with many weapons.
The most powerful of these weapons...
patience
Wait for it...
Dad... I can't finish my pizza.
okay, go play.
chomp chomp chomp

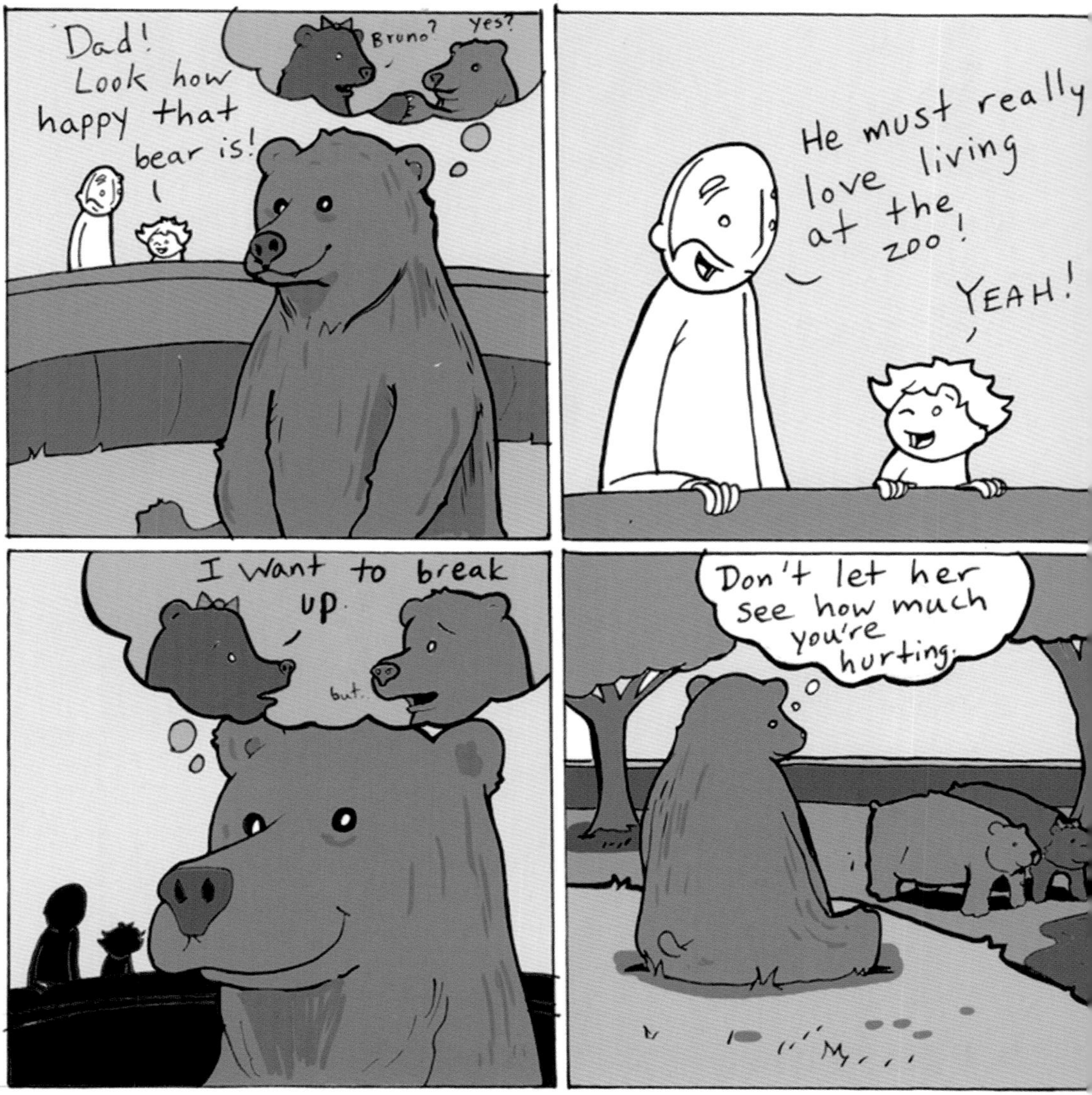
Dad! Look how happy that bear is!
Bruno?
yes?
He must really love living at the zoo!
YEAH!
I want to break up.
but.
Don't let her see how much you're hurting.

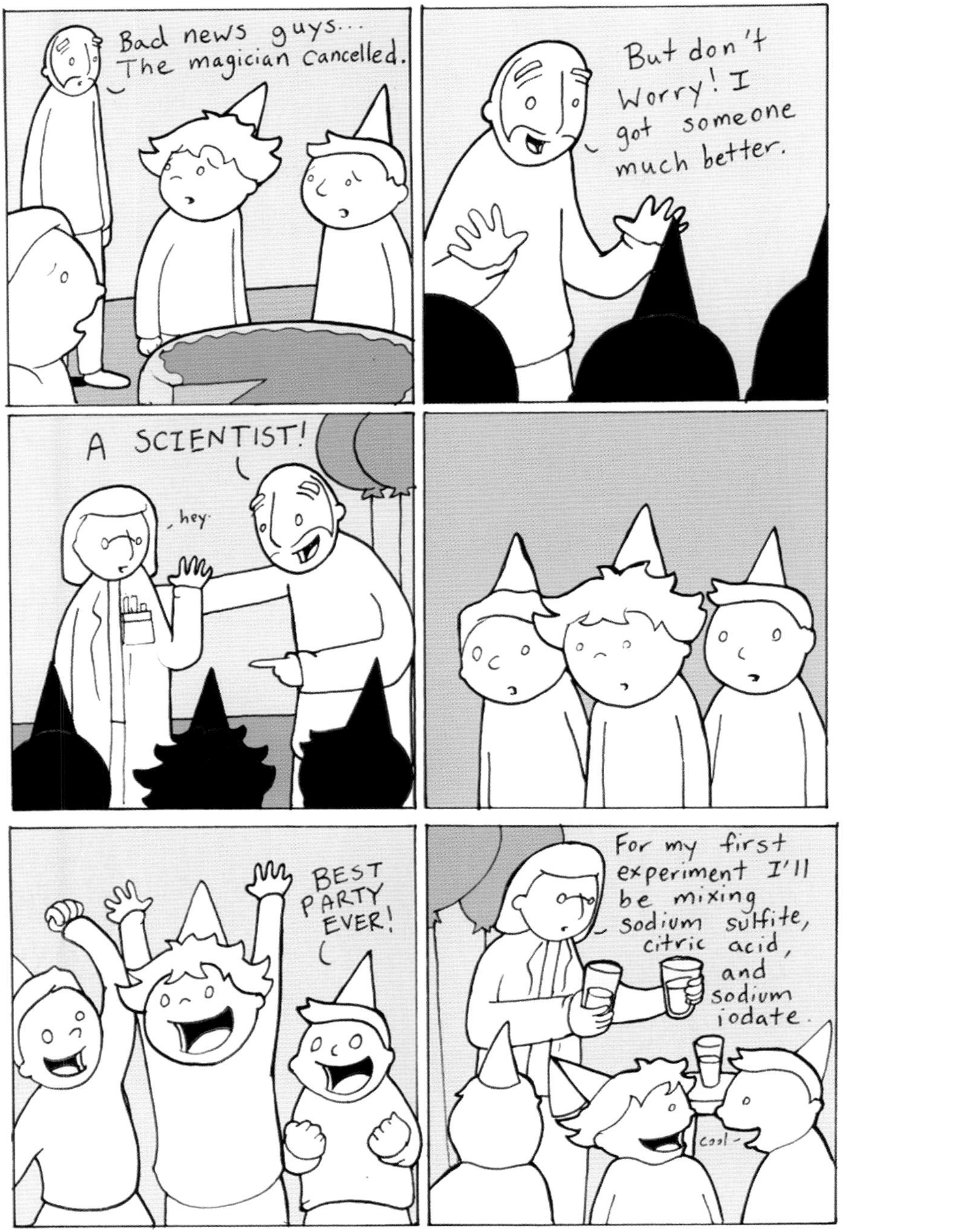
Bad news guys... The magician cancelled.
But don't Worry! I got someone much better.
A SCIENTIST!
hey.
BEST PARTY EVER!
For my first experiment I'll be mixing sodium sulfite, citric acid, and sodium iodate.
cool

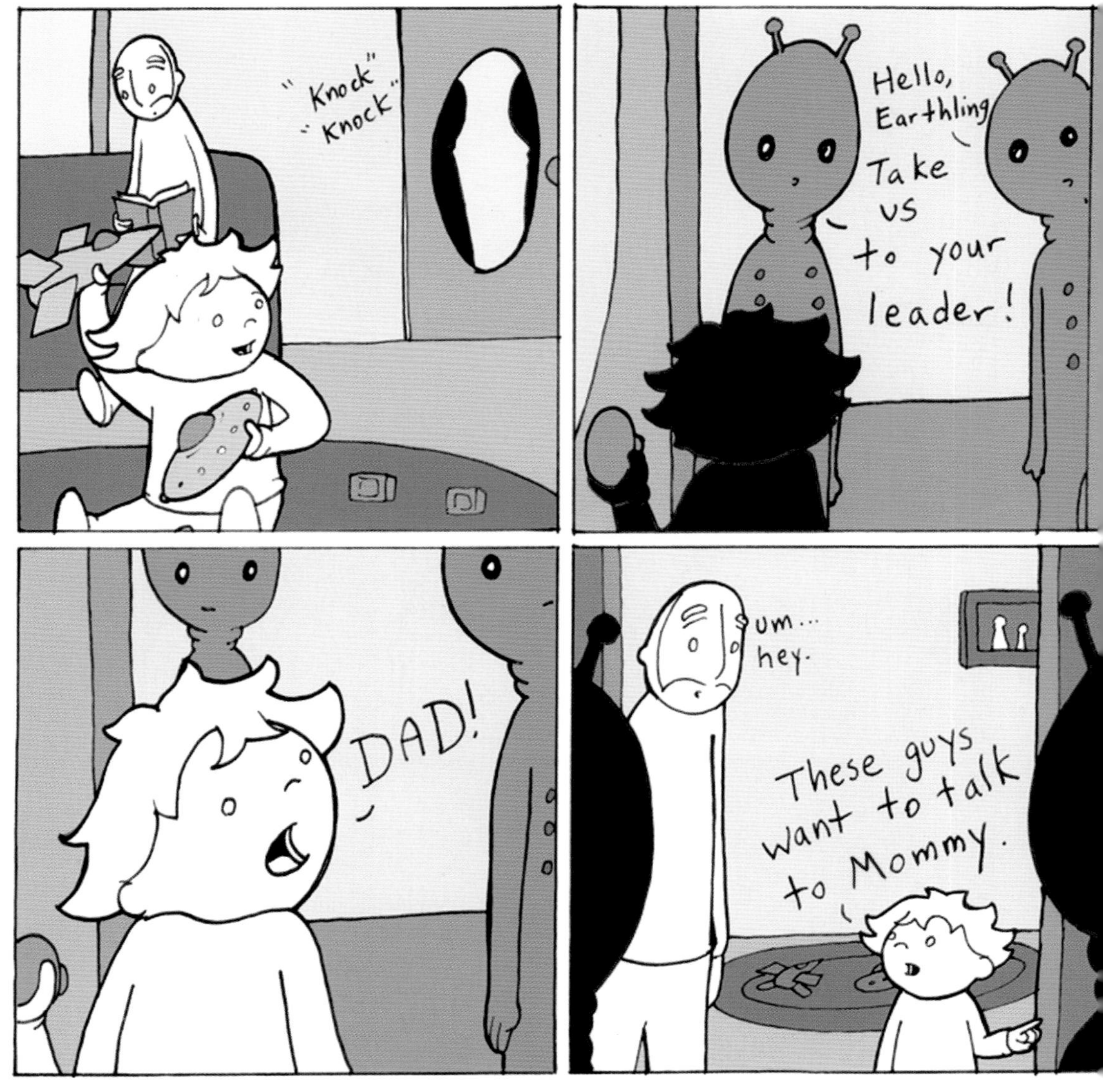
"Knock" "Knock"
Hello, Earthling
Take us to your leader!
DAD!
um... hey.
These guys want to talk to Mommy.

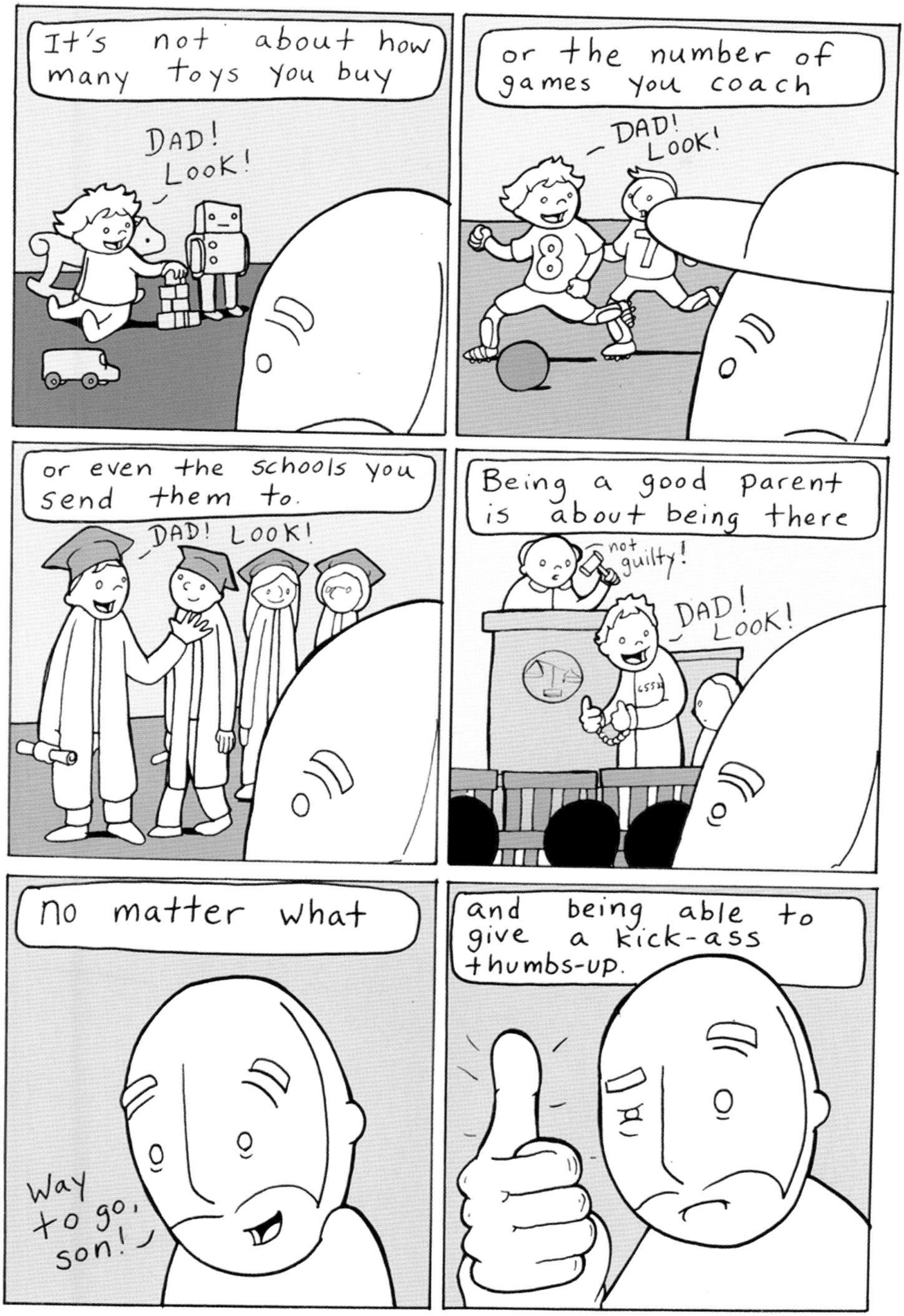

It's not about how many toys you buy
DAD! LOOK!
or the number of games you coach
DAD! LOOK!
or even the schools you send them to.
DAD! LOOK!
Being a good parent is about being there
not guilty!
DAD! LOOK!
no matter what
Way to go, son!
and being able to give a kick-ass thumbs-up.

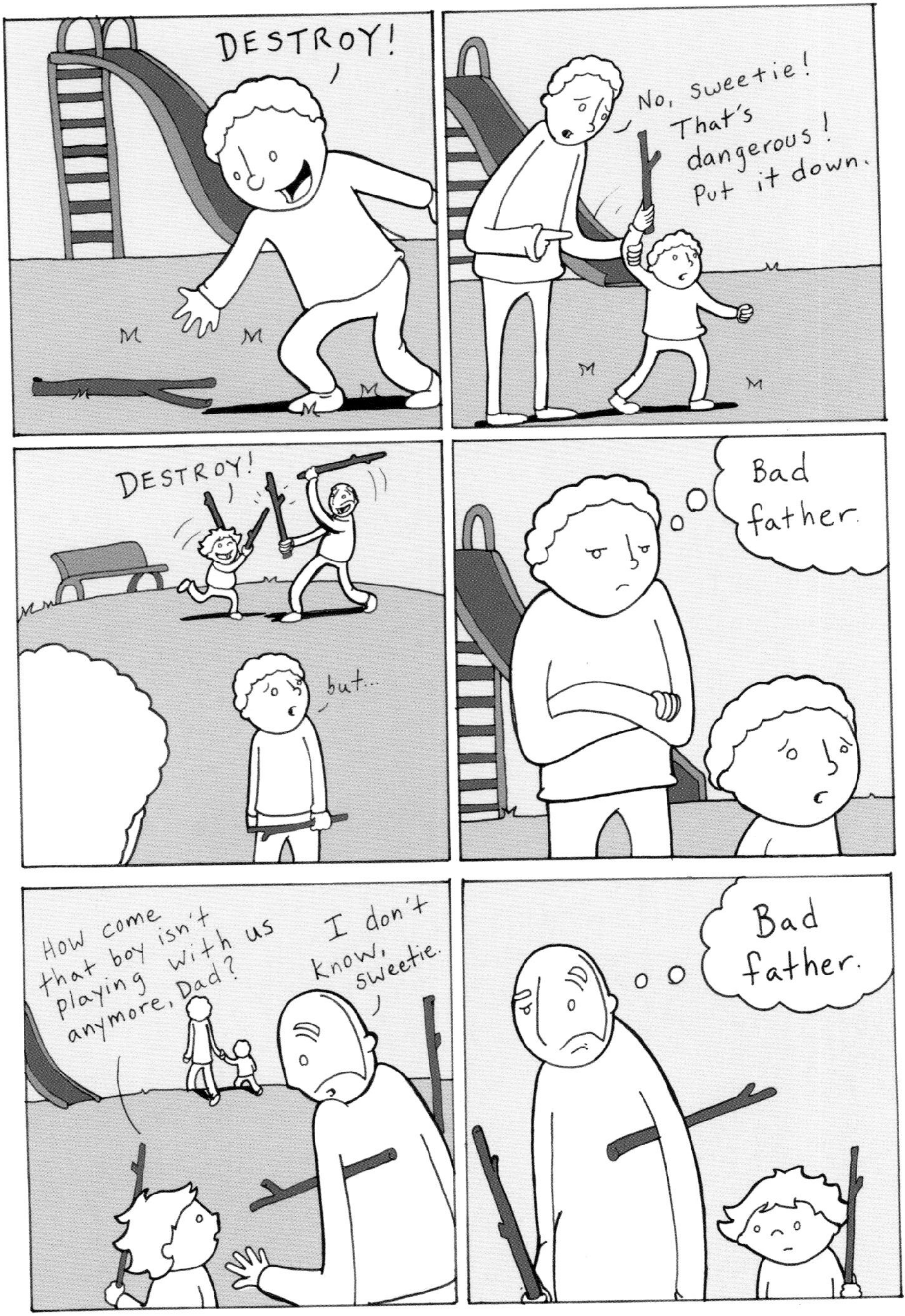
DESTROY!
No, sweetie! That's dangerous! Put it down.
DESTROY!
but...
Bad father.
How come that boy isn't playing with us anymore, Dad?
I don't know, sweetie.
Bad father.

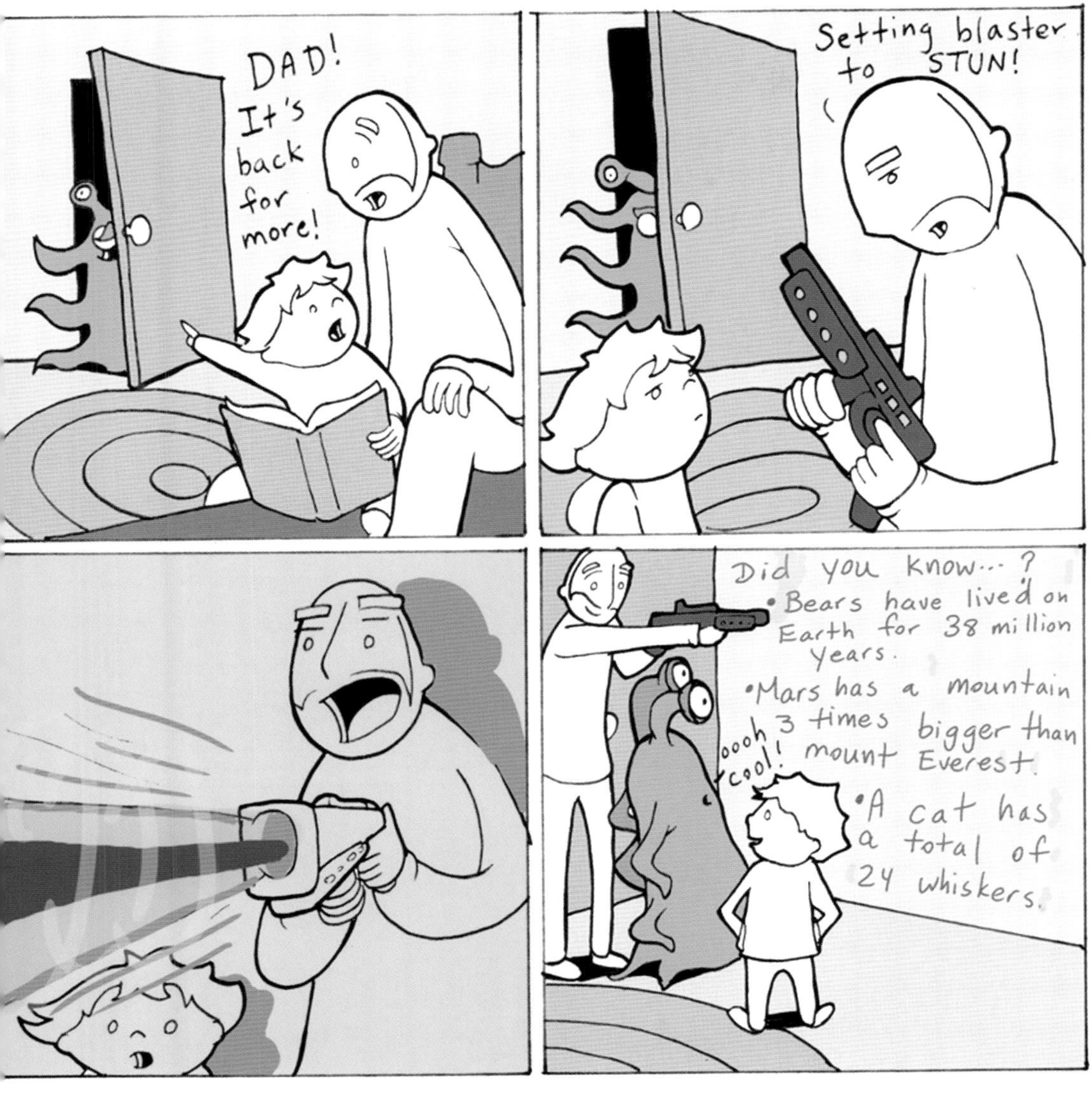
DAD! It's back for more!
Setting blaster to STUN!
Did you know...?
•Bears have lived on Earth for 38 million years.
•Mars has a mountain 3 times bigger than mount Everest.
•A cat has a total of 24 whiskers.
oooh cool!

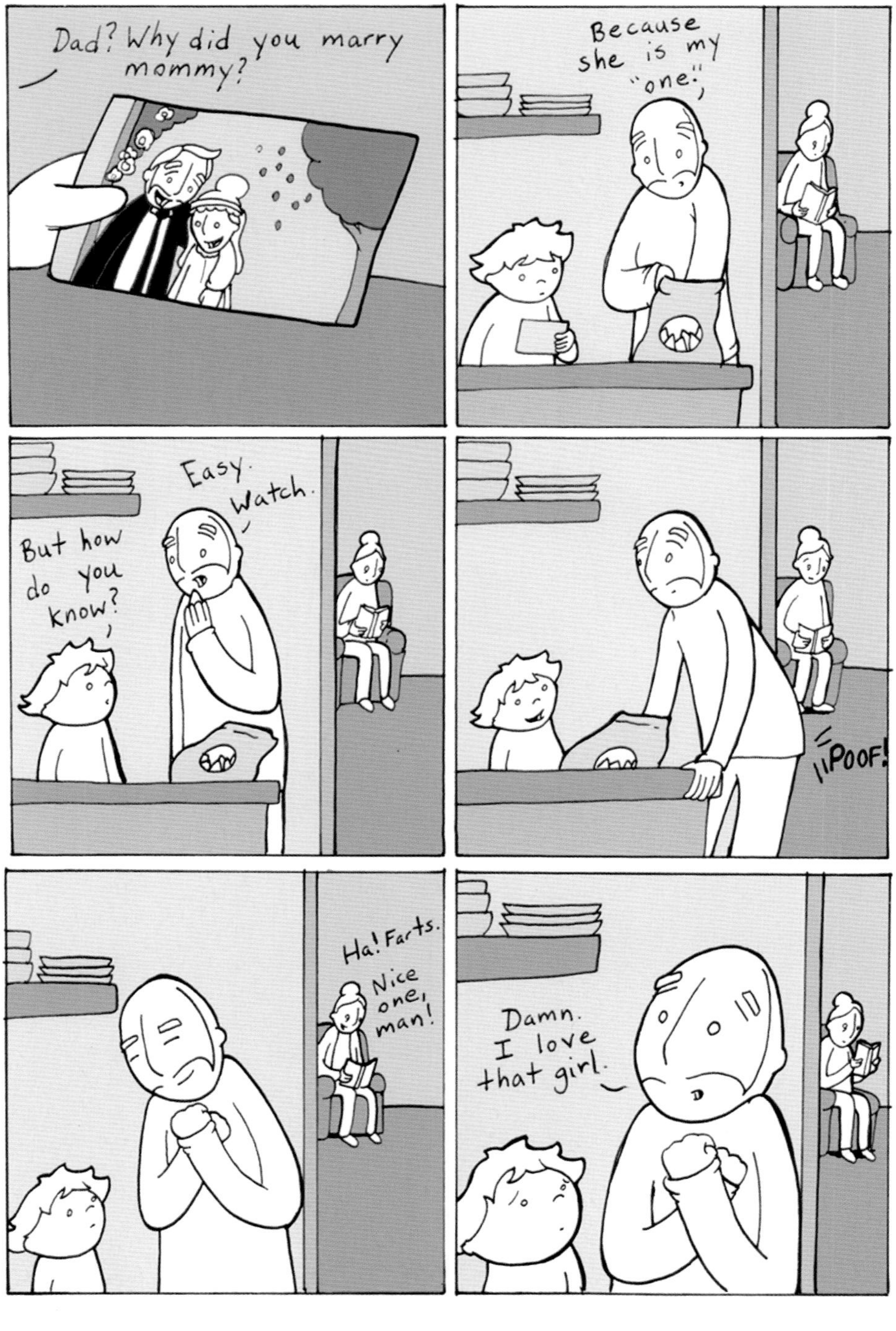
Dad? Why did you marry mommy?
Because she is my "one."
But how do you know?
Easy. Watch.
POOF!
Ha! Farts.
Nice one, man!
Damn. I love that girl.

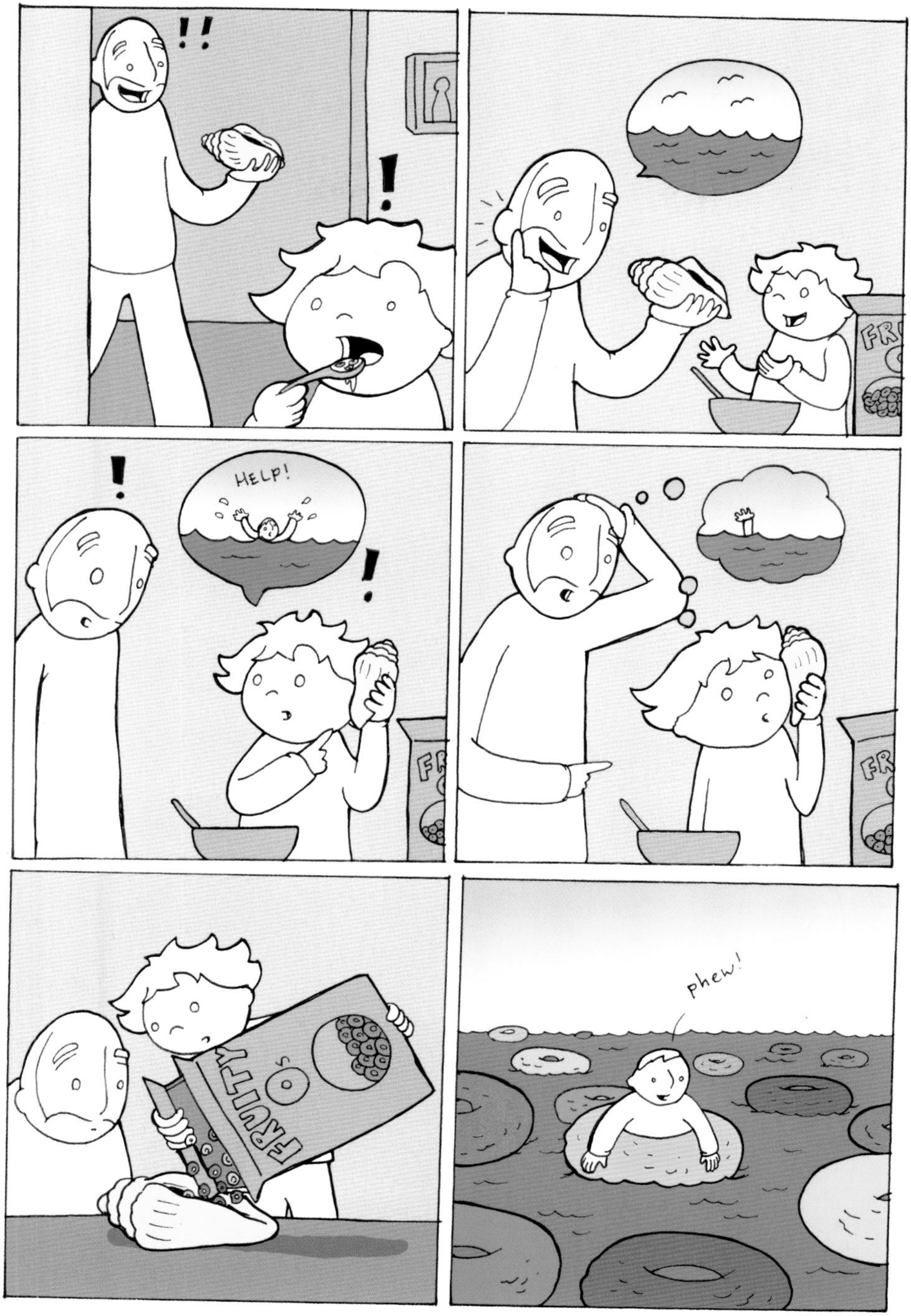
!!
!
HELP!
!
!
FRUITY
O's
FR
phew!

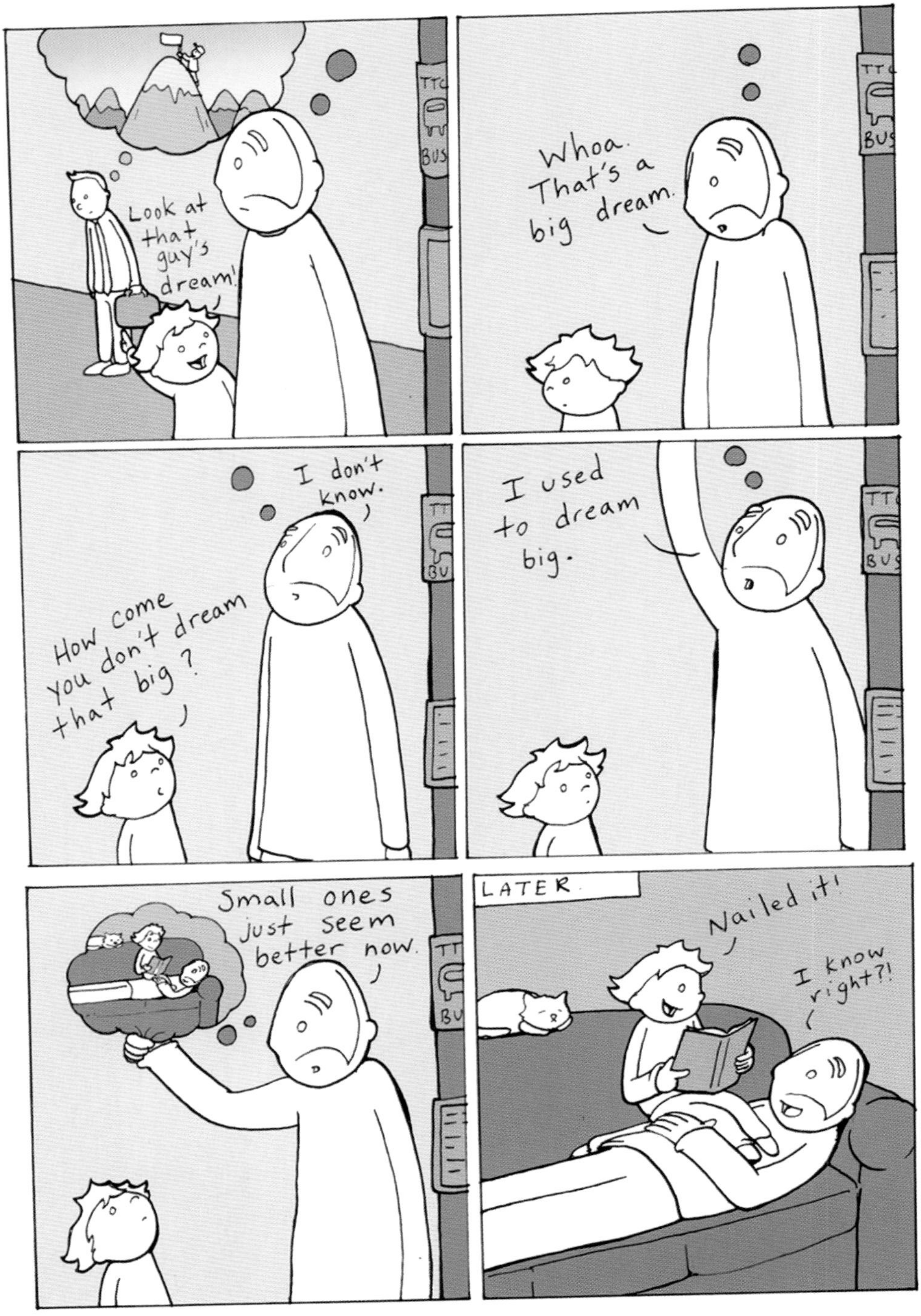
Look at that guy's dream!
Whoa. That's a big dream.
How come you don't dream that big?
I don't know.
I used to dream big.
Small ones just seem better now.
LATER.
Nailed it!
I know right?!

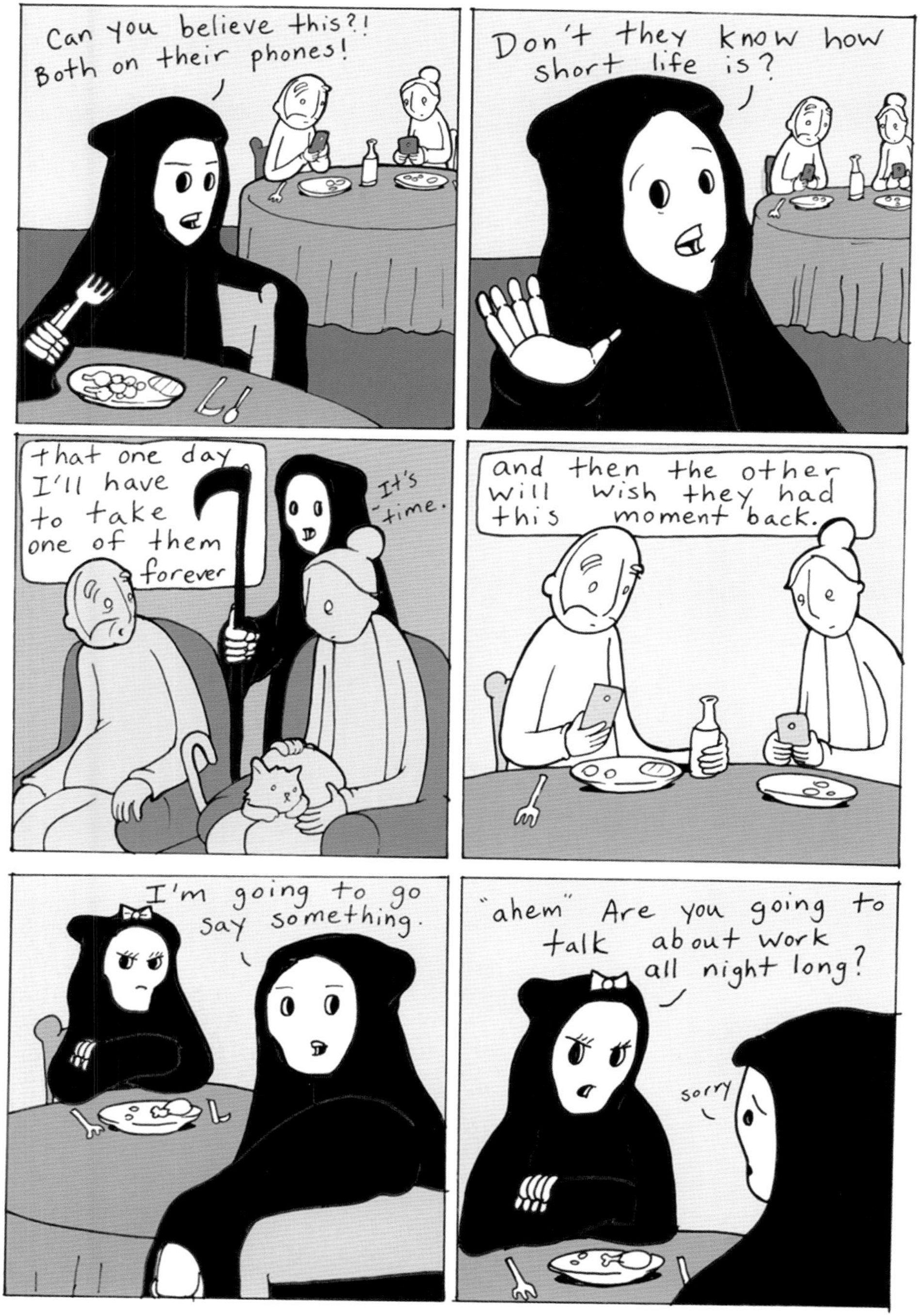
Can you believe this?! Both on their phones!
Don't they know how short life is?
that one day I'll have to take one of them forever
It's time.
and then the other will wish they had this moment back.
I'm going to go say something.
"ahem" Are you going to talk about work all night long?
sorry

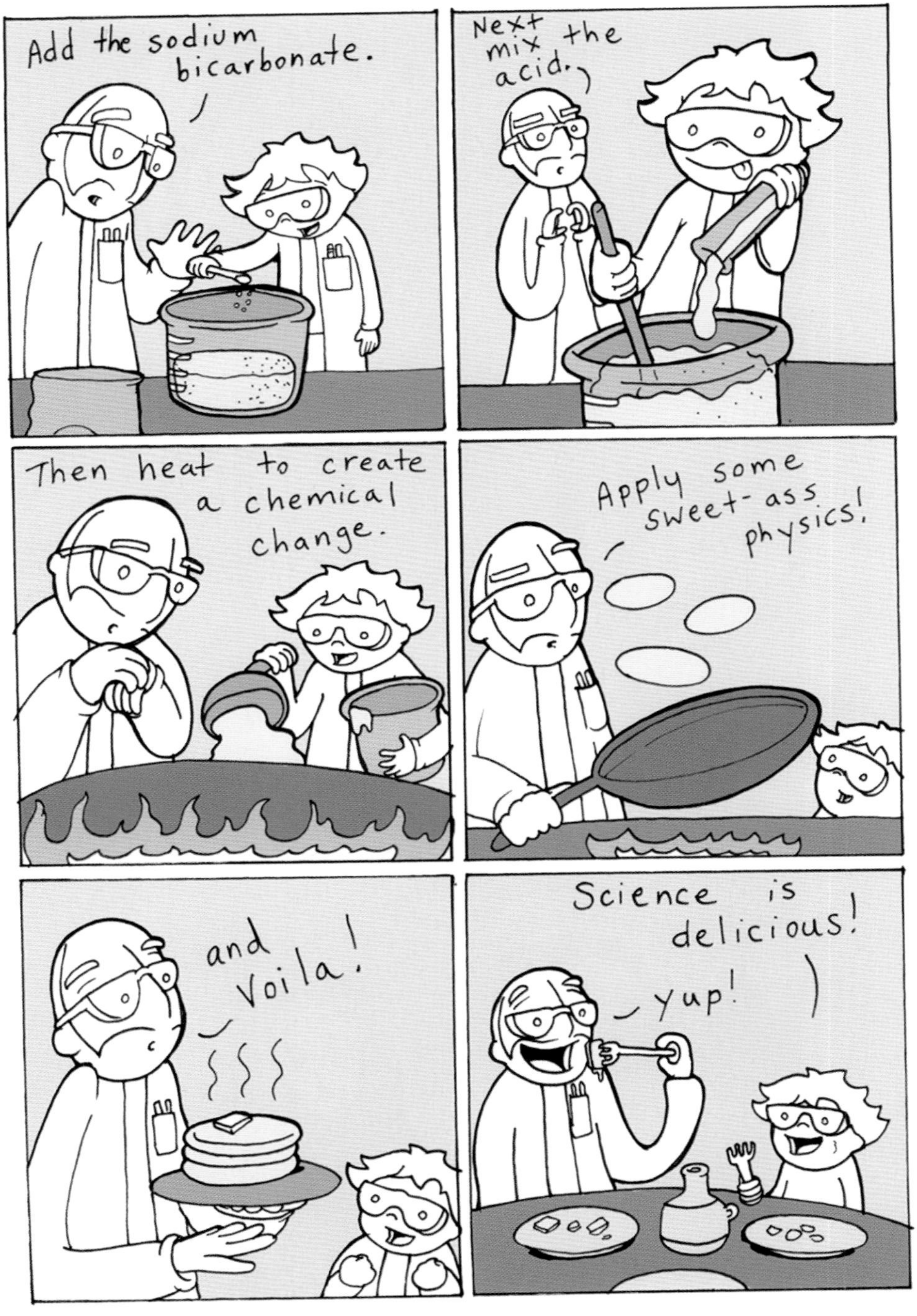
Add the sodium bicarbonate.
Next mix the acid.
Then heat to create a chemical change.
Apply some sweet-ass physics!
and Voila!
Science is delicious!
yup!

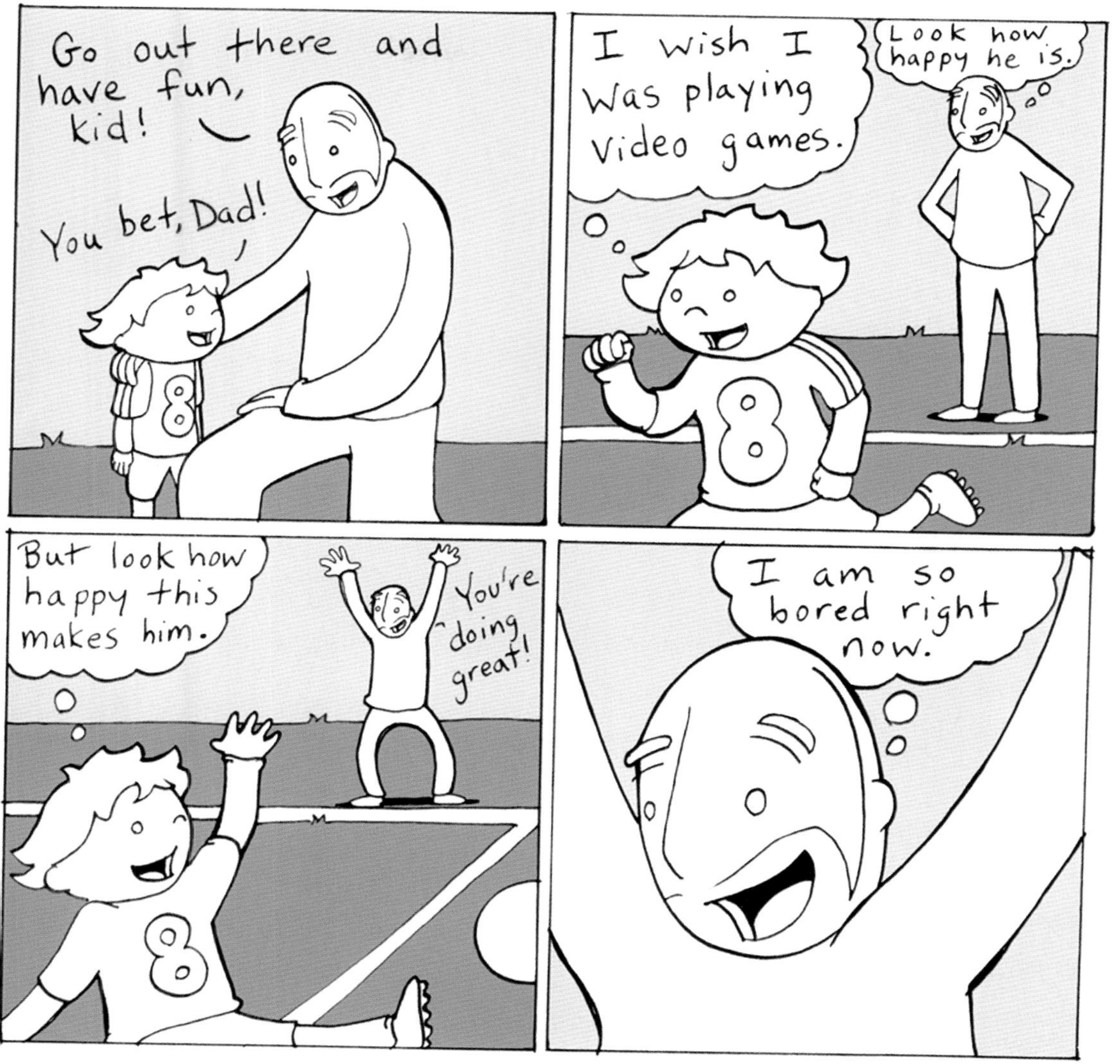
Go out there and have fun, kid!
You bet, Dad!
I wish I was playing video games.
Look how happy he is.
But look how happy this makes him.
You're doing great!
I am so bored right now.

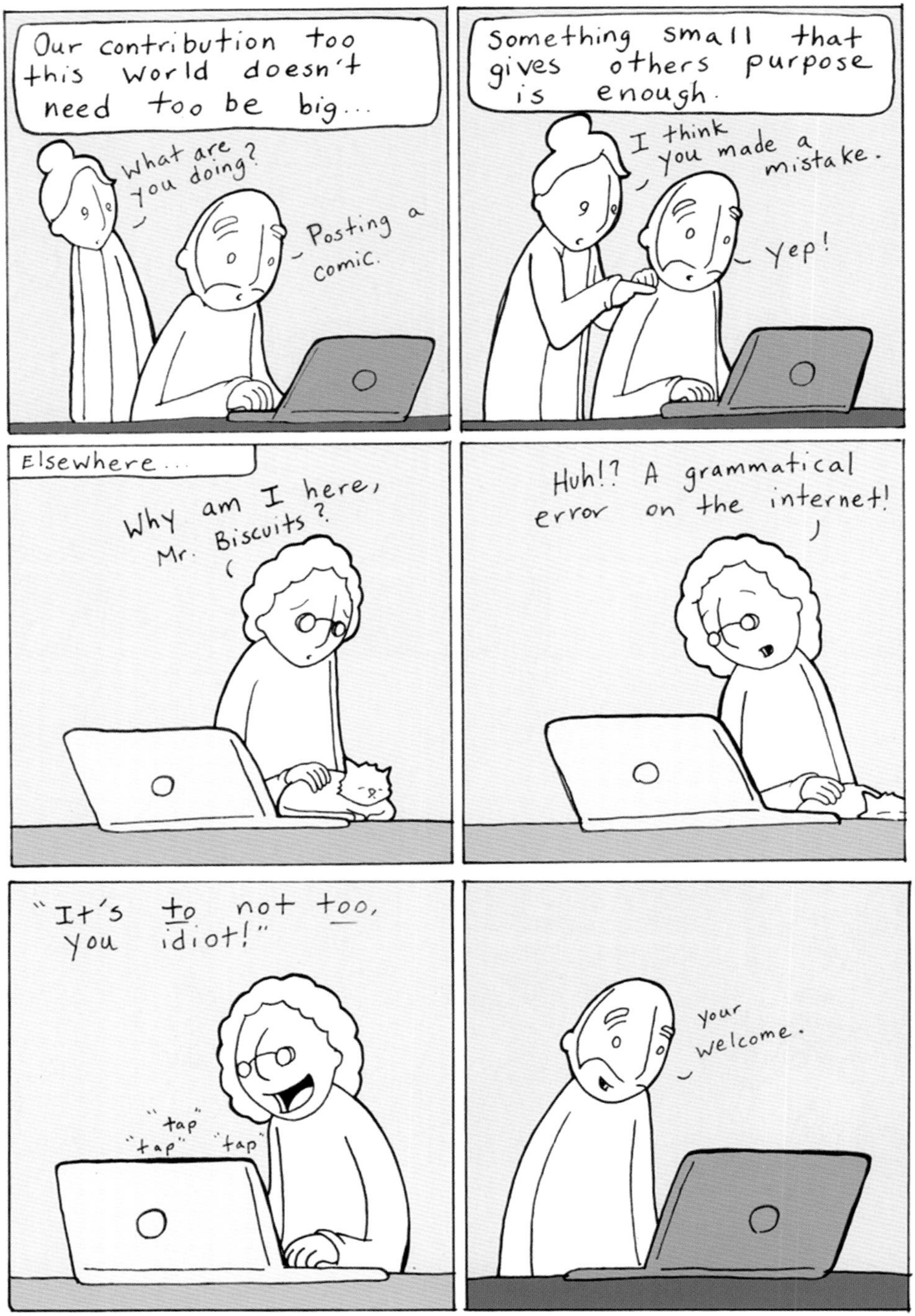

Our contribution too this world doesn't need too be big...
What are you doing?
Posting a comic.
Something small that gives others purpose is enough.
I think you made a mistake.
Yep!
Elsewhere...
Why am I here, Mr. Biscuits?
Huh!? A grammatical error on the internet!
"It's to not too, you idiot!"
"tap" "tap" "tap"
your welcome.

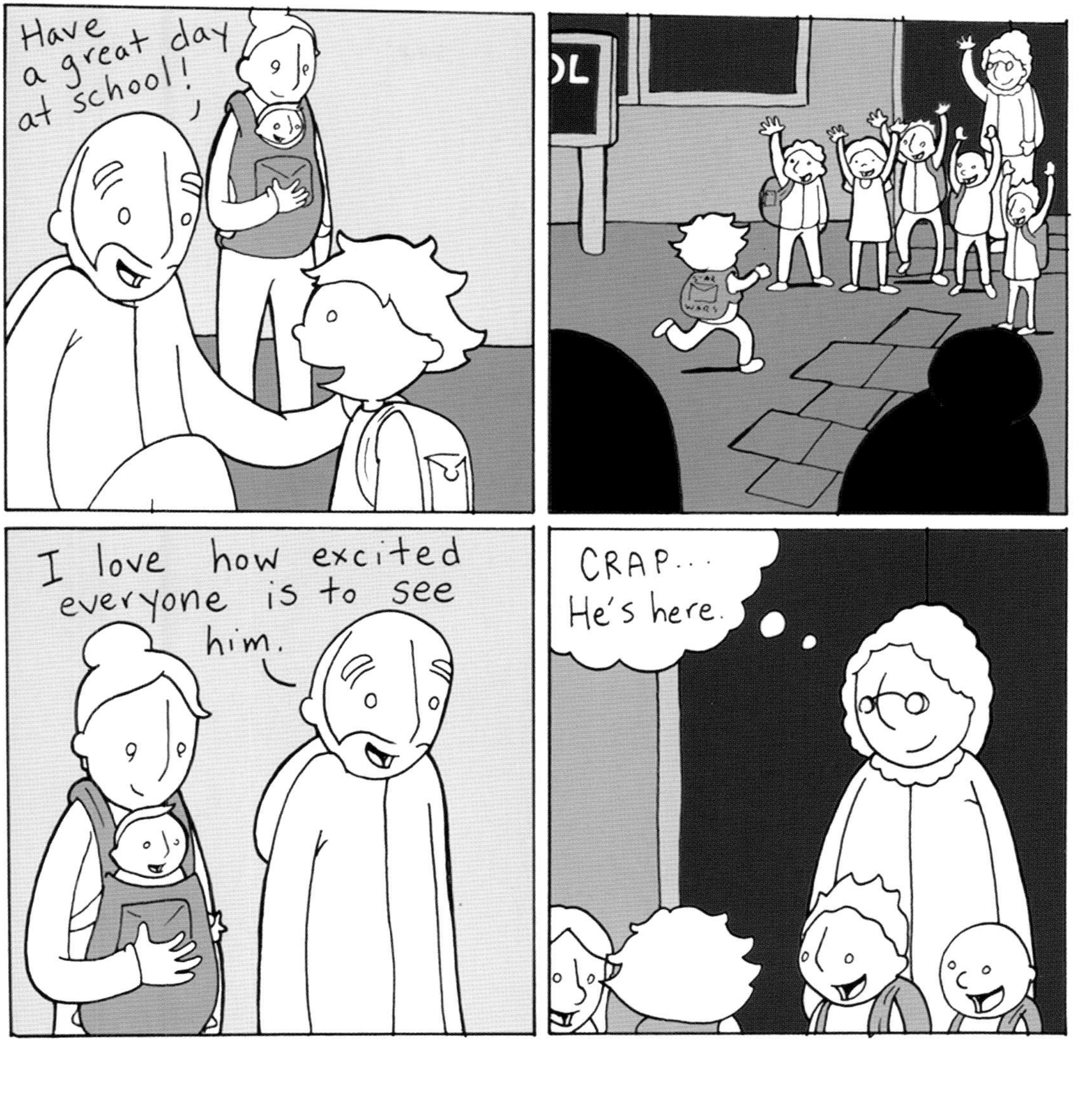
Have a great day at school!
OL
STAR WARS
I love how excited everyone is to see him.
CRAP... He's here.

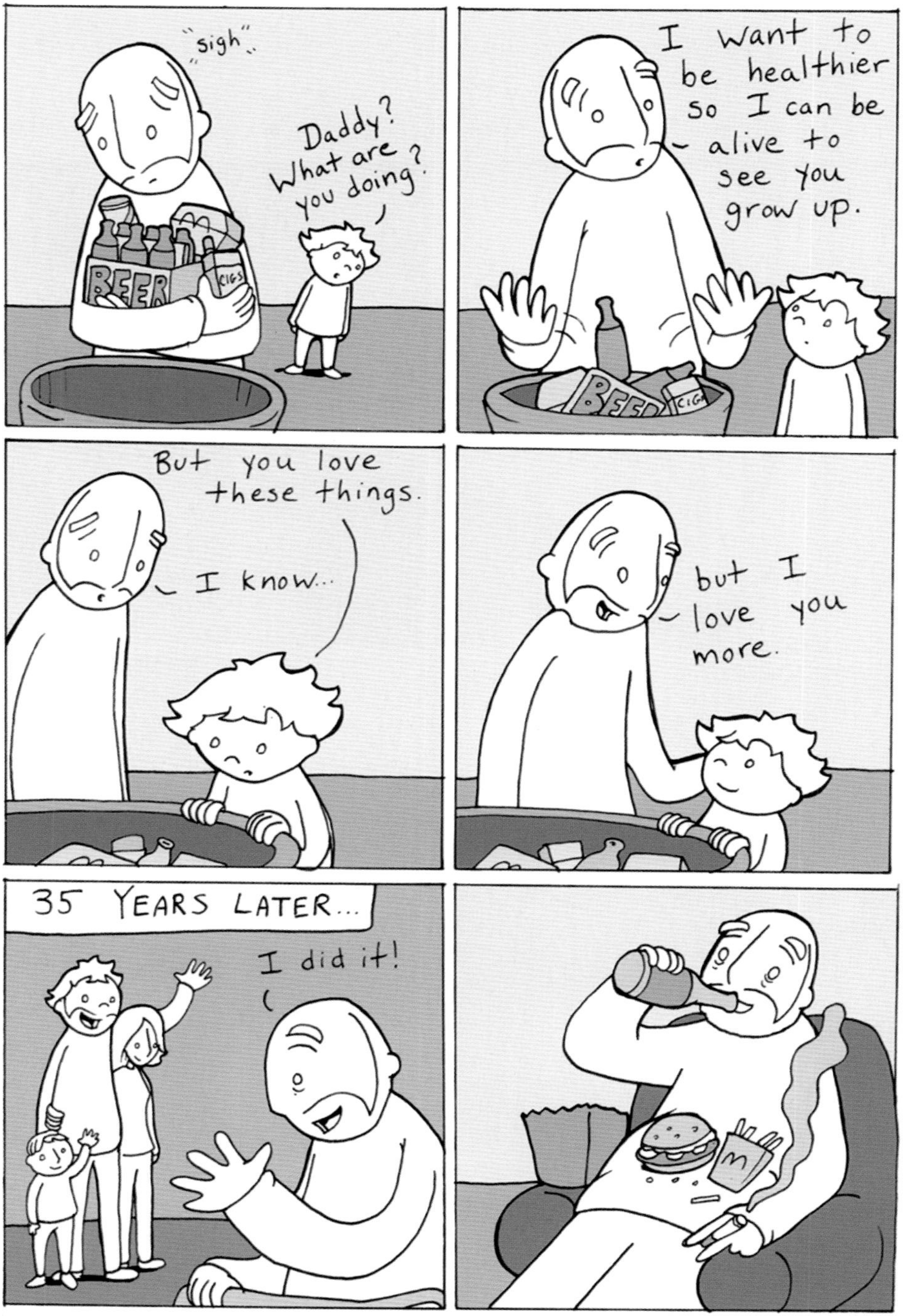
"sigh"
Daddy? What are you doing?
BEER
CIGS
I want to be healthier so I can be alive to see you grow up.
But you love these things.
I know...
but I love you more.
35 YEARS LATER...
I did it!

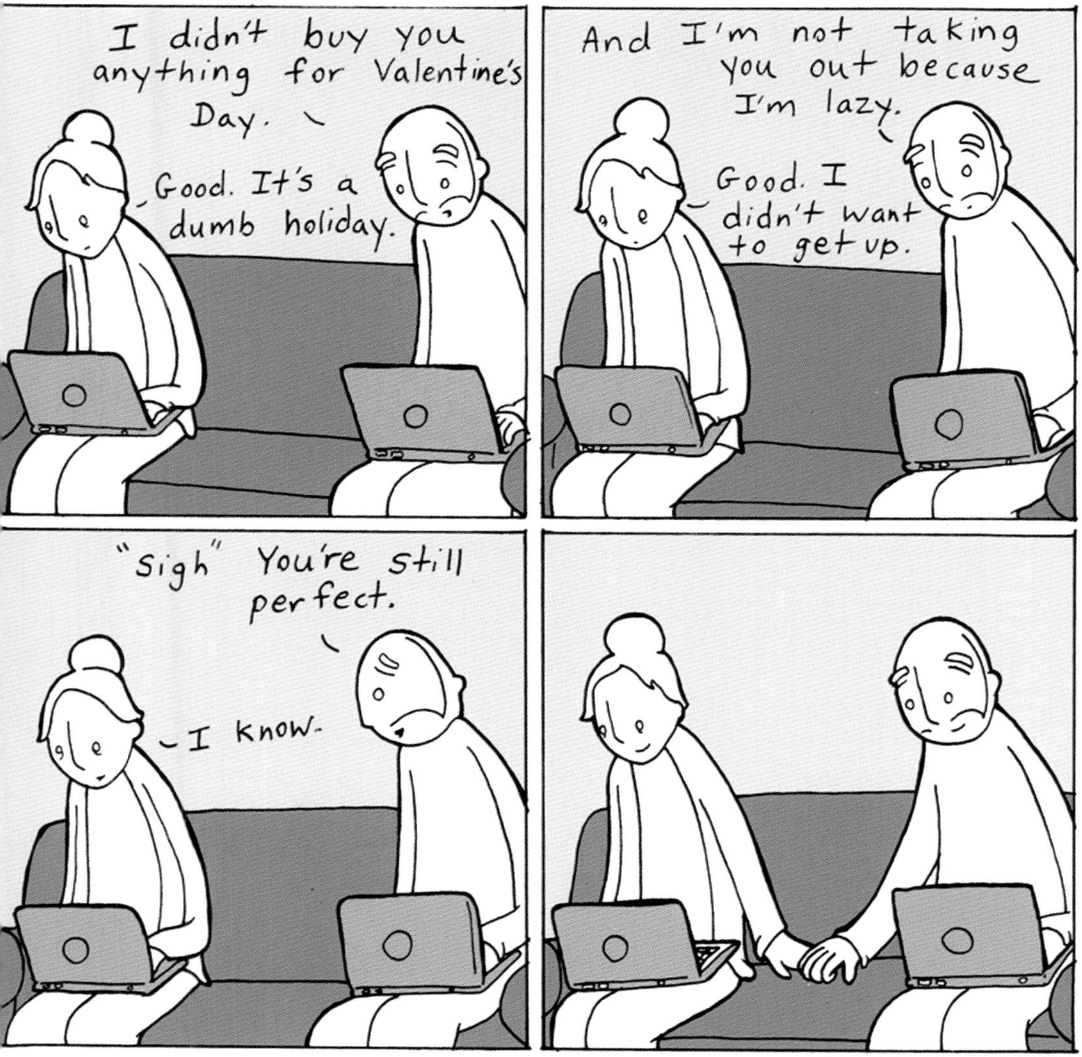
I didn't buy you anything for Valentine's Day.
Good. It's a dumb holiday.
And I'm not taking you out because I'm lazy.
Good. I didn't want to get up.
"Sigh" You're still perfect.
I know.

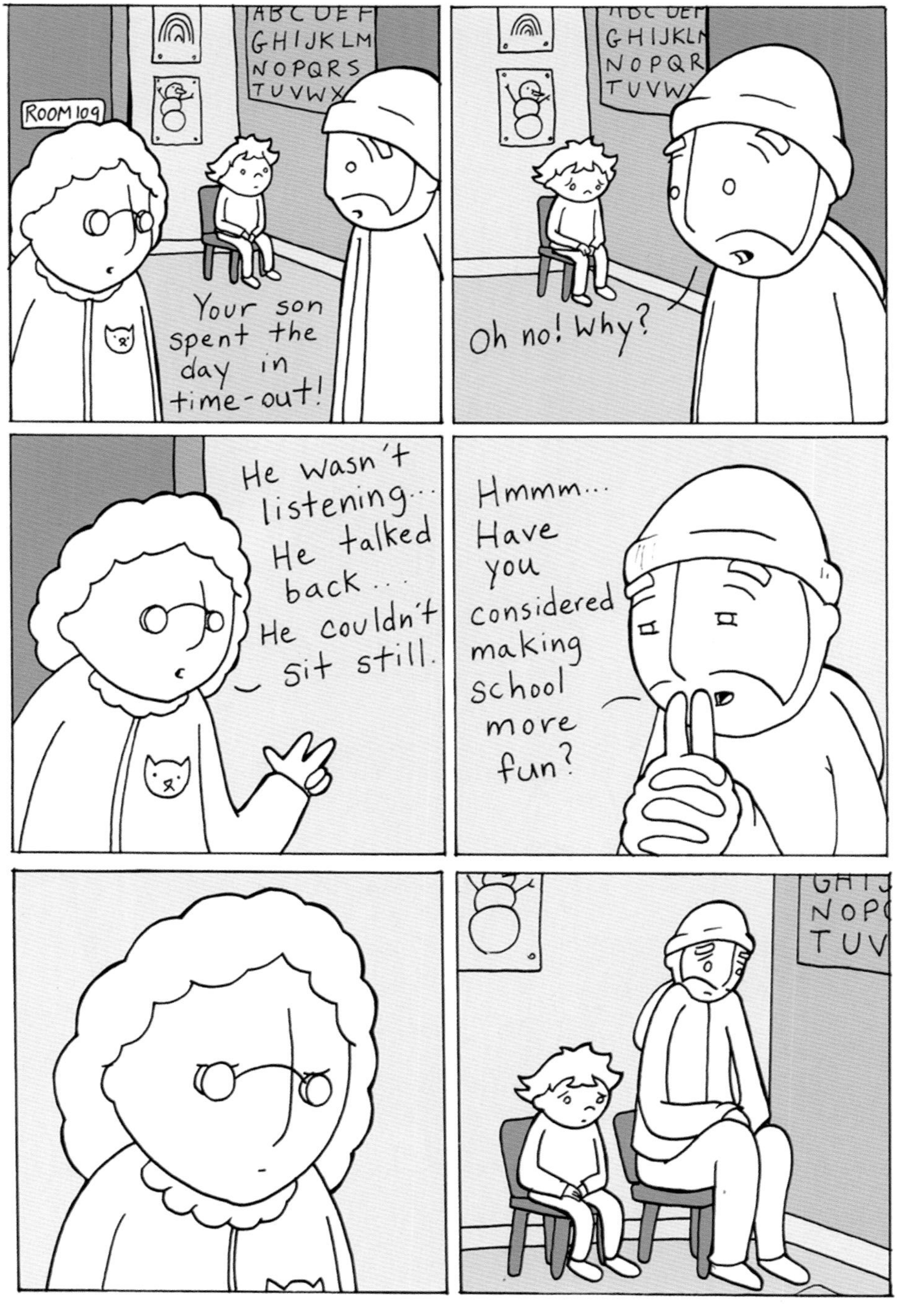
ROOM 109
ABCDEF
GHIJKLM
NOPQRS
TUVWX
Your son spent the day in time-out!
Oh no! Why?
He wasn't listening... He talked back... He couldn't sit still.
Hmmm... Have you considered making school more fun?

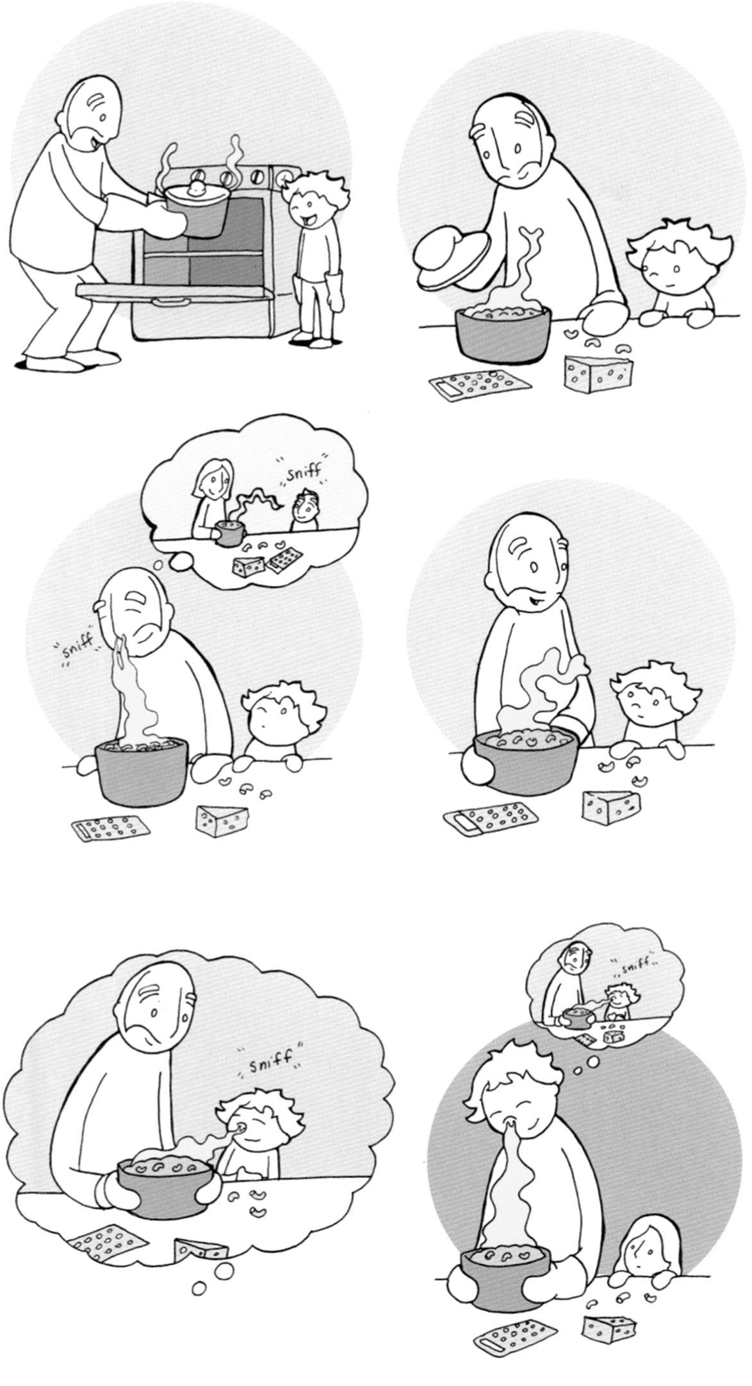
sniff
sniff
sniff
sniff

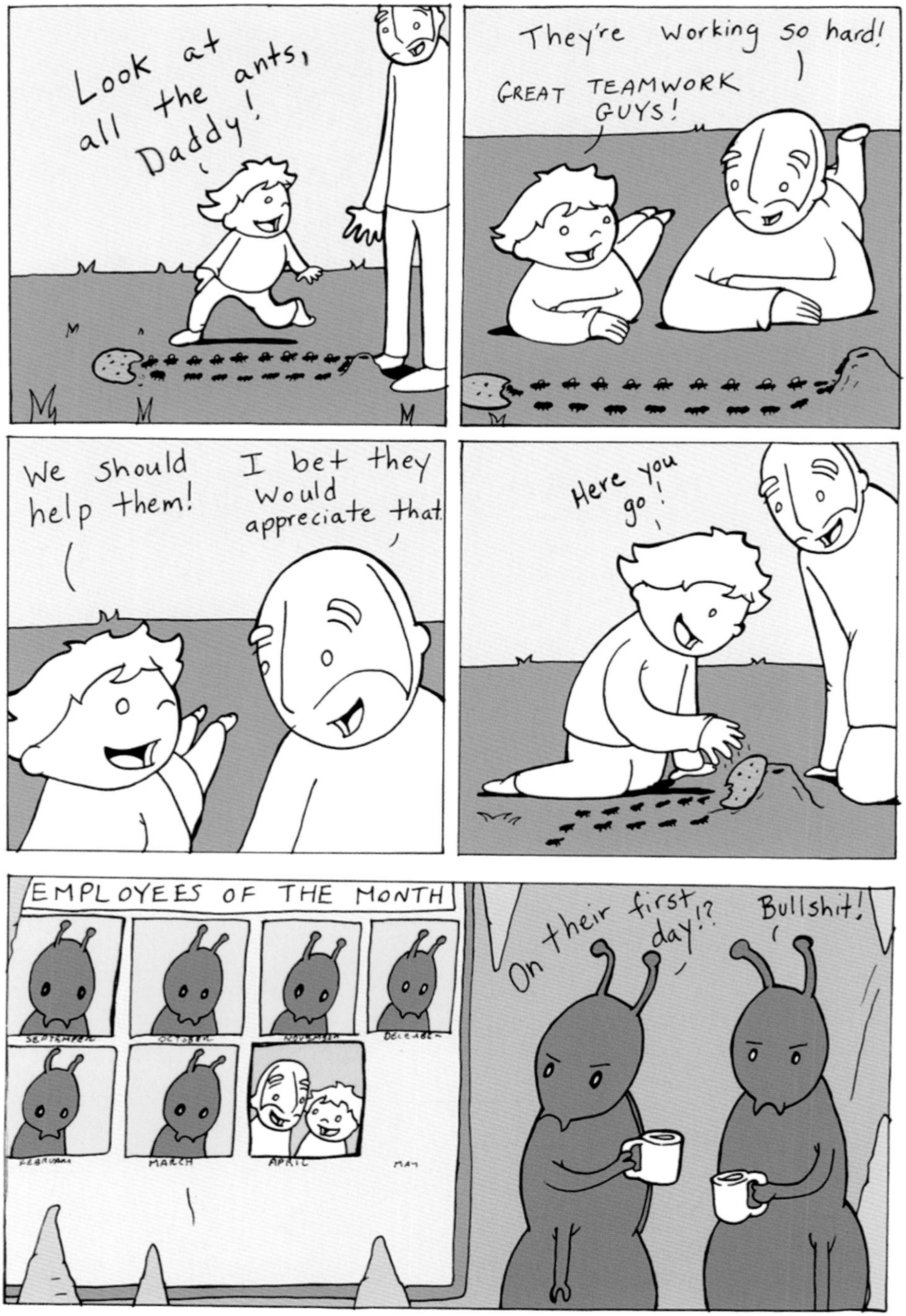
Look at all the ants, Daddy!
They're working so hard!
GREAT TEAMWORK GUYS!
We should help them!
I bet they would appreciate that.
Here you go!
EMPLOYEES OF THE MONTH
MARCH
APRIL
MAY
On their first day!?
Bullshit!

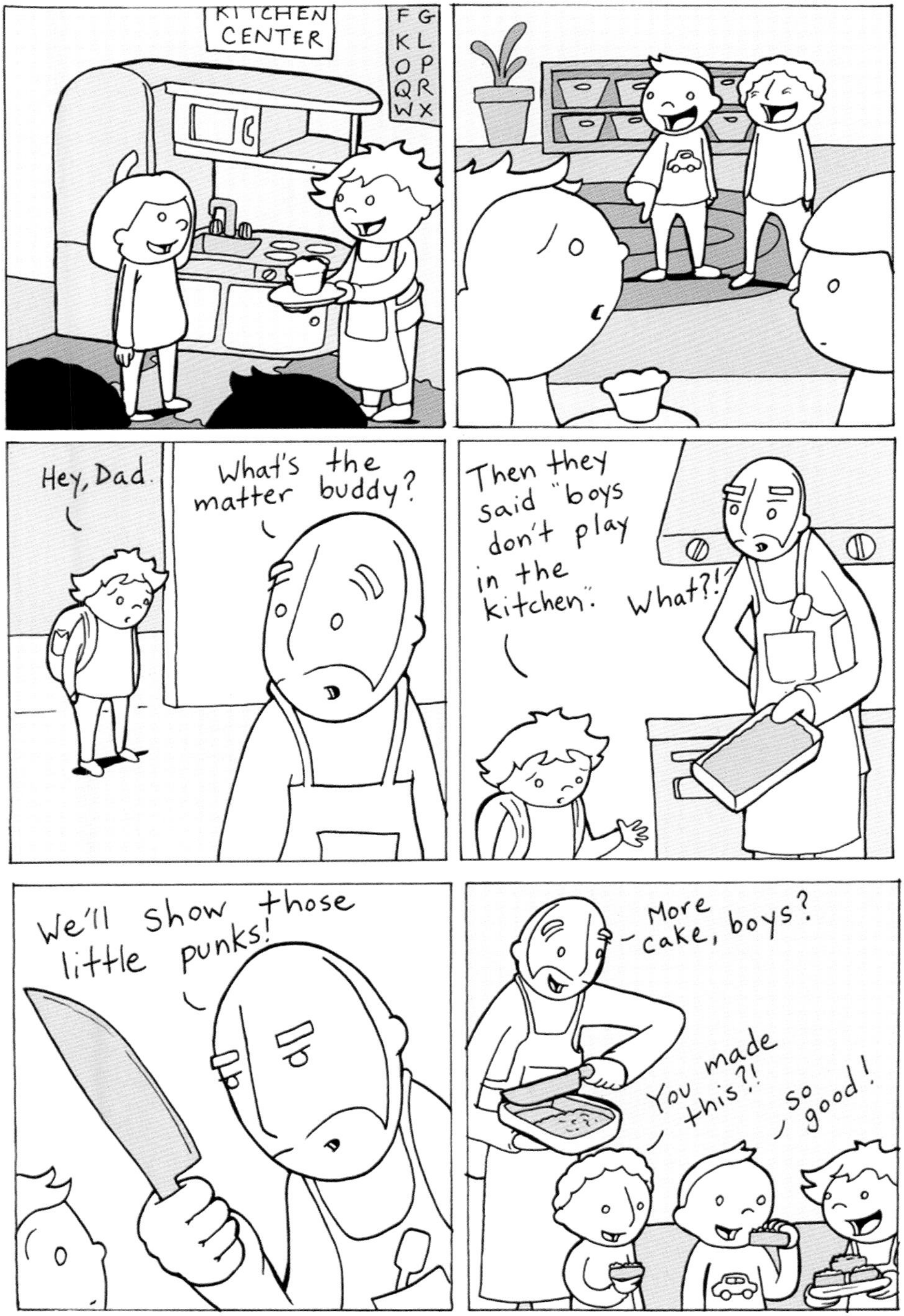
KITCHEN CENTER
F G
K L
O P
Q R
W X
Hey, Dad.
What's the matter buddy?
Then they said "boys don't play in the kitchen".
What?!
We'll show those little punks!
More cake, boys?
You made this?!
So good!

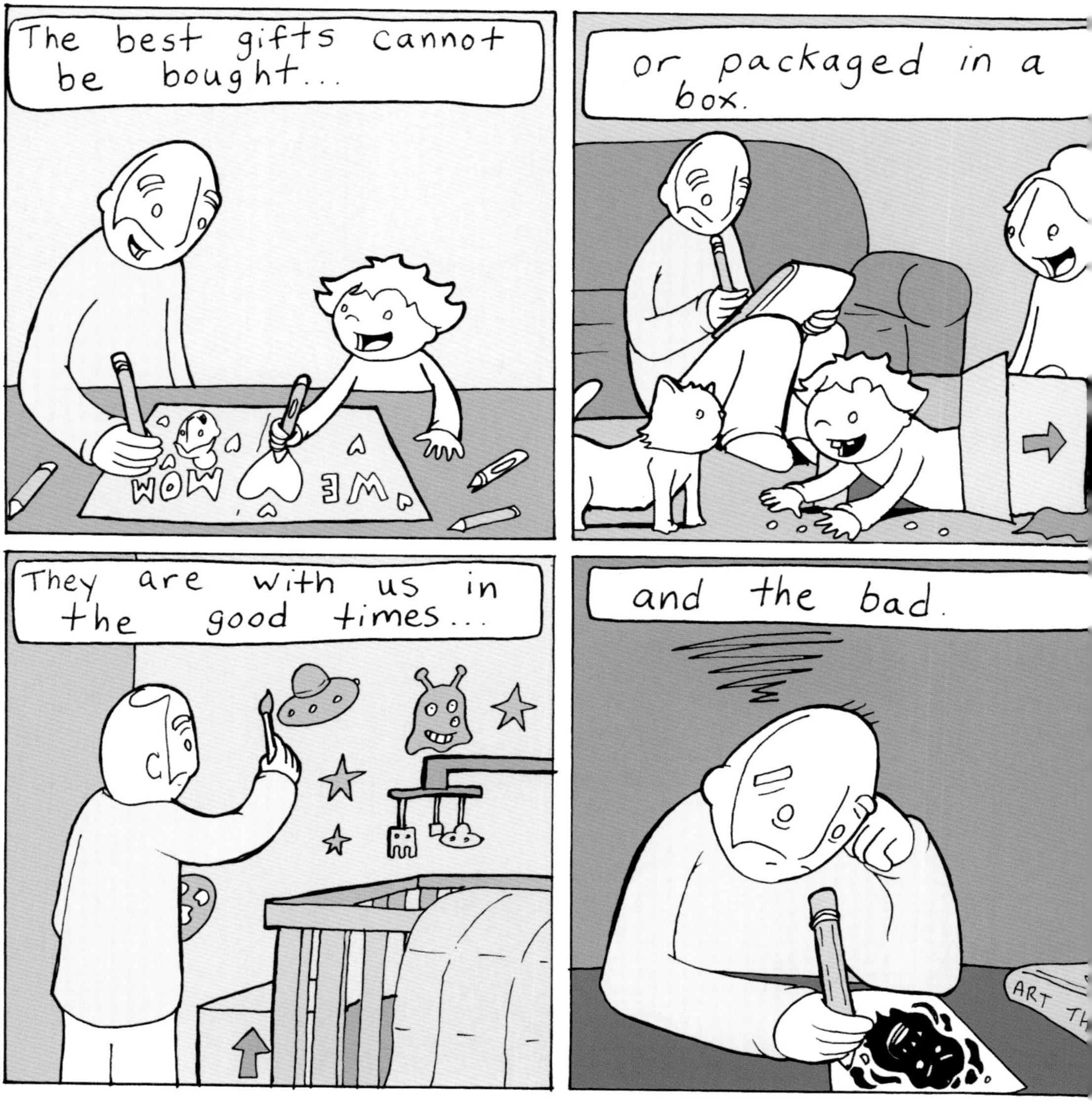
The best gifts cannot be bought...
or packaged in a box.
They are with us in the good times...
and the bad.

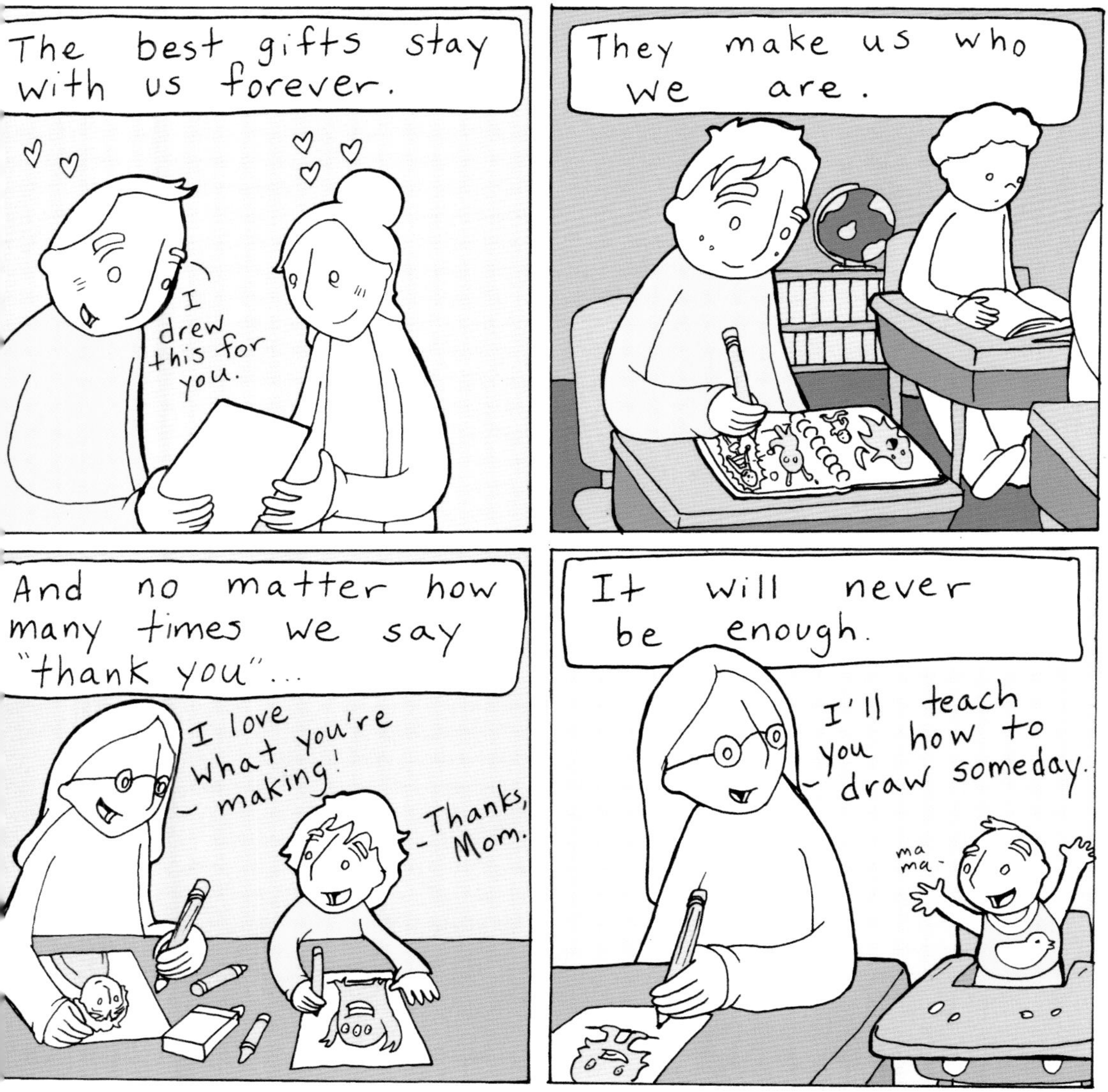
The best gifts stay with us forever.
I drew this for you.
They make us who we are.
And no matter how many times we say "thank you"...
I love what you're making!
Thanks, Mom.
It will never be enough.
I'll teach you how to draw someday.
ma ma-

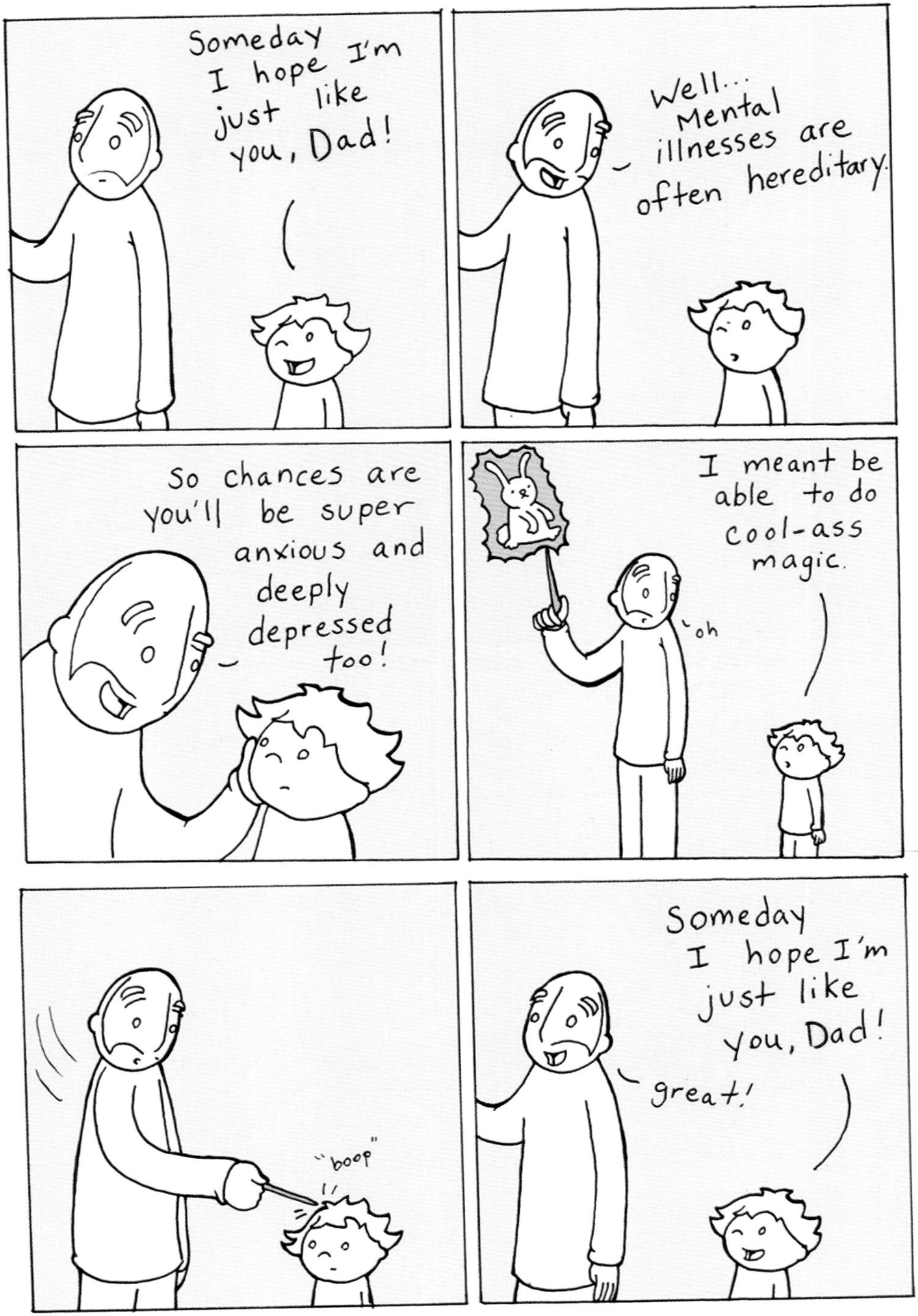

Someday I hope I'm just like you, Dad!
Well... Mental illnesses are often hereditary.
So chances are you'll be super anxious and deeply depressed too!
I meant be able to do cool-ass magic.
oh
"boop"
Someday I hope I'm just like you, Dad!
great!

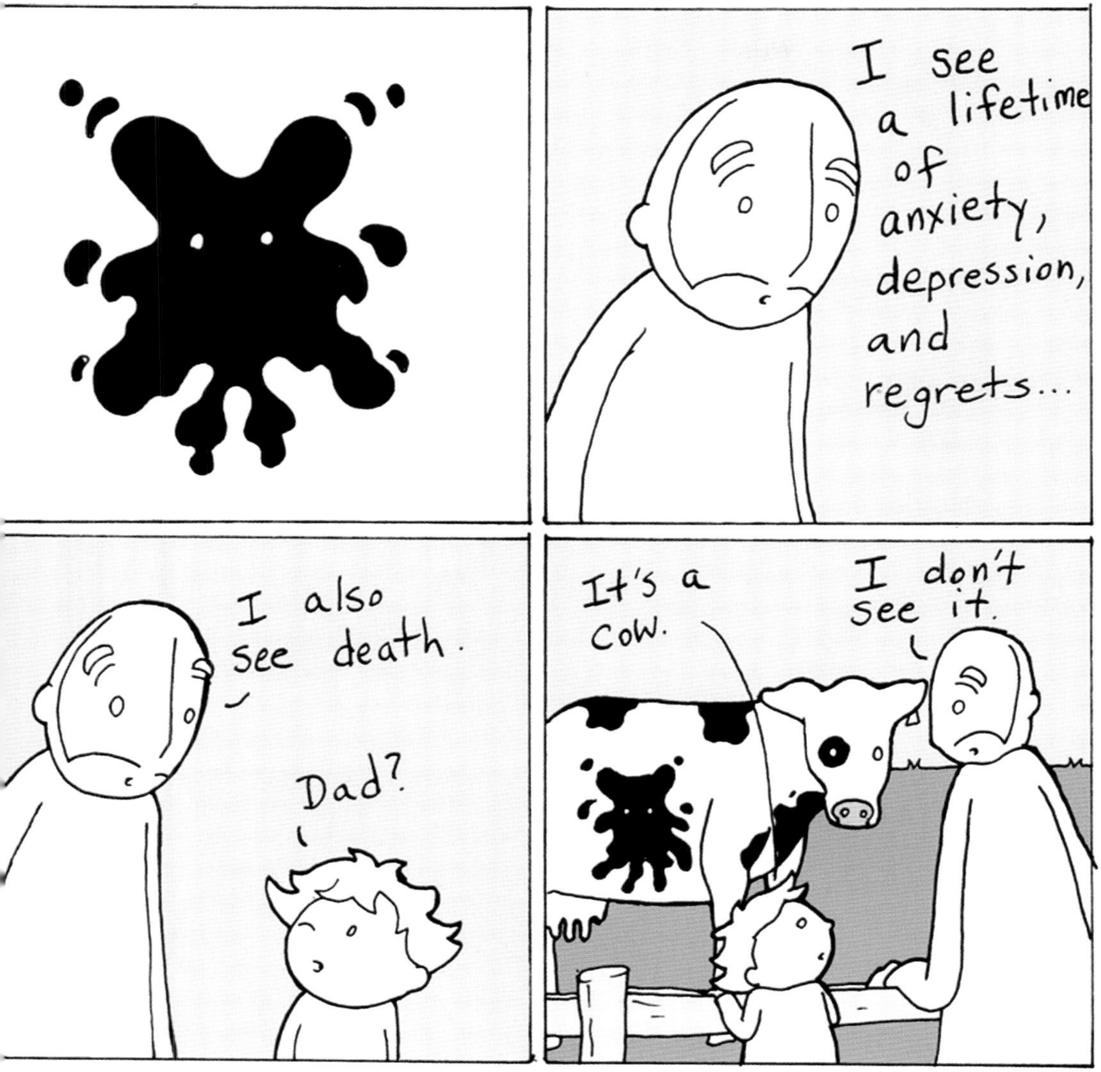
I see a lifetime of anxiety, depression, and regrets...
I also see death.
Dad?
It's a cow.
I don't see it.

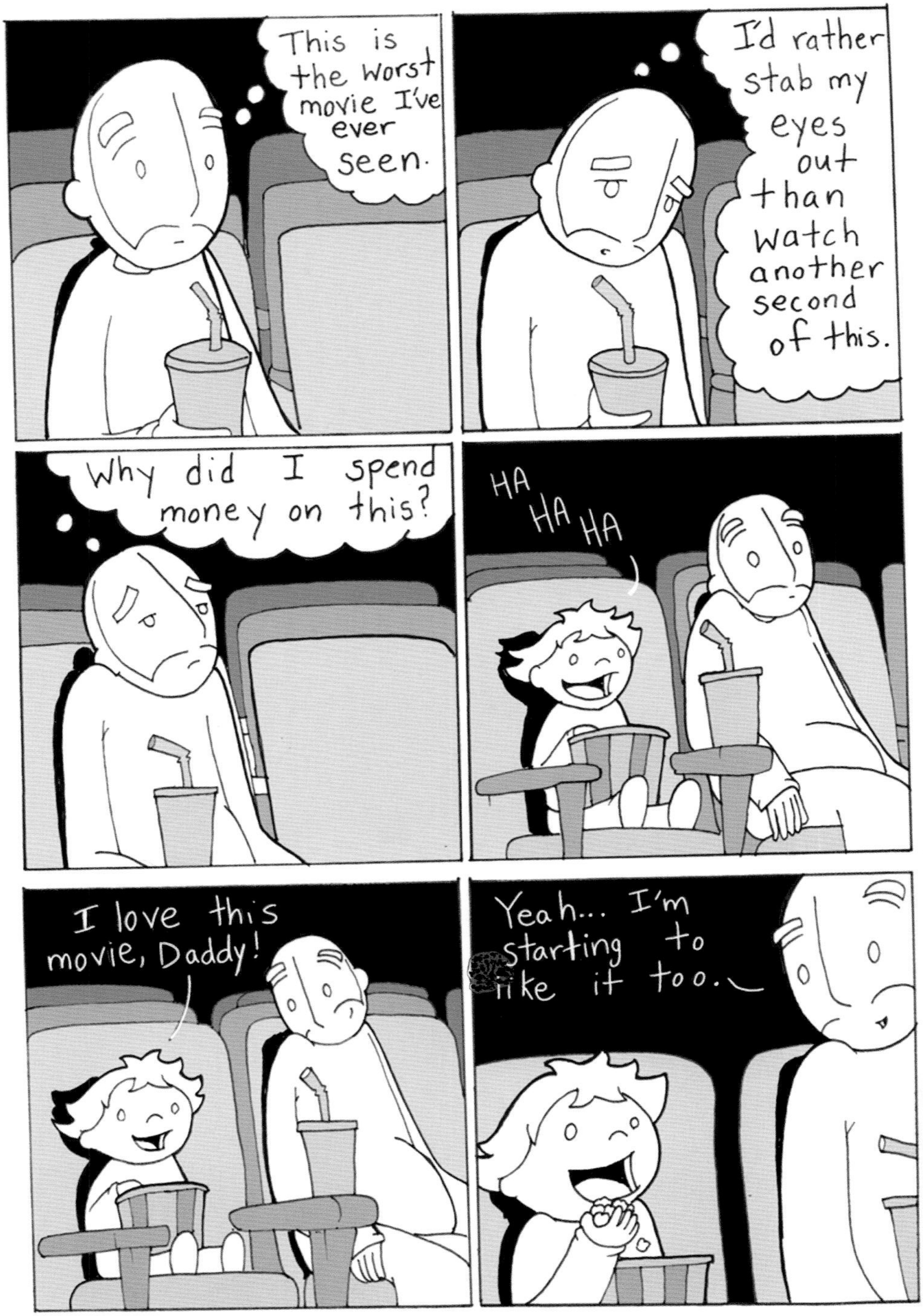
This is the worst movie I've ever seen.
I'd rather stab my eyes out than watch another second of this.
Why did I spend money on this?
HA HA HA
I love this movie, Daddy!
Yeah... I'm starting to like it too.

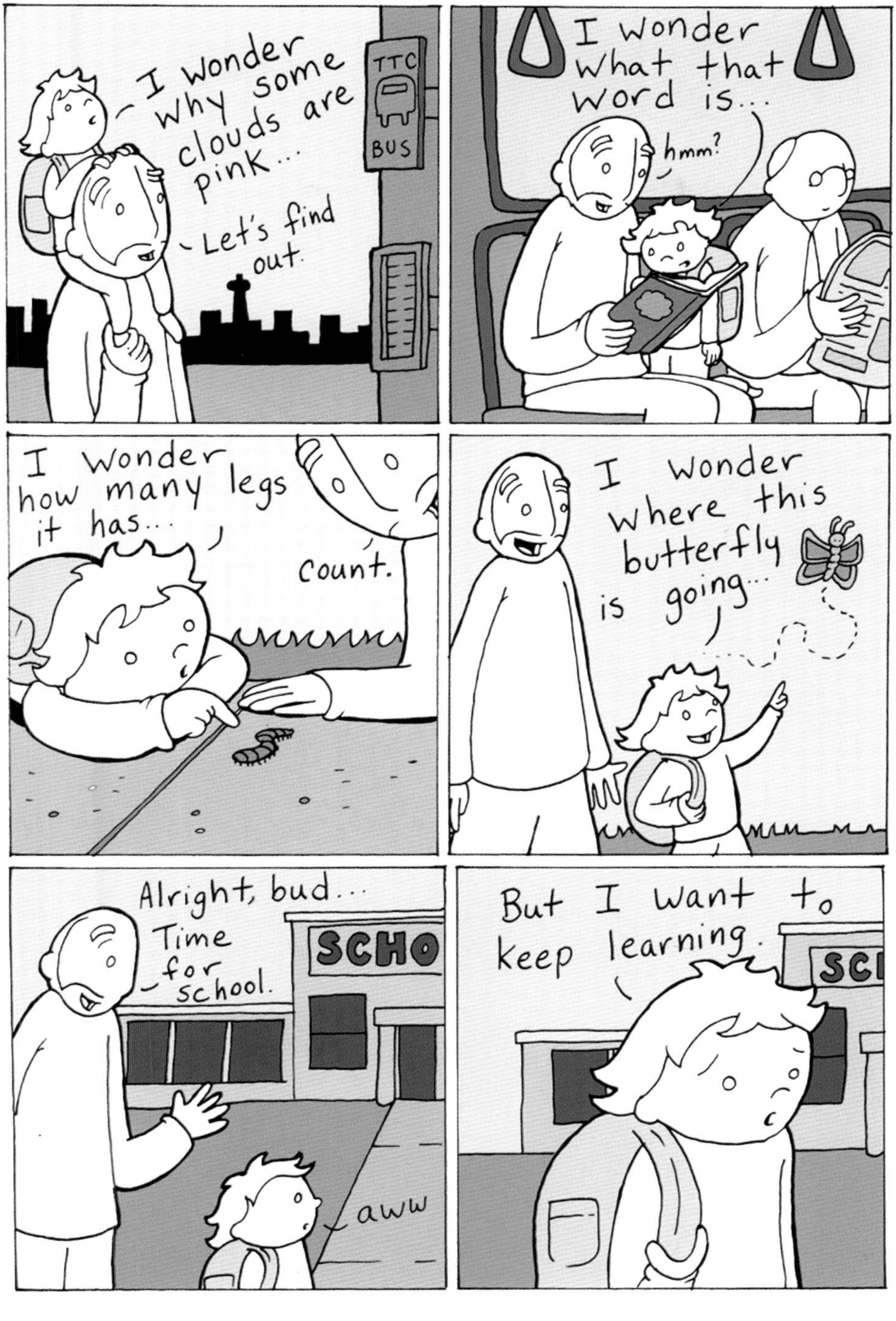
I wonder why some clouds are pink...
Let's find out.
TTC
BUS
I wonder what that word is...
hmm?
I wonder how many legs it has...
Count.
I wonder where this butterfly is going...
Alright, bud... Time for school.
SCHO
aww
But I want to keep learning.
SC

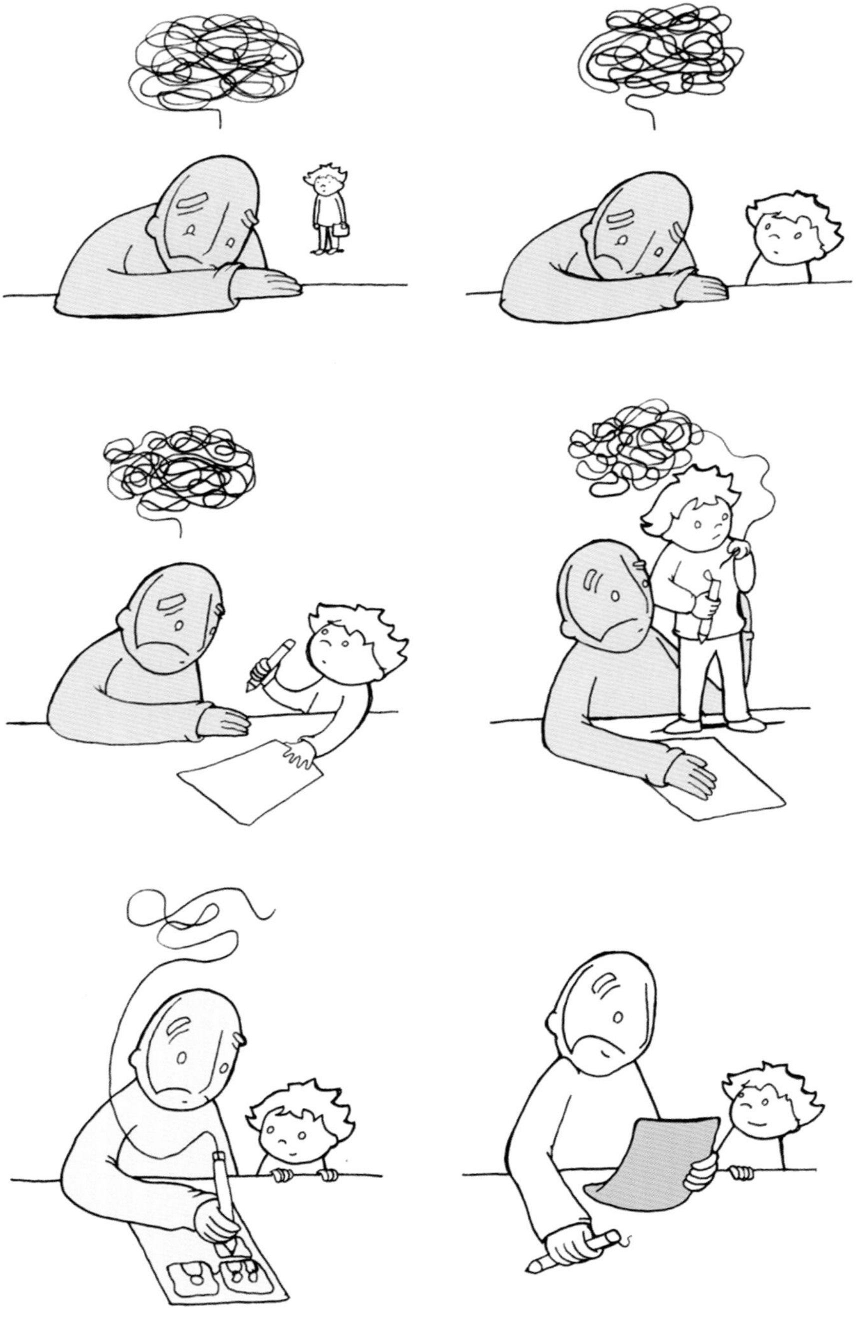

Andrews McMeel Publishing
a division of Andrews McMeel Universal
1130 Walnut Street, Kansas City, Missouri 64106

www.andrewsmcmeel.com

17 18 19 20 21 TEN 10 9 8 7 6 5 4 3 2 1

ISBN: 978-1-4494-7993-0

Library of Congress Control Number: 2016952053

Editor: Patty Rice
Art Director: Tim Lynch
Production Editor: Erika Kuster
Production Manager: Tamara Haus

ATTENTION: SCHOOLS AND BUSINESSES

Andrews McMeel books are available at quantity discounts with bulk purchase for educational, business, or sales promotional use. For information, please e-mail the Andrews McMeel Publishing Special Sales Department: specialsales@amuniversal.com.